SETTLING THE BORDERLAND

Other Voices in Literary Journalism

Jan Whitt

University Press of America,® Inc.

Lanham · Boulder · New York · Toronto · Plymouth, UK

Copyright © 2008 by
University Press of America,® Inc.
4501 Forbes Boulevard
Suite 200
Lanham, Maryland 20706
UPA Acquisitions Department (301) 459-3366

Estover Road
Plymouth PL6 7PY
United Kingdom

Library of Congress Control Number: 2008926050
ISBN-13: 978-0-7618-4093-0 (paperback : alk. paper)
ISBN-10: 0-7618-4093-1 (paperback : alk. paper)
eISBN-13: 978-0-7618-4260-6
eISBN-10: 0-7618-4260-8

♾™ The paper used in this publication meets the minimum
requirements of American National Standard for Information
Sciences—Permanence of Paper for Printed Library Materials,
ANSI Z39.48—1984

For

Sherry Boyd Castello

and

Rachel Hunter Moore

Contents

Preface

I became interested in literary journalism when I began to understand its role in awakening the social consciousness of readers. Literary journalists convey emotion, personal voice, contextualization, and commentary in addition to providing the factual underpinnings of an event. Literary journalism, like all narrative genres, depends upon the essential nature and function of storytelling in a society and often relies upon an extended symbolic system of meaning.

In *Waterland,* Graham Swift argues that human beings inevitably tell stories. He writes:

> But man—let me offer you a definition—is the story-telling animal. Wherever he goes he wants to leave behind not a chaotic wake, not an empty space, but the comforting marker-buoys and trail-signs of stories. He has to go on telling stories, he has to keep on making them up. As long as there's a story, it's all right. Even in his last moments, it's said, in the split second of a fatal fall—or when he's about to drown—he sees, passing rapidly before him, the story of his whole life. (62-63)

Having majored in journalism and English and having received master's and doctoral degrees in English, I didn't need to be convinced of the significance of storytelling. I had read the classics of American literature and journalism, convinced that, as Roger Rosenblatt argues in "Once Upon a Time," we tell stories "because it is in us to do so—like a biological fact—because story-telling is what the human animal does, to progress, to learn to live with one another" (n.p.). What I didn't yet understand was that journalism—like American literature and art—was dominated by men. To be more specific, stories were often those created by, valued by, and communicated to others by particular men whose work makes up the canon of American journalism history.

Upon completing my doctorate in English at the University of Denver in 1985, I treated myself to a trip to the campus bookstore. I purchased the new and hefty *Norton Anthology of Literature by Women,* edited by Sandra M. Gilbert and Susan Gubar (New York: W.W. Norton, 1985), and walked to a nearby restaurant to begin reading.

As I scanned the table of contents, I confronted names and works of literature I barely recognized. Certainly, I would have felt somewhat inadequate scanning any anthology of literature (a doctorate in English does not guarantee that one has read *everything),* but I could cite readily and confidently from the works of Jorge Luis Borges, William Faulkner, Herman Melville, Mark Twain, Walt Whitman, and others. Why had I studied Emily Dickinson, Margaret Fuller, Carson McCullers, Flannery O'Connor, Katherine Anne Porter, and Eudora Welty but missed so many other women writers?

Today, of course, students in graduate programs in English are exposed to writing by women and people of color much more often than were students in the 1980s. However, what I experienced on that day drives much of this study: Women continue to be underrepresented in the literary and journalistic canon. Furthermore, as I moved from the department of English to a department of mass communication at the University of Denver and later to a School of Journalism and Mass Communication at the University of Colorado, I relived my earlier experience. Preparing for courses in journalism, media history, and literary journalism, I confronted the standard cast of characters: Truman Capote, William Randolph Hearst, Ernest Hemingway, Norman Mailer, Adolph Ochs, Joseph Pulitzer, Lincoln Steffens, Hunter S. Thompson, Mark Twain, Tom Wolfe, and others.

Where were the women?

Over the years, I have wondered how to address the lack of information about and access to the work of women journalists and women literary journalists. The way I dealt with my curiosity about women in journalism was to write *Women in American Journalism: A New History* (Champaign, Ill.: U of Illinois P, 2008). The way I am dealing with the dearth of information about women literary journalists is to embark on this study. So much more remains to be done, but much is being written by my colleagues in schools and departments of journalism and mass communication and departments of English across the country. Many of those who have spent their lives filling in the gaps are celebrated in *Women in American Journalism* and in this book as well.

A media history scholar, Nancy Roberts, correctly defines journalism as "one of the few socially acceptable ways for women in radical movements to function as activists"; she cites writer Dorothy Day as someone who believed that a story should exist "to move the heart, stir the will to action, to arouse pity, compassion, to awaken the conscience" *(Sourcebook* 179). Roberts' work in media history and in literary journalism is a lamp lighting the way for the others who have followed; the social impact of literary journalism so central to her research is addressed throughout this study.

Settling the Borderland: Other Voices in Literary Journalism deals with the intimate connection between journalism and literature, both fields in which work by women has been underrepresented. The study has a twin focus: the work of journalists who became some of the greatest novelists and poets and short-story writers of the nineteenth and twentieth centuries in America, several of whom are men, and contemporary journalists (previously referred to as "New Journalists"), who best exemplify the effective use of literary techniques in news coverage. *Settling the Borderland* relies upon an analysis of the increasingly indistinct lines between truth and fiction and between fact and creative narrative in contemporary media.

The often false dichotomy between literature and journalism is evident in the critical texts themselves. The dedication to R. Thomas Berner's book *Writing Literary Features* (Mahwah, N.J.: Lawrence Erlbaum, 1988) reads: "This volume is dedicated to the late Joseph Jay Rubin, Professor Emeritus of American Literature, whose course on Masters of American Literature included journalists, which encouraged me" (n.p.). The fact that the two fields are so consistently separated in American literature survey courses merits serious examination, although that is not Berner's goal in his dedication. The term he prefers in his book designed for journalism students is "literary newswriting" (1).

Other pioneers in criticism of literary journalism also address the thin line between literature as art and journalism as practice. Ronald Weber entitled his book *The Literature of Fact* but subtitled it *Literary Nonfiction in American Writing* (Athens: Ohio UP, 1980). He describes the field as "nonfiction with a literary purpose" (1). Thomas B. Connery separates The New Journalism and literary journalism in *A Sourcebook of American Literary Journalism* (New York: Greenwood Press, 1992). He defines the genre as "nonfiction printed prose whose verifiable content is shaped and transformed into a story or sketch by use of narrative and rhetorical techniques generally associated with fiction" (xiv).

And, finally, John Hellmann's *Fables of Fact: The New Journalism as New Fiction* (Champaign: U of Illinois P, 1981) provides a provocative discussion of a journalist's responsibility to provide a personal explanation for events instead of a corporate one and restates the impossibility of objectivity as the public and the media once understood it. His prose is clear and direct: "Almost by definition, new journalism is a revolt by the individual against homogenized forms of experience, against monolithic versions of truth" (8).

Unfortunately, Hellmann is not alone when he deals extensively with only male literary journalists (Norman Mailer, Hunter S. Thompson, Tom Wolfe, and Michael Herr). Connery's collection—an essential resource—documents the work of 35 literary journalists, of whom four are women (Dorothy Day, Lillian Ross, Joan Didion, and Jane Kramer). Shelley Fisher Fishkin's *From Fact to Fiction: Journalism and Imaginative Writing in America* (New York: Oxford UP, 1985) chronicles the news and fiction writing of only Walt Whitman, Mark Twain, Theodore Dreiser, Ernest Hemingway, and John Dos Passos. Norman Sims's two books *The Literary Journalists* (New York: Ballantine, 1984) and

Literary Journalism in the Twentieth Century (New York: Oxford UP, 1990) feature two sets of writers who belong under the broad banner of literary journalism. In the former, Sims showcases contemporary literary journalists (three of the thirteen are women) and lists five characteristics of literary journalism. In the latter, he features essays by scholars interested in Ernest Hemingway, John McPhee, Joseph Mitchell, and John Steinbeck (An essay by Fishkin does deal with work by W.E.B. Du Bois, James Agee, Tillie Olsen, and Gloria Anzaldúa).

Literary Journalism in the Academy

Discovering that women in literary journalism have been sidelined in much the same way they have been in other disciplines came as no real surprise to me in 1985. However, gradually discovering that literary journalism itself is controversial and often disregarded in academic circles was another case entirely.

I have studied literary journalism since 1990—when I presented a paper about Carson McCullers, Eudora Welty, and Katherine Anne Porter entitled "The Pathway Between Journalism and Fiction" at the American Journalism Historians Association (AJHA) conference in Couer d'Alene, Idaho. Since joining the Association for Education in Journalism and Mass Communication (AEJMC) and other leading professional organizations, I have discovered that reviewers often argue that papers about literary journalism are not appropriate for the history, cultural and critical studies, or newspaper divisions of AEJMC. If literary journalism is literature, they seem to ask, why are its proponents not part of conferences more appropriate to a study of the humanities?

Certainly, my experience with professional organizations has highlighted the "borderland" into which literary journalism falls. Scholars of literary journalism sometimes have opted to submit papers about literary journalism to American literature conferences, conferences on nonfiction, popular culture conferences, American history conferences, and American studies conferences and have been welcomed in these venues. However, like John C. Hartsock in his chapter entitled "The Critical Marginalization of American Literary Journalism," I argue that scholarship concerning literary journalism is broadly significant and illuminates many areas of critical inquiry, including but not restricted to the study of cultural and critical studies, journalism, history, literature, and media. I'm indebted to David Abrahamson, Thomas B. Connery, John C. Hartsock, John J. Pauly, Michael Robertson, Norman Sims, and other established scholars in the field for proposing, moderating, and participating on panels on literary journalism at AEJMC and AJHA and for being astute and caring mentors to those of us who have sought to write about women in literary journalism.

When I began this study, I grappled with the title. If a primary focus of the book was to be women literary journalists, could I afford to employ a word such as "settling" in the title? Didn't it play into the stereotype of men as adventurers, explorers, conquerors and into the stereotype of women as the colonized, the settlers? The concept suggested women who sit, who wait, who ponder, who might write but never publish and never influence their readers in significant ways.

However, as I thought about the men who shaped American literature in the nineteenth and twentieth centuries and the male academicians who carved out the field of literary journalism, I realized that—in some cases—men were the settlers and women the revolutionaries. Women literary journalists would adapt to the definitions of literary journalism. They would study its rituals and imitate its celebrities. Then, quietly—without visible disruption—some of them would begin to subvert the accepted tenets and transform the genre.

Allegory would be one of the primary devices these women would employ. Reliance upon description, appropriation of narrative forms, heavy use of dialogue, emphasis on character: These were the techniques of literary journalism already in use by the men who represented the genre. But to employ these strategies in the service of rich symbolism—for Joan Didion to tell a tale of middle-class America in which a seemingly content woman would burn her husband to death in a Volkswagen on a street called "Bella Vista"—well, that is allegory. This use of narrative taps into the wellspring. The accomplishment of women practitioners of literary journalism would rival the realism of *The Right Stuff* (Tom Wolfe); the naturalism of *In Cold Blood* (Truman Capote); the raw, hard power of *Dispatches* (Michael Herr).

Sara Davidson would tell the story of friendship and betrayal and forgiveness and despair in *Loose Change: Three Women of the Sixties.* Joan Didion would write about eerie music piped into a deserted mall during war in *Salvador.* And in *Orchid Thief* Susan Orlean would marvel at people who devote their lives to finding a symbol—a sign of beauty and perfection—in a tormented and imperfect world. These tales by women literary journalists would reflect humility, indecision, compassion, and mystery. And they would—as William Faulkner said of Dilsey in *The Sound and the Fury* (348) and of humankind in his "Nobel Prize Acceptance Speech"—both endure and prevail.

The subtitle of *Settling the Borderland* is *Other Voices in Literary Journalism.* Although the study will emphasize five women who unsettled the settlers (Katherine Anne Porter, Eudora Welty, Joan Didion, Sara Davidson, and Susan Orlean), three men whose work was profoundly influenced by journalism also are included in Chapter 2: From Straight News to Literary Journalism and Fiction. Edgar Allan Poe, Walt Whitman, and John Steinbeck are well known as writers of poetry, short stories, and novels, but they, too, are among the "other voices" rarely included in studies of literary journalism.

Settling the Borderland alludes often to the explorers who carried the lantern and to the critics who collected and critiqued their work, most of whom are men. But with patience, the stories women tell will achieve prominence, and *Settling the Borderland* is a place to begin.

Jan Whitt
Boulder, Colorado
September 2007

Acknowledgements

I would like to acknowledge the friendship, scholarship, and support of several people deeply invested in literary journalism as a field of study. Several of them are critics of the genre; a few are literary journalists as well as scholars. They include David Abrahamson, Thomas B. Connery, Sara Davidson, John C. Hartsock, John J. Pauly, Michael Robertson, and Norman Sims. I treasure their energy, their commitment to teaching, their love of literature, and their optimistic spirits.

I thank Sherry Boyd Castello and Rachel Hunter Moore of Baylor University for encouraging my love of journalism and literature, respectively. The book is dedicated to them with love and gratitude.

I thank Diane L. Borden, director of the School of Journalism and Media Studies at San Diego State University. At an American Culture Association of the South conference in Columbia, S.C., in 1997, Diane asked about women literary journalists after my panel presentation on Edgar Allen Poe and Walt Whitman. When I found it difficult to respond to her question by citing anyone but Joan Didion, I realized how much more research remained to be done, not only about women in literary journalism but about men who have not received the recognition they deserve.

I thank the editors and production staff at University Press of America, especially Patti Belcher, acquisitions editor, and Brian DeRocco, editorial administrator. I owe a great deal to my friend and colleague Elizabeth Skewes, who proofread a draft of this manuscript. Conversations with my friend Len Ackland, a scholar and investigative reporter, kept me grounded. His skepticism about some of the techniques employed by literary journalists cautioned me to remember that the "best" story might not be a human interest profile but a well-researched city council story that provokes community response.

In *Settling the Borderland: Other Voices in Literary Journalism*, I have drawn on my work that has been published in other venues. My knowledge about allegory and literary journalism, some of which is included in Chapter 1, is rooted in research I conducted for *Allegory and the Modern Southern Novel* (Macon, Ga.: Mercer UP, 1994). Sections of Chapter 2 and 3 are included in *Women in American Journalism: A New History* (Champaign: U of Illinois P, 2008). I thank Willis G. (Bill) Regier, director of the University of Illinois Press, for his ever-present support and encouragement.

Part of my work on John Steinbeck, included in Chapter 2, has been published as "Final Letters to the World: Mark Twain, F. Scott Fitzgerald, John Steinbeck, and Artistic Entropy" in *Journal of the American Studies Association of Texas* 38 (November 2007): 1-19 and as "'To Do Some Good and No Harm': The Literary Journalism of John Steinbeck," *Steinbeck Studies* 3.2 (Fall 2006): 41-62.

Previous articles on Eudora Welty and Katherine Anne Porter have been published as "Portrait of an Artist as a Young Woman: Eudora Welty's Early Years in Media" in *Southwestern Mass Communication Journal* 15 (1999): 26-38 and as "'The Truth About What Happens': Katherine Anne Porter and Journalism," *Journal of the American Studies Association of Texas* 26 (October 1995): 16-35. I thank the editors and publishers of these journals for their permission to use substantial sections of my articles in this and other venues.

My interest in Edgar Allan Poe began when I wrote a paper about Poe and Walt Whitman for presentation in a 1997 American Culture Association of the South conference. Before that paper, which is updated and included in *Settling the Borderland*, I published "'The Very Simplicity of the Thing': Edgar Allan Poe and the Murders He Wrote" in *Clues* 15 (Spring/Summer 1994): 29-47. That article was reprinted in *The Detective in Fiction, Film, and Television*, ed. Jerome P. Delamater and Ruth Prigozy (Westport, Conn.: Greenwood, 1998): 111-21.

Finally, and most importantly, I would like to thank Willard D. (Wick) Rowland Jr., dean emeritus of the School of Journalism and Mass Communication at the University of Colorado at Boulder (1987-1999). Without him, I would not have attended the American Journalism Historians Association conference in Coeur d'Alene, Idaho, in 1990. As an untenured instructor with a Ph.D. in English, I was relatively unaware of the emerging field of literary journalism and would most certainly not have sought out Wick's friends and colleagues in AJHA who are cited in this book. Wick is now president and CEO of Colorado Public Television (KBDI-TV/12) in Denver and continues to be a caring and effective mentor to many of us in public broadcasting and in the academy.

Introduction

I'm a journalist at heart; even as a novelist, I'm first of all a journalist. I think all novels should be journalism to start, and if you can ascend from that plateau to some marvelous altitude, terrific. I really don't think it's possible to understand the individual without understanding the society. (92)

Tom Wolfe
"Master of His Universe"

Tom Wolfe's words about the definition and purposes of journalism and about literature as art lie at the heart of *Settling the Borderland: Other Voices in Literary Journalism.* Closely connected to the distinctions we will make between these literary enterprises is their role in describing the individual as a player in the larger society. When scholars discuss literary journalism, they often do so by listing words and phrases that are sometimes synonymous and sometimes oppositional; furthermore, the terms are sometimes laudatory and sometimes tinged with contempt, depending both on the word choice and on the context. They include:

Art-journalism
Artistic nonfiction
Creative nonfiction
Essay-fiction
Fact as fiction

Faction
Factual fiction
Immersion journalism
Intimate journalism
Journalit
Literary journalism
Literary nonfiction
Literature as fact
Narrative nonfiction
The New Journalism
New reportage
Nonfiction with a literary purpose
The nonfiction novel
Novelistic journalism
Participatory journalism
Parajournalism
Personal journalism
Witness literature
Writerly nonfiction

In *A History of American Literary Journalism: The Emergence of a Modern Narrative Form,* John C. Hartsock says he prefers the terms "narrative journalism" or "narrative literary journalism": "Finally," he writes, "I prefer 'journalism' as the last element for three reasons. First, to define the form as a 'nonfiction' reinscribes its status as a 'nought,' thus reenacting an elitist literary conceit that has long consigned such writing as a 'non' 'essential' literature" (12).

The task involved in identifying and celebrating those we now call "literary journalists" has just begun. Critics such as Shelley Fisher Fishkin *(From Fact to Fiction: Journalism and Imaginative Writing in America)* and Norman Sims *(Literary Journalism, The Literary Journalists,* and *Literary Journalism in the Twentieth Century)* waded in years ago, and a few hardy professors have built fences around small sections of the vast territory and have taught classes in the "new" genre. Still, critics must wrestle with semantics and must continue to deal with the distinctions among the terms that describe a field of academic inquiry increasingly referred to simply as "literary journalism."

How convenient it would be at the beginning of a study of the emergence and development of literary journalism to argue that the terms listed in this introduction exist in harmony, but, in fact, when one has many words for "snow," each signifies at least a slightly different understanding of the white flakes that fall to earth in winter. In the borderland between genres is precisely where those interested in this particular literary phenomenon must begin.

How convenient, too, if we could pretend that literary journalism is a genre that those in the news business, those in departments and schools of journalism and mass communication, and those in departments of English debate good-naturedly. However, certain techniques employed in literary nonfiction raise doubt about accuracy among working journalists and scholars of journalism; these techniques include the revelation of interior states of mind, the re-creation of a scene, manipulation of timelines, and other issues to be addressed in this and subsequent sections of *Settling the Borderland: Other Voices in Literary Journalism.*

Those who love literary journalism and those who have begun to explore it realize that discussion about literary journalism is rarely neutral. In the Winter 2006 issue of *Journalism and Mass Communication Educator* appeared an article by David Abrahamson entitled "Teaching Literary Journalism: A Diverted Pyramid?" The teaser on the cover of the publication reads "Is There a Conflict Between Literature and Journalism?" Although Abrahamson concludes that there is "a clear trend in the mainstream press away from the formulaic strictures of the inverted pyramid" (430) and although he celebrates timelessness, the individual over the institution, and the talent exhibited by literary journalists, a subtext remains: There exists suspicion between traditional journalists espousing news values and literary journalists redefining what is newsworthy.

Some journalism practitioners and scholars are put off by what they perceive to be a cavalier way of manipulating chronology, dialogue, and character description by some literary journalists. Those in literary studies sometimes object to literary journalism's reliance upon actual events and real figures. Fortunately for the scholarly pilgrimage itself, though, literary journalism texts provide those in both literature and journalism with a rich continuum for academic and personal inquiry.

Literary journalism *is* a borderland, and as we have noted, it is a borderland that makes some academicians in both English departments and schools and departments of journalism and mass communication very nervous. If literary journalists themselves acknowledge that they are writing a type of nonfiction that makes the mainstream journalism establishment edgy, shouldn't we be honest enough to admit that our *critical* study of *their* work makes some of *our* colleagues edgy as well? Literary journalism is not fiction—because the people are real and the events occurred—nor is it journalism in a traditional sense—because there is interpretation and a personal point of view and (often) experimentation with structure.

Several characteristics of literary journalism surprise some educators and practitioners in the news industry: For example, not all literary journalists have written for or write for newspapers or magazines; they may employ literary techniques, including stream of consciousness; they may experiment with chronology and rename sources, etc. Other characteristics of literary journalism concern those in departments of English, most especially what they consider to be the secondary nature of nonfiction in literary studies (never mind the place of daily journalism in the estimation of some literary scholars).

Another essential element of literary journalism is its focus. Rather than emphasizing government institutions, literary journalism explores the lives of those who are affected by those institutions. "Rather than hanging around the edges of powerful institutions," Norman Sims writes, "literary journalists attempt to penetrate the cultures that make institutions work" *(The Literary Journalists* 3).

This study will not produce what one literary journalism scholar calls "critical closure"; instead, it will focus on a series of challenging questions in a literary landscape about which we have just begun to ask the important questions. *Settling the Borderland: Other Voices in Literary Journalism* deals with the definitions, characteristics, contributions, and future of studies in literary journalism, and much of the manuscript highlights contributions by the women in the field who are changing the genre in significant ways.

Part of the debate about literary journalism centers upon the characteristics of the genre that are generally acknowledged by students, media scholars, and industry professionals. In *Fables of Fact: The New Journalism as New Fiction,* John Hellman is one of those who ventures to list some of the techniques common to literary journalism, although not all of them are employed by all literary journalists and not all may be employed in one literary journalism text: Literary journalists may frame their narratives with forewords, afterwords, and other devices; they often employ a self-conscious (sometimes "highly obtrusive") narrator; they alter punctuation and may experiment with composition; they use episodic structure; they introduce allegorical or mythic patterns; they use parody and satire; and they believe that the center of the work must be philosophical and should highlight social concerns (13-14). An afterword might emphasize the factual nature of the piece and might draw attention to its "fictional shape" and to the author's "organizing consciousness" (14), according to Hellman.

Other characteristics, according to Sims in "The Literary Journalists," include immersion in the story one is covering; thematic, not necessarily chronological, structure; accuracy (no made-up dialogue, no composite characters, and evidence of the authority of the author's voice); personal voice (incorporating first-person perspective as opposed to the institutional voice of newspapers); a sense of responsibility to the reader; and "symbolic realities" and resonance (8-25).

Rather than listing specific characteristics of the genre, Thomas B. Connery goes to the heart of the issue in the introduction to his collection about literary journalism entitled "Discovering a Literary Form." The focus of the debate between proponents and opponents of literary journalism is the uneasy merging of retelling facts (nonfiction) with the use of literary techniques (fiction). Citing James Agee, R. Thomas Berner, Edwin Ford, Jon Franklin, John Hollowell, Barbara Lounsberry, James E. Murphy, Norman Sims, Ronald Weber, and Tom Wolfe, Connery maneuvers through myriad perspectives on the merging of literature and journalism and establishes a central premise that governs his collection. Connery writes:

Use of the word "journalism" is preferred over "nonfiction" because the works assigned to this literary form are neither essays nor commentary. It also is preferred because much of the content of the works comes from traditional means of news gathering or reporting, including interviews, document review, and observation. Finally, journalism implies an immediacy, as well as a sense that what is being written about has a relevance peculiar to its time and place.

Use of the word "literary" is more problematic than the use of "journalism." The word "literary" is not meant to suggest that journalism is not a part of literature, or that literary journalism is literature and most daily journalism and magazine journalism is not. Nor should it be thought of as an attempt to categorize a specific kind of journalistic writing as more artistic, and perhaps elite, although occasionally that may be the case. "Literary" is used because it says that while the work considered is journalistic, for the reasons just cited, its purpose is not just informational. A purely journalistic work is structured to convey information, primarily facts and authoritative viewpoints, clearly and efficiently. In a literary work, and in literary journalism, style becomes part of the meaning conveyed; the structure and organization of language interpret and inform. (15)

In defining terms in this way, Connery allows for what he and Joseph Webb have called the "Romantic Reporter" (17-18), a poetic recorder of events who is invested in human experience. Connery acknowledges the importance of immersion, description, narration, and other techniques familiar to those who study literary journalism and makes them more than strategies. The techniques become vehicles to move a writer—and, by implication, a reader—toward what T.S. Eliot would call in *Four Quartets* the "still point of the turning world" (15), one's personal center.

As Connery and many of his essayists know well, news is not a collection of facts, no matter how finely arranged, and newsgathering is not merely the recording of a source's words. Dismissing the importance of a writer's vantage point and personal perspective makes possible the false polarities of fiction and nonfiction on a complex continuum of storytelling. Furthermore, within each human event is meaning, meaning that sometimes propels those involved in it toward other events, or toward a governing philosophy, or into relationship. Exterior events contain images and symbols that participants and observers transform into interior reality. And if the events and people with whom we come in contact transform us, they most assuredly transform the reporters who cover the news.

What follows Connery's introduction to *A Sourcebook of American Literary Journalism: Representative Writers in an Emerging Genre* are 35 representatives of literary journalism and the critics who have begun to carve out the "emerging genre" of literary journalism. They are George Ade, James Agee, C.D.B. Bryan, Abraham Cahan, Truman Capote, Stephen Crane, Richard Harding Davis, Dorothy Day, Joan Didion, Theodore Dreiser, Joe Eszterhas, Bob Greene, Hutchins Hapgood, and William Hard. Others are Ernest Hemingway, Michael Herr, John Hersey, Jane Kramer, Richard Ben Cramer, Tracy Kidder, Ring Lardner, Norman Mailer, Joe

McGinniss, John McPhee, Joseph Mitchell, John Reed, Jacob Riis, Lillian Ross, Damon Runyon, Lincoln Steffens, John Steinbeck, Gay Talese, Hunter S. Thompson, Mark Twain, and Tom Wolfe.

Certainly, Connery's list is not exhaustive. *Settling the Borderland: Other Voices in Literary Journalism* will both add to the list of characteristics generally understood to contribute to the study of literary journalism and add to the list of names in studies by Connery and others. In addition, the study will suggest the importance of allegory in literary journalism and highlight the work of Sara Davidson, Joan Didion, Adrian Nicole LeBlanc, Susan Orlean, and others. Like literary journalism, allegory is in disrepute in some academic circles because, as this study will suggest in a most preliminary way, it is misunderstood and often misdefined.

In the postmodern universe, we need more than facts. Daily, there is evidence that human beings crave what Wallace Stevens called the "blessed rage for order" (292) in his poem "The Idea of Order at Key West." Readers want stories in which characters move from innocence to experience because readers themselves move from innocence to experience. Women and men in contemporary society don't cry out for press releases but for what Hellman calls the "penetration of mystery." According to Hellman, "Almost by definition, new journalism is a revolt by the individual against homogenized forms of experience, against monolithic versions of truth" (8).

Hellman cites Robert Scholes, whom he calls "one of our most lucid theoreticians of narrative" (17). Scholes argues that the dichotomy between "fact" and "fiction" is artificial: The word "fact" comes from the Latin *facere,* meaning "to make or do," while "fiction" comes from *fingere,* meaning "to make or shape" (17-18). New journalists and fiction writers, he contends, share "an emphasis upon the perceiving consciousness as a transforming power, and a desire to avoid the distortion caused by an attempt to disguise that power" (13).

Contributing to what many newspaper and news magazine readers want in order to make sense of their world is a mistrust of conventional journalism. What many perceive to be "corporate fiction" (4), as Hellman suggests, increases the distance between a reader's need for verifiable information upon which to make life-altering decisions and the desire of owners of media outlets to survive economically and to make profits. For many Americans, the battle is not between objectivity and subjectivity or between fact and fiction but between a "disguised perspective and an admitted one," between a "corporate fiction" and a "personal one" *(Fables* 4).

And, lest we be confused, readers can and do tell the difference, can and do distinguish among reportorial techniques and textual subtleties. They understand, as Daniel Boorstin argues, that "pseudo-events" *(Fables* 5) can be manufactured by the media and that, as Hellman writes, "even the most delicate instrument of observation necessarily alters the phenomenon observed" (6). This study suggests that many readers respond favorably to a text with admitted biases and an acknowledged point of view. It is easier for many readers to accept that there is a personal voice behind a story than that the story is objective.

Into the mire of controversy involving point of view and the literary techniques that permeate and help to define the genre of literary journalism step proponents of the genre, who argue that literary journalism is at root a political and social movement. At its heart is the belief that a disclosed point of view is everything and that readers will trust a personal voice, informed commentary, and thorough research more than they will trust many of the texts produced by mainstream media. In an essay entitled "The Other Side," Richard D. Manning writes, "Reporters keep their distance from community, and reporters think they like that. We call it objectivity. It is the myth that organizes our subculture, a naïve belief that we are better observers because we are separate" (13). Separate is not equal, and equal is not corporate-generated stories about those who run a transportation system. Readers demand stories in which reporters talk with those who ride city buses at least as often as they talk to those who manage the transportation system. It bears repeating that readers understand a personal voice and can distinguish it from an institutional one.

In popular culture, reporters and editors often are portrayed as vultures, as automatons who care only about the story, as human beings whose allegiances are primarily to corporate media. Films such as "Absence of Malice," "Broadcast News," "The Insider," "Network," "The Paper," and "Wag the Dog" highlight these portrayals. One of the most important books to deal with the public perception of the reporter as "other" is Janet Malcolm's *The Journalist and the Murderer.* In it, Malcolm asks hard questions about the role of journalism and about the tendency of some reporters to manipulate their sources to get a story. (The same issue is explored in the 2006 films "Capote" and "Infamous," both of which deal with Truman Capote's relationship with one of his two primary sources, Perry Smith, as he conducted research for *In Cold Blood.*) One of Malcolm's most damning comments appears on the first page of her book. There, she focuses on the source, who must realize that the reporter's first obligation is to the story and not to the assumed relationship established between the reporter and the source during the interview: "On reading the article or book in question, he has to face the fact that the journalist—who seemed so friendly and sympathetic, so keen to understand him fully, so remarkably attuned to his vision of things—never had the slightest intention of collaborating with him on his story but always intended to write a story of his own" (3).

Unlike corporate journalism and reporters who exploit their sources in order to get the story first, literary journalists immerse themselves in the worlds of those whom they cover. They build extended relationships with their sources, making it unlikely that they can avoid bias and making it even more unlikely that they would want to do so. They relay dialogue and use description in a way that makes it clear that they are a part of the world they describe. Does their work contain bias? Certainly. Do they write from their own point of view and "distort" the news by being too close to the events and sources? Most assuredly. But literary journalists count on readers to understand their vantage point and to trust their narrative precisely *because* they confess their preconceptions and their points of view.

The Development of Literary Journalism

The roots of literary journalism go back to eighteenth-century British litera-ture (some say the Bible), but this study focuses on the evolution of "The New Journalism" into what we understand as "literary journalism" today. Studies that are essential for those interested in the extended history of liter-ary journalism are Michael Johnson's *The New Journalism: The Under-ground Press, the Artists of Nonfiction, and Changes in the Established Media* (1971), John Hollowell's *Fact and Fiction: The New Journalism and the Nonfiction Novel* (1977), and John C. Hartsock's *A History of American Literary Journalism: The Emergence of a Modern Narrative Form* (2000).

The purpose of this chapter is not to provide a comprehensive history of the field, as these scholars and others have done, but to highlight the de-velopment of the principles of literary journalism as they affect the women and men who are and should be considered literary journalists. As editor and author of *A Sourcebook of American Literary Journalism,* Connery is nothing if not courageous in the quest to establish the core values in literary journalism. The very title of his 1992 book testifies to the difficulties inher-ent in writing about a group as diverse as Stephen Crane, Theodore Dreiser, Joan Didion, John McPhee, Mark Twain, Tom Wolfe, and others. Literary journalism is in no way an "emerging genre" when one remembers its earli-est practitioners; critics are, however, only beginning the struggle to catego-rize, to understand, and to do justice to the men and women who 1) began their literary careers working for American newspapers and/or 2) who em-ploy the literary techniques defined and described during the time of "The New Journalism."

The 1960s and 1970s, writes Ronald Weber, were a pragmatic, issue-oriented time period in America. Literary models were not William Faulk-ner or James Joyce, he suggests, but George Orwell and James Baldwin, whom he considers proponents of "passionate and personal journalism" (9). "The realistic novel, or that part of the novel that was realistic, had been pre-empted by visual and verbal forms that brought us the world more di-rectly and with greater immediacy" (10), he writes. Suggesting a kind of cultural allegory or "irrealism," Weber states that the "only hope of making literary sense of such a society was through indirect, nonrealistic means" (11).

In 1962, Tom Wolfe was writing for the *New York Herald Tribune.* "The feature writers had freedom from rhetorical and space restrictions or-dinary reporters did not have, and those working for the faltering *Herald Tribune* had the additional freedom to experiment with methods and materi-als in the hope that something would rescue the paper," Wolfe said. Wolfe called the journalism he practiced "Saturation Reporting" or "reporting that went to the bottom depths of the material and sought out not only what was said and done but what was thought and felt, reporting that got inside character and scene the way novelists did but without the invention they employed" *(The New Journalism* 52).

By 1973, Wolfe had introduced several tenets of literary journalism as it became more and more popular. He argued that journalists should engage in scene-by-scene construction, depicting people in dramatic scenes as traditional storytelling did; should present dialogue as recorded and remembered rather than journalism's selective quotations; should vary the points of view; and should include "status" details, or the habits, mannerisms, gestures, etc., that distinguish people, societies, and subcultures (Connery 3; Wolfe, *The New Journalism* 31-33).

In his landmark book *The New Journalism,* he argues that there were three classes of writers before the new nonfiction genre became popular. The "literary upper class," he suggests, were the novelists. "They were regarded as the only 'creative writers,' the only literary artists," Wolfe writes. "They had exclusive entry to the soul of man, the profound emotions, the eternal mysteries, and so forth and so on" (25). The middle class were the essayists, the critics, the biographers, and the historians. "The lower class," Wolfe continues, "were the journalists, and they were so low down in the structure that they were barely noticed at all. They were regarded chiefly as day laborers who dug up slags of raw information for writers of higher 'sensibility' to make better use of" (25).

Since the time Wolfe sought to define the techniques of those who called themselves "The New Journalists" and since the time many others have distinguished themselves as practitioners of the form, a generation of writers has taken the stage and another has joined it. "Drilling Into the Bedrock of Ordinary Experience" by Robert S. Boynton, who has served as director of the magazine journalism program at New York University, deals with those Boynton calls the "New New Journalists." He lists Ted Conover, William Finnegan, Jonathan Harr, Alex Kotlowitz, Jon Krakauer, William Langewiesche, Adrian Nicole LeBlanc, Michael Lewis, Susan Orlean, Richard Preston, Eric Schlosser, Lawrence Weschler, Lawrence Wright, and others. Obviously, their emergence has altered the literary journalism paradigm in discernable ways.

Boynton's argument is that a new generation of writers is experimenting with the form made popular by The New Journalists of the 1960s and 1970s to "speak to social and political concerns" (B10) resembling those of nineteenth-century writers such as Stephen Crane, Jacob A. Riis, and Lincoln Steffens. "Rigorously reported, psychologically astute, sociologically sophisticated, and politically aware" (B10), these New New Journalists have capitalized on what Boynton calls "the literature of the everyday" (B10):

> Of course, the New New Journalists do not constitute a coherent group. Some of them know each other, but most do not. They don't live in

any one city or part of the country. They write for magazines—primarily *The Atlantic Monthly, The New York Times Magazine, The New Yorker, Rolling Stone*—but mostly make their living writing books. What they do share is a devotion to close-to-the-skin reporting as the best way to bridge the gap between their subjective perspective and the reality they are observing. (B10)

Although Boynton's list is most assuredly not intended to be comprehensive, it is important to a study of women in literary journalism to note that only Adrian Nicole LeBlanc and Susan Orlean are mentioned. The dearth of women's names is significant and troubling, as is Boynton's celebration of Lincoln Steffens as the best example of the nineteenth-century form of American journalism. The exclusion of Ida Tarbell, a woman equal to Steffens in every way, is typical and problematic. And while LeBlanc and Orlean are significant in *Settling the Borderland: Other Voices in Literary Journalism,* they are only two in a growing group of talented contemporary women who also are transforming the genre as we know it.

The Art of Literary Journalism

If Wolfe is correct that journalists have been seen as "day laborers who dug up slags of raw information for writers of higher 'sensibility' to make better use of" *(The New Journalism* 25), and I suspect he is, then it is important to re-examine the kinship between journalism as practice and literature as art. Literary journalism lives in the borderland between them, and the lines are so indistinct as to be oftentimes invisible.

Ronald Weber's *The Literature of Fact: Literary Nonfiction in American Writing* is a standard text when one addresses the emergence and development of American literary journalism. Introducing the ideas of Donald Pizer, Weber argues that there are two kinds of documentary narrative (and by extension two kinds of journalism). The first explores a factual event as an event, as documentary narrative presumes to do. The second explores a factual event as meaning (Pizer considers documentary narrative to be art). In the first kind of documentary, the point is accuracy, "or at least verisimilitude." In the second, the point is simply a means to an end, and the end is interpretation or experience (2-3).

Weber introduces the feature writers on the "Style" section at the *Washington Post* during the late twentieth century into his discussion of literary journalism. Quoting Richard Poirier, he writes, "Rather than try to turn journalism into art, they sought instead to 'mesh traditional reporting disciplines of research, accuracy, moral objectivity and clear thinking with a new freedom of literary expression'" (23). He said what was practiced at the *Post* was not literary nonfiction as much as "distinguished" journalism (23). He argues that the reporter "was never a totally neutral figure" and said "to deny the shaping presence of the reporter because of rhetorical demands of detachment and objectivity was to be fundamentally dishonest with the reader as well as oneself" (23). Weber then added: "Literature, as opposed to journalism, is always a refracting rather than reflecting medium; it always to some degree distorts life, if only in giving it a shape or clarity that otherwise cannot be detected" (27).

It is important that Weber quotes Truman Capote—who said that "reporting can be made *as* interesting as fiction and done *as* artistically"—and, significantly, Weber says that Capote doesn't "mean to say that one is a superior form to the other" (21). This clears the way, of course, for a broader conversation about the purpose and nature of literature and the function and character of journalism, while still acknowledging that storytelling binds them together and that readers can entertain the differences and similarities without feeling compromised.

Two books are pivotal in the discussion about the kinship between the journalist and the writer of literature. One is Shelley Fisher Fishkin's *From Fact to Fiction,* mentioned earlier in the introduction. In it Fishkin explores the ways in which journalism has contributed to the life of a fiction writer: "It forced him to become a precise observer, nurtured in him a respect for fact, and taught him lessons about style that would shape his greatest literary creations," she writes. "It taught him to be mistrustful of rhetoric, abstractions, hypocrisy, and cant; it taught him to be suspicious of secondhand accounts and to insist on seeing with his own eyes" (4). The other book is Barbara Lounsberry's *The Art of Fact: Contemporary Artists of Nonfiction.* In it, she lists the characteristics for compelling literary journalism: They include "documentable subject matter," "exhaustive research" (immersion and saturation reporting), description of the scene, and "fine writing" (xiii-xv). For both Fishkin and Lounsberry, The New Journalism is characterized by internal consciousness, while traditional journalism concerns itself with the external world.

The contribution that journalism makes to the writing of fiction and that writers of fiction make to journalism lies at the heart of the study of literary journalism. Into this mix we must add the purpose and ultimate goal of both journalism and literature: to entertain, challenge, and educate the reader. Literary journalism, according to John J. Pauly, goes a step further and can encourage civic engagement. Arguing that literary journalism is part of a social movement intended to improve people's lives, Pauly writes about two paths that emerged in journalism in the late nineteenth century and suggests what traditional contemporary journalism may be lacking:

> What we sometimes forget is that the late nineteenth century drove newspapers in two somewhat opposite directions. One path led journalism toward the ethereal goal of objectivity and reduced reporting to a bureaucratic function within the new system of economic and political administration. The other path led into the streets and plunged the reporter into the myriad forms of city life. The contemporary newspaper plods along that first wide, flat, and dusty path. The beauty of [a literary journalist's] work is that it leads us back to the second path. And along the way we begin to understand what journalism has lost in its rush for certainty. ("Damon Runyon," *Sourcebook* 176)

Settling the Borderland: Other Voices in Literary Journalism relies upon Pauly's "The Politics of The New Journalism" in which he suggests that New Journalism (and presumably literary journalism) should be studied as social—not simply as aesthetic—discourses. He argues that the aesthetic revolution of The New Journalism was a direct result of its social setting. The New Journalism, he claims, was a "generational manifesto" *(Literary Journalism in the Twentieth Century* 119) in that it devalued investigative reporting; resurrected what he calls the "romantic vision of the writer" *(Literary Journalism in the Twentieth Century* 119); fueled nonfiction; made the study of culture valid work; attacked established journalism's "fact-fetish" *(Literary Journalism in the Twentieth Century* 121); raised a new central issue, suggesting that "the truth of all writing is a matter for social negotiation" *(Literary Journalism in the Twentieth Century* 122); and set up a new social contract *(Literary Journalism in the Twentieth Century* 124).

The Techniques of Literary Journalism

When a reporter does her or his job well, social and political contexts become clear and the underpinnings of the day's news are within view. The "true reporter's eye" *(Sourcebook* 228) does indeed provide "those telling bits of reality that lend scale and texture to the larger picture" *(Sourcebook* 228-29), as Giles Fowler writes. Fowler ultimately argues that the journalist and novelist often merge into a single person *(Sourcebook* 228-29). Whether literary journalists consider themselves first and foremost journalists (as do Tom Wolfe and others), they must nonetheless accept the honor and the responsibility of helping their readers move into an interior world, to see into what poet William Wordsworth once called "the life of things" ("Lines Composed a Few Miles Above Tintern Abbey" 153).

Scholars of literature and journalism and practitioners of journalism often demand more from journalism than it can provide, and their calls to arms become significant as we acknowledge the higher purpose of literature and of literary journalism. In *Fame and Obscurity: Portraits,* Gay Talese writes, "The new journalism, though often reading like fiction, is not fiction. It is, or should be, as reliable as the most reliable reportage although it seeks a larger truth than is possible through the mere compilation of verifiable facts, the use of direct quotations, and adherence to the rigid organizational style of the older form" (vii). The "larger truth," of course, suggests a reader's response to the text, a response that presumably drives her or him into the community to alter and improve it. For example, Richard D. Manning, angry about massive destruction of virgin forest and the media that he believes allowed it to occur, condemns conventional news coverage and challenges reporters and editors to be more than they are and to commit themselves to social and political change: "It would be journalism. It would be balanced, fair and irrelevant. It would be yet another example of the bipolar, fill-in-the-blanks, objective, alienated journalism that has fueled our homeland's controversies lo these many years" (14).

And Michael Herr, who reports on Vietnam in *Dispatches,* introduces his own concerns as he challenges journalists to fulfill their responsibilities by understanding the possible contributions of their craft: "The press got all the facts (more or less), it got too many of them," he writes. "But it never found a way to report meaningfully about death, which of course was really what it was all about" *(Sourcebook* 7; *Dispatches* 214-15). Writing meaningfully about death and other universal issues—translating everyday event and providing context for readers and viewers—is precisely what many scholars challenge media practitioners to do. And it is the goal to which literary journalists in general have committed themselves.

In "A Third Way to Tell the Story: American Literary Journalism at the Turn of the Century," Connery discusses a news story as a cultural artifact and says that literary journalism is not fiction because the people are real and the facts occurred and is not journalism because it is interpretive and incorporates a personal point of view. He singles out Stephen Crane as an example and celebrates his use of dialogue, concrete description, detailed scene setting, imagery, irony, etc. Immersion, Connery suggests, includes the belief that the reader wants to identify with a subject rather than watch her or him from an intellectual or ideological distance *(Literary Journalism in the Twentieth Century* 3-20). Although this definition, of course, does not preclude the possibility that a reader may identify closely with the subject of a conventional news story, it suggests that connection between a reader and the subject of the story is one of the primary goals espoused by a literary journalist. The text, then, becomes a catalyst for change and for human relationship.

The debate about the virtues of literary journalism explodes again with the publication of every successful example of the genre embraced by the public. When Truman Capote published *In Cold Blood* in 1965, he considered it the first nonfiction novel. Journalists accused him of having gambled with the integrity of news by employing literary techniques such as stream of consciousness; literary critics accused him of glorifying sensationalism and of violating the high calling of fiction. The controversy that followed *In Cold Blood* erupted again with the 1994 publication of *Midnight in the Garden of Good and Evil.* In an "Author's Note," John Berendt acknowledged that he took "certain storytelling liberties" but that his book remained "faithful to the characters and to the essential drift of events as they really happened" (n.p.). Certainly, the nonfiction novels of Capote and Berendt are catalysts for what Sims, a former United Press International reporter, calls an exploration of the "borderlands between fact and fiction" *(Literary Journalism in the Twentieth Century* v).

Literary journalism does not gain its name or its identity from being the only lyrical or creative prose in the field of journalism. It does, however, differ significantly from everyday journalistic stories published in newspapers and magazines. It requires immersion in an event. It presumes a point of view. It also employs the techniques of literature without apology, making rich use of stream of consciousness, metaphor, symbol, description, point of view, narration, dialogue, and other techniques considered by many to lie in the province of literature.

Some literary journalists experiment with chronology and/or change the names of characters, but most adhere to rigid journalistic practices while writing an extended narrative that captures the reader's interest and builds suspense and an investment in the development of complex characters. Literary journalism also is often interdisciplinary and a combination of genres. In "The Art of Literary Journalism," Sims writes: "The liveliness of literary journalism, which critics compare to fiction, comes from combining this personal engagement with perspectives from sociology and anthropology, memoir writing, fiction, history, and standard reporting . . . Literary journalists are boundary crossers in search of a deeper perspective on our lives and times" *(Literary Journalism* 19). Literary journalist Tracy Kidder also defends literary journalism against the charge that its practitioners use literary techniques (presumably thereby violating journalistic ethics) by saying: "Some people criticize nonfiction writers for 'appropriating' the techniques and devices of fiction writing. Those techniques, except for invention of character and detail, never belonged to fiction. They belong to storytelling. In nonfiction you can create a tone and a point of view. Point of view affects everything that follows" *(Literary Journalism* 19).

Since the 1960s and 1970s, the orthodoxy of news—most especially the concept of "objectivity"—has been under fire. Tom Wolfe's *The New Journalism* shattered forever the notion that inverted pyramid, "just-the-facts-ma'am" journalism could meet the deeper needs and the intellectual demands of readers in America. Like Norma M. Schulman, I argue that it is no accident that the phrase "just the facts, ma'am" became an industry cliché. Schulman's suggestion is that because of cultural stereotypes, the men who control news flow believe that women digress when telling stories and that they must be brought up short and be required to talk or write concisely and within clear parameters (55-67). These parameters are, presumably, to be set by law enforcement officials and newspaper editors.

Literary journalism refutes this claim. For literary journalists, whether male or female, "understanding begins with emotional connection" and "quickly leads to immersion" *(Literary Journalists* 10), Sims writes. Hartsock, too, highlights the point of view essential to the literary journalist: "It should come as no surprise then that narrative literary journalists who did not 'leave' their material but instead engaged their subjectivities in it found themselves having to take sides" (79).

Rather than distancing themselves from the subjects of their stories and striving to maintain objectivity, literary journalists immerse themselves in the lives and the environments of their subjects and, while they strive for balance and fairness, trust the reader to realize that their stories are bounded by time, space, and human limitation. There is no place for omniscient point of view in literary journalism. Again, Hartsock is helpful in understanding these concepts, although he rightly refuses to privilege literary journalism over traditional objective journalism:

> In addition, we can see at work in the two strains of journalism the kinds of ideological concerns that would eventually be reflected in the development of objective objectified news and narrative literary journalism, and that raise a fundamental epistemological question, How best can one account for the phenomenal world? In principle, objective news would seem to serve the purpose better because of its announced intention to exclude partisanship. But as several critics have noted, objective news paradoxically disempowers readers by excluding their participation in such discourse. Narrative literary journalism offers more of an opportunity for reader engagement precisely because its purpose is to narrow the distance between subjectivity and the object, not divorce them . . . Nor is this to suggest that one form of journalism is superior to the other. That has been precisely the problem in the historic privileging of the information or discursive model over the story model, and more specifically of objective news over narrative literary journalism in our own century. Rather, given that the strengths of both are also their liabilities, such a conclusion argues in favor of a diversity of journalisms in the problematic attempt to interpret the phenomenal world. (132-33)

Presented earlier in this chapter, Boynton's analysis of the importance of the new generation of literary journalists focuses on their primary motivation in relaying information about the lives of others. Boynton notes a key difference between their craft and Wolfe's: "Wolfe said he went inside his characters' heads; the New New Journalists become part of their lives" (B10). Boynton writes:

> The New New Journalism may well be the most popular and influential development in the history of American literary nonfiction. Neither frustrated novelists nor wayward newspaper reporters, today's authors tend to write magazine articles or nonfiction books that benefit from both the legitimacy that Wolfe's legacy has brought to literary nonfiction and from the concurrent displacement of the novel as the most prestigious form of literary expression. ("Drilling" B10)

It is the implied social contract between reporter and source and the emphasis on allegory and principles of storytelling that will interest us as we celebrate the work of Sara Davidson, Joan Didion, Adrian Nicole LeBlanc, Susan Orlean, and others. All seek to transform the world in which they live by challenging their readers to explore new ideas and values. They do so without artifice, although they employ literary techniques considered by some to be manipulative.

Those who mistrust literary journalism—perhaps because they consider its techniques to be contrivances (and therefore misleading)—may find the plain style of a straight news story comforting. But these readers may have trouble with Hugh Kenner's opinions in "The Politics of the Plain Style" and with one of the premises of *Settling the Borderland.* Kenner argues that plain style is a "perfect medium for hoaxes" and is a "vehicle for profitable lies" (186) precisely because readers trust it more. "Handbooks and copy editors now teach journalists how to write plainly, that is, in such a manner that they will be trusted," Kenner writes. "You get yourself trusted by artifice" (187).

Second, those who mistrust literary journalism because its disciples rely upon symbol and metaphor and strive for a thematic center may have trouble with another premise of *Settling the Borderland,* one best expressed by David Eason in "The New Journalism and the Image-World." This study argues that—after all is said and done—reporting is storytelling and its goal is to captivate the reader. Eason places mainstream newspapers in a category he calls "realist" and alternative media in a category he terms "modernist." "Realist" publications (mainstream newspapers) rely upon assumed values, a "consensus about a frame of reference" and a community of readers, and traditional models of interpretation (meaning) and expression (story form). Alternative media (modernist texts), according to Eason, connect writers and readers in creating reality in a new community (192-93).

Alternative media practitioners and by implication literary journalists understand that traditional cultural distinctions cannot order all experience. Replacing the phrase "alternative media" with "literary journalism" serves us well in this introduction. Literary journalism practitioners seek to create new communities and rely on a reader's understanding that, as Eason suggests, both what is reported and the report itself are social constructions (201).

This study is divided into three parts: Chapter 1, which deals with the development of literary journalism and its place as a borderland between fiction and nonfiction, which introduces writers who made their professional homes in American newsrooms before building their reputations as writers of fiction (Willa Cather, Stephen Crane, Edna Ferber, and others fall into this category), which suggests the importance of allegory in a study of literary journalism, and which introduces the "classics" of American literary journalism (the instantly successful 2005 memoir *The Year of Magical Thinking* by Joan Didion is one such work); Chapter 2, which presents the work of Edgar Allan Poe, Walt Whitman, Katherine Anne Porter, Eudora Welty, and John Steinbeck and argues for their inclusion in the canon of American literary journalism; and Chapter 3, which delves into the contributions made by women in literary journalism, especially Joan Didion, Sara Davidson, and Susan Orlean.

As we move into a discussion of the works generally agreed to be the best literary journalism has to offer, it is appropriate to return to Hellman, who argues that The New Journalism and literary journalism are not "realistically dramatized documentaries" (x) or "absurdist transcriptions of fact" (x) but "profoundly *transforming* literary experiments embodying confrontations between fact and mind, between the worlds of journalism and fiction" (x). Literary journalism is dangerous precisely because it challenges us to rethink what we believe about the lines between fact and fiction and between truth and falsehood and because it redefines and expands the idea of truth beyond the definitions of "objectivity," "veracity," or "accuracy."

Authors of literary journalism, Hellman suggests, "attempt to 'make up' or construct meaningful versions of the 'news' that continually threatens to overwhelm consciousness" (x). He treats literary journalism as a "genre of the new fiction" and says "the form should be approached as primarily literature—indeed as a genre of fiction—despite its adherence to the factual criteria of journalism" (xi). This way of looking at literary journalism can be shocking, troubling, frustrating, challenging, and revolutionary. Critics of the genre know that there is a great deal to lose in the maelstrom between journalism and literature; some of them also know there is a great deal to be gained, including a better understanding of ourselves and of the world we seek to understand and transform.

Some of the questions raised by *Settling the Borderland* include: Is there room for various "journalisms?" Is it possible for the academy—both departments and schools of journalism and mass communication and departments of English—to acknowledge what Sara Davidson calls "The Gray Zone" and embrace literary journalism as journalism, as literature, and as a symbolic genre all its own? Will we be able to address and redefine the practices of news reporting and writing in the new century? What does our understanding of literary journalism suggest about "fact" and "fiction," as we have traditionally understood them, and about the nature of "truth?" Is there a place in daily news reporting for stories that don't stop with a description of our worst selves but challenge us to exemplify courage and commitment and concern for others? And finally, as news consumers and media scholars, can we—beyond analyses in our news writing and reporting classes of the emblematic figures that appear in *Wall Street Journal* leads—begin to address the profoundly allegorical quality of news?

Most importantly, in the chapters that follow we will explore the failure of scholars to recognize the women who have built their careers as literary journalists. A few critics—such as Julia M. Klein, who wrote a review of Boynton's *The New New Journalism: Conversations with America's Best Nonfiction Writers on Their Craft* (2005)—acknowledge the emphasis on males in the field, but their voices are too often lost in the wind. Klein writes:

> Why is it that just three of the nineteen writers in this book—[Adrian Nicole] LeBlanc, Susan Orlean, and Jane Kramer—are women? It can be argued that Boynton's choices merely reflect the predominance of male voices in the prestigious U.S. magazines that publish both narrative and opinion journalism. *The New Yorker* has recently been criticized for this tendency. *The New Republic, The Washington Monthly,* and *The American Prospect* have long been led and dominated by men. And the much-praised *Atlantic* is no exception. Excluding poetry, the January/February issue has thirty-two bylines by men, including the prolific [William] Langewiesche, and just five by women, a ratio that is typical for the magazine.

But why? Is the culprit rank sexism? Male editors hiring their male buddies? Or else the magazine's preference for subjects such as war and politics that draw more male writers? Do women writers, facing rejection, discourage more easily? (I've heard that thesis proposed.) Or, as devoted mothers and daughters and wives, are they simply unavailable to devote the months and years of zealous, almost superhuman effort required by immersion journalism? There is surely no single, and no easy, answer. But it would have been nice if Boynton, in this otherwise probing book, had thought to raise the question. (n.p.)

Whatever the explanation, the gang's all here, and the clubhouse is full of men such as Ted Conover, Jon Krakauer, Ron Rosenbaum, Gay Talese, and 12 others. Although these writers are to be celebrated, their contributions do not constitute the full story.

Settling the Borderland: Other Voices in Literary Journalism will place women writers in the historical context of the men who were gaining recognition during the time they, too, were writing. While celebrating the achievements made by men such as Truman Capote and Ernest Hemingway, it is dedicated to the recognition of the women who were equally talented but who were often overlooked or relegated to the footnotes. In some cases, male writers such as Edgar Allan Poe and John Steinbeck will be granted significant space in a book that is ostensibly about women: This occurs because, although they have not suffered from a lack of critical acclaim, their reliance on journalism perpetually takes a back seat to an interest in their production of fiction.

A study of literary journalism is not complete, of course, without a discussion of those who either worked for American newspapers and then built their reputations by writing fiction or those who moved comfortably between nonfiction and fiction, as did John Steinbeck and others. Most scholars of literary journalism think primarily of Joan Didion, Norman Mailer, Hunter S. Thompson, Tom Wolfe, and others when they consider the other thread of literary journalism, a thread that features print journalists who opted to write extended nonfiction. Certainly, Didion, Mailer, Thompson and Wolfe have written successful extended nonfiction and have become well-known because of the quality of their work and because of the circulation and reputation of publications such as *The New Yorker*, but they are not alone.

Chapter 1 explores works by the giants of American literary journalism such as Truman Capote, John Berendt, Tom Wolfe, and Joan Didion that represent the classics in the field of literary journalism. Capote's *In Cold Blood* deals with the murder of a Kansas farm family; Berendt's *Midnight in the Garden of Good and Evil* portrays life and death in Savannah, Georgia; Wolfe's *The Right Stuff* provides insight into the life of astronauts, into the definitions of masculinity, and into the myth of American heroism; and Didion's *The Year of Magical Thinking* is an example of memoir and its powerful hold on contemporary American readers. Her book *Salvador,* too, is historically and artistically significant when one considers the landmark texts in literary journalism.

In addition to the classics that are representative of the best in literary journalism, *Settling the Borderland: Other Voices in Literary Journalism* is devoted to those too often omitted or minimalized, including Edgar Allan Poe, Walt Whitman, Katherine Anne Porter, and Eudora Welty who, like John Steinbeck, worked in journalism before becoming known for their fiction. It is also committed to telling the stories of Sara Davidson and Susan Orlean who, like Joan Didion, continue to expand both the reputation and range of literary journalism.

Chapter 1.
Literary Journalism as a Borderland

> It forced him to become a precise observer, nurtured in him a respect for fact, and taught him lessons about style that would shape his greatest literary creations. It taught him to be mistrustful of rhetoric, abstractions, hypocrisy, and cant; it taught him to be suspicious of secondhand accounts and to insist on seeing with his own eyes. (4)
>
> Shelley Fisher Fishkin
> *From Fact to Fiction:*
> *Journalism and Imaginative Writing in America*

Experience in journalism helped many men and women of letters to find topics worthy of extended coverage, helped them focus their writing, and provided them with material that had social, political, and economic impact. However, being trained in journalism and moving into fiction writing had its downsides as well, especially for the self-conscious, self-critical, and self-aware writers whose work comprises this study. Although it would be arrogant to suggest that the final answers to ongoing controversies about the increasingly indistinct lines that separate journalism as a profession from literature as art lie in these pages, it would be dishonest and cowardly to avoid raising them.

The issues are, of course, rooted in what constitutes fiction and nonfiction, how to negotiate the borderland between them, what the advantages of nonfiction might be, what the advantages of fiction might be, what liberties (if any) that literary journalists take with the truth, what constitutes the "truth" (and whose truth), how human perception determines narrative, and what literary techniques affecting both structure and content can be employed in writing nonfiction without violating reader expectations and without compromising decisions readers make based on the veracity of what they read.

The space between journalism and literature is considered by many to be an ocean; by others, a river; and by others, merely a rivulet. This study is a celebration of the space between. Texts are slippery; definitions of genre, imprecise. Scholars who struggle with shifting definitions of fiction and nonfiction wrestle with angels.

Chapter 2 of *Settling the Borderland* deals with Edgar Allan Poe, Walt Whitman, Katherine Anne Porter, Eudora Welty, and John Steinbeck, well-known writers in American literature who are too often omitted from studies of literary journalism and who learned much of their craft through the discipline of journalistic writing. In fact, although these authors are included as examples of those who left journalism and made their reputations writing fiction, Steinbeck and Porter never abandoned nonfiction entirely.

In addition to the five writers featured in this study, it is important to acknowledge others who began their professional careers by working for daily newspapers or by working as war correspondents or by using the news of the day to construct essays and short stories, although they may have received more critical attention. For them, too, the differences between fiction and nonfiction, between fiction and journalism, must have been intriguing indeed. The stories of Willa Cather, Stephen Crane, Theodore Dreiser, Ernest Hemingway, Upton Sinclair, Mark Twain, and others are a cautionary tale about writers who experimented with the text and who were in practice—if not in theory as well—reluctant to categorize their narratives. All of them worked as journalists; all of them are best known for their fiction.

As Thomas B. Connery and many of the writers included in *A Sourcebook of American Literary Journalism* know well, news is not a collection of facts, no matter how finely arranged, and newsgathering is not merely the recording of a source's words or the description of chronological events. As noted in the introduction to this study, within human events are meanings, meanings that sometimes propel those involved in them toward other events, or toward a governing philosophy, or into relationship with the characters who drive the action. External events contain images and symbols that participants and observers transform into interior reality. And if the events and people with whom we come into contact transform us, they most assuredly transform the reporters who cover the news.

That the journalist and the writer of fiction are sometimes one and the same person is a concept that lies at the center of *Settling the Borderland,* but it is a notion that troubles those who prefer a cleaner demarcation between fact and fiction. In *From Fact to Fiction: Journalism and Imaginative Writing in Amer-*

ica, Shelley Fisher Fishkin echoes other literary critics who argue that training in journalism contributed to the skills of the writer of fiction: "It forced him to become a precise observer, nurtured in him a respect for fact, and taught him lessons about style that would shape his greatest literary creations. It taught him to be mistrustful of rhetoric, abstractions, hypocrisy, and cant; it taught him to be suspicious of secondhand accounts and to insist on seeing with his own eyes" (4). John McPhee, a prolific literary journalist and environmentalist, goes a step further than Fishkin by affirming the intimate relationship between journalism and fiction. He also reassures those who rely upon journalism to make decisions about the world around them: "Things that are cheap and tawdry in fiction work beautifully in nonfiction because they are *true.* That's why you should be careful not to abridge it, because it's the fundamental power you're dealing with. You arrange it and present it. There's lots of artistry. But you don't make it up" *(The Literary Journalists* 3).

Several characteristics of literary journalism send up red flags for traditional journalists. As noted earlier, for example, not all literary journalists have written for or write for newspapers or magazines; they may employ literary techniques, including stream of consciousness; they may experiment with chronology; they may rename sources, etc. Literary journalism flies in the face of accepted notions of "objectivity." While acknowledging that "all writing, including objective news, reflects a shaping consciousness," Hartsock argues that the difference for literary journalism is "one of degree": "In contrast to narrative literary journalism, objective news reflects an attempt to *deny* a shaping consciousness by means of the pose of objectivity reflected in a distilled and abstracted language. Objective journalism attempts to transcend or elide subjectivity as one contributing means of production" (165). Hartsock explains the development of the concept of objectivity:

> This "objectification" of news is central to demonstrating a modus by which I suggest narrative literary journalism operates. By the "objectification" of news or journalism I mean disengaged journalisms that objectify the world as something different or alien from the viewing subject, namely either that of author or reader. This applies to the evolution in the late nineteenth century of a factual news style that in the twentieth century came to be called objective journalism, and of sensational yellow journalism, which in its own way also objectifies the experience of the world. Indeed, while objective journalism and yellow sensational journalism are often represented as being in opposition to each other, they share a common epistemological problem. (17)

To support his point, Hartsock cites James Agee, who published the notable *Let Us Now Praise Famous Men,* as Agee remembers one of his subjects: "George Gudger is a man, et cetera. But obviously, in the effort to tell of him (by example) as truthfully as I can, I am limited. I know him only so far as I know him, and only in those terms in which I know him; and all of that depends as fully on who I am as on who he is" (x). In this reference, of course, Agee admits that even the creation of character resides in large part in the author's experience of that character and not on an omniscient, objective truth.

The writers featured in this section are representatives of the nineteenth and twentieth centuries, but Richard D. Manning is a twenty-first-century writer facing the demons they faced and intellectualizing the issues they confronted. "I want to tell why I have left behind fourteen years of commitment to daily newspaper journalism to sit here, instead, quiet and unemployed, chasing a new line of words that I hope will illuminate it all. I mean all" (12), writes Manning in "The Other Side." And he is far from alone.

Literary critics are profoundly aware of the borderland in which Cather, Crane, Dreiser, Hemingway, Poe, Porter, Sinclair, Steinbeck, Twain, Welty, Whitman, and others lived and wrote. Their words remind us that the issues are not peripheral to our lives because distinguishing between truth and falsehood, between nonfiction and fiction, and between fact and inexactitude is at the heart of the decisions we make and the communities we build. Gary L. Whitby proudly summarizes the work of Truman Capote by writing: "What glitters most, perhaps, is Capote's remarkable memory for dialogue and scene. The former is rendered so convincingly as to make the reader believe that the author used a tape recorder. He did not" *(Sourcebook* 241). If he did not, how much can we believe his re-creation of scene in *In Cold Blood?* How much weight can we put on the stream of consciousness that pervades the nonfiction novel? How well can we know Perry Smith or Dick Hickock, the unlikely killers of a farm family in Kansas?

The Bible-thumping intensity of the critics who deal with acclaimed writers from the nineteenth and twentieth centuries suggests the importance of the study of this category of literature. Jack A. Nelson's prose, for example, is infused with the energy of Twain's own convictions: "He burns with mining fever like the other early prospectors in Nevada; he exults in owning his own timber tract before burning it down out of carelessness; he imbibes the invigorating life of Virginia City and the madness of speculation in mining stocks; he is aghast at territorial government" *(Sourcebook* 51). Nelson's enthusiasm for his subject matches the enthusiasm of many readers who encounter storytelling that connects fact with the techniques of fiction.

American Literary Giants and Journalism

Readers are captivated by the prose of writers such as Twain, enticed by the intellectual issues, and drawn to the controversies in the narratives themselves. Cather, Crane, Dreiser, Hemingway, Poe, Porter, Sinclair, Steinbeck, Twain, and Whitman have already earned their status as authors of some of the finest American prose and poetry. They are counted as literary journalists only insomuch as Poe and Whitman relied upon news stories to frame their prose and poetry, respectively; as Twain built his reputation as a humorist and was syndicated in American newspapers before publishing his greatest novels; as Hemingway covered the Spanish-American War and drew from his experiences and his news stories to create *For Whom the Bell Tolls;* as Porter recast her years as a reporter for the *Rocky Mountain News* in *Pale Horse, Pale Rider;* and as Steinbeck danced between encounters with real people such as Tom Collins, director of a migrant camp, and fictional people in *The Grapes of Wrath.* Knowing more about their abilities to move among the sometimes arbitrary boundaries of genre will be useful as we deal with each writer and with several generally accepted classics in literary journalism.

The study of those who began their careers in American newsrooms and later made their reputations as writers of fiction must begin with this observation: Women such as Edna Ferber might have had long and profitable careers in journalism, but the prejudice against their doing a "man's job" was palpable. Known today as a novelist, a playwright, and a writer of short stories, Ferber serves as an effective symbol of many others like her.

In her autobiographies, Ferber recounts that she was unable to attend Northwestern University because of her family's financial situation; she opted instead to work at the *Appleton* (Wisconsin) *Daily Crescent,* where no editor had ever hired a woman reporter. Although she did not enjoy writing the society column, a position relegated to women, she worked hard. However, after 18 months, Ferber was fired by a new city editor. She was hired by the *Milwaukee Journal* as a court and police reporter where she was expected to provide a woman's perspective on the news. Forced to leave the *Journal* because of illness, she later applied for a job at the *Chicago Tribune* and was told there were no women reporters.

Ferber's time in journalism differs from that of Willa Cather in two ways: 1) Cather was able to work as a reporter longer than Ferber, largely because of her time at *McClure's,* a well-known muckraking magazine; and 2) Cather never wanted to remain in newspaper work, while Ferber might have done so if she had been afforded the opportunity. For all the authors whose lives are featured here, the borderland between fiction and nonfiction on occasion became indistinguishable. As Giles Fowler writes, the purpose of narratives by reporters and writers of fiction is similar. In an essay about John Steinbeck, Fowler writes:

> Here is evidence, surely, of the true reporter's eye for those telling bits of reality that lend scale and texture to the larger picture. Such an eye belongs also, of course, to the true literary writer, which is one reason we are not surprised when journalist and novelist merge in a single person. *(Sourcebook* 228-29)

Willa Cather

Because several scholars have evaluated Cather's time in journalism and have drawn the important connections between her journalistic career and her writing of fiction, this study will simply introduce her contributions. Surprisingly, given Cather's lack of respect for the hack writing she believed permeated American journalism, in a 1915 interview in the *Lincoln Sunday Star,* Cather is quoted as valuing the real-life experience journalism afforded her: "If I hadn't again grasped the thrills of life, I would have been too literary and academic to ever write anything worthwhile" (Bohlke, *Willa Cather in Person* 15). However,

Cather wrote an obituary about fellow journalist Eugene Field that reflects her negative view of her early experience in journalism:

> Eugene Field was only a journalist. The American newspaper was his task and his curse, as it has been of so many brilliant men. Journalism is the vandalism of literature. It has brought to it endless harm and no real good. It has made an art a trade. The great American newspaper takes in intellect, promise, talent; it gives out only colloquial gossip. No man can write long for any journal in this country without for the most part losing that precious thing called style. Newspapers have no style and want none. (Slote, *Kingdom of Art* 332)

Although it is true that Cather's journalism became a focus of scholarly inquiry only recently, historians and literary critics have been diligent in their scholarship about the Nebraska native. Some of the critics who have conducted in-depth research about Cather and her life in the borderland between fact and fiction are William Curtin, Carolyn Kitch, Pamela C. Laucella, and James Woodress.

It is Woodress who provides the thesis for all four critics: Cather's time in the newspaper industry—although disparaged by herself and some of her peers—was time well spent and contributed to her prose style and to her choice of topics. "When she died in 1947," Woodress writes, "her public was virtually unaware of this foreground as a newspaper and magazine writer, [but] it is the long apprenticeship that led to her mature artistry" (88). Laucella argues similarly when in an unpublished essay she writes that "Cather's journalism clearly reflected an artist in waiting. She embodied not only a talented journalist with her eye for objectivity and detail, but her writings clearly exhibited her potential as an artist" (23).

Curtin, who collected Cather's work from several newspapers and magazines, believes that her journalism allowed her to take on the personas of varieties of people, something he argues makes her fiction more compelling. Curtin's *The World and the Parish* (1893-1902), Volumes I and II, are collections of Cather's work from the *Nebraska State Journal*, the *Lincoln Courier, The Home Monthly*, the *Index of Pittsburgh Life*, and the *Pittsburgh Gazette*. Curtin called Cather "a chameleon journalist who assumes many roles and speaks many voices" (xiii).

In "The Work That Came Before the Art: Willa Cather as Journalist (1893-1912)", Carolyn Kitch discusses Cather's transformation from a journalist to a writer of fiction. Emphasizing the journalism Cather produced, Kitch reminds us that Cather spent two decades as a journalist, working as a newspaper and magazine writer and editor in Lincoln, Pittsburgh, and New York. She worked for five newspapers and four magazines. She was managing editor of *McClure's* from 1908 to 1912. As a junior at the University of Nebraska, Cather began writing for the *Nebraska State Journal*. She wrote nearly 300 articles, many of them about the arts, for the *Journal* and the *Lincoln Courier* during this time.

Cather's commitment to the journalistic enterprise began early. On March 26, 1995, Rhonda Stansberry published an article in the *Omaha Sunday World-*

Herald entitled "Scholars Often Overlook Miss Cather as Journalist." According to files at the *World-Herald,* Cather was introduced to journalism less than a year before she moved to Lincoln to attend college. Charles Cather purchased the *Red Cloud Republican,* and his daughter worked as an editor and business manager, according to a resumé she sent to the *World-Herald* in 1925.

Her commitment to journalism continued into and beyond her college years. For example, one of her professors at the University of Nebraska submitted a paper she wrote on Thomas Carlyle to the *Nebraska State Journal.* Also, Cather contributed to the student magazine, the *Hesperian,* and was literary editor for the *Sombrero,* the college yearbook. Kitch writes that by the time Cather was invited to talk to the women of the Nebraska Press Association, she was well established as a journalist (428).

Living in Pittsburgh from 1896 to 1906, Cather had already begun writing short stories and poetry. She supported herself through journalism. "For the first time she demonstrated her true range in the field," Kitch writes. "She worked as an editor for two publications and a reporter for at least eight. Wanting a break from the demands of daily journalism as well as time to concentrate on her fiction, Cather taught English in a high school for five years, but still managed to freelance newspaper and magazine articles" (429).

Originally, Cather had moved to Pittsburgh to accept the editorship of *The Home Monthly,* a women's magazine. Kitch said she was hired because she was a "hard-working, prolific, eager professional" (429). Cather wrote features and criticism for *The Home Monthly,* the Lincoln newspapers, and a Pittsburgh newspaper.

One of Cather's most significant contributions is her reporting and editing for *McClure's,* one of the most famous and respected publications in American history. In 1903, Cather met S.S. McClure, editor of the muckraking magazine that altered the course of journalism history. In 1908, Cather became managing editor of *McClure's* and would remain there for six years. In a 1921 letter to his wife, McClure wrote that the "best magazine executive I know is Miss Cather" (Lyon, *Success Story* 390). She was a "magazine executive," but she was also invested in journalism that transformed society.

In an article that resembles the muckraking journalism familiar to reporters and editors at *McClure's,* Cather wrote about Homestead, Pennsylvania, a town near Pittsburgh where a strike occurred in 1892. The article followed that strike and a July 1901 steelworkers' strike against the U.S. Steel Corporation. Woodress writes that, ironically, Cather "found social reformers very dull people," although she clearly contributed to activist journalism. "She did not despise the expert investigative reporting that *McClure's* published, but her eye was always on art" (188), Woodress argues.

In addition to her 20-year career in journalism, Cather wrote 12 books of fiction, 10 collections of short stories, six nonfiction works, and a volume of poetry. Cather is best known for *My Antonia, O Pioneers!, the Song of the Lark, One of Ours, A Lost Lady, The Professor's House, My Mortal Enemy, Death Comes for the Archbishop,* and *Lucy Grayheart.* Many of these works rely upon the precise detail and ability to create dialogue that are at the center of good journalistic writing; many also rely upon issues of the time, including immigration and class systems, topics that interested Cather as a reporter and as a writer of fiction.

Like Cather, three men who depended upon their background in journalism for their works of fiction are especially worthy of note. Stephen Crane, Theodore Dreiser, Upton Sinclair, and Ernest Hemingway have been blessed with critical acclaim. Critics have often noted the contributions of their journalistic training, both on the styles they developed and on the topics that interested them.

Stephen Crane

Stephen Crane was the fourteenth child of a pastor who died when Crane was nine. The family was poor, and Crane developed early his identification with and compassion for the impoverished. Issues of class became central to his work, and he wrote about groups of Americans, such as farmers, who were victims of natural forces no matter how hard they toiled. If God existed at all in Crane's world, he was blind to their fate and had no pity for humanity.

Crane began his journalistic career in his teens, writing sketches for a school newspaper. Having dropped out of Syracuse University, he worked for the *New York Tribune,* the *New York Herald,* the *New York Journal,* the *New York Press,* the *New York World,* the *Philadelphia Press,* and the *Newark Daily Advertiser.*

Known primarily for his novel *The Red Badge of Courage*, Crane served as a war correspondent for the *New York Journal* and the *New York World* in Greece and Cuba. He later went to Lincoln, Nebraska, where he met Cather at the *Lincoln State Journal.* "Bitter about his double life as poet and journalist," R.W. Stallman said, Crane wrote "tirades against journalism" *(Stephen Crane* 131). His destiny as a writer of fiction is clear: When he wrote of the drought of July 1894 and the snowstorm of February 1895 for the *State Journal,* Crane said, "The farmers—helpless, with no weapon against this terrible and inscrutable wrath of nature—were spectators at the strangling of their hopes, their ambitions, all that they could look to from their labor." He added: "It was as if upon the massive altar of the earth, their homes and their families were being offered in sacrifice to the wrath of some blind and pitiless deity" (132).

One of his most powerful works, *Maggie: A Girl of the Streets,* focuses on the chaos of life among the poor of New York City. Moral confusion, sadness, and chaos permeate the novel and provide evidence of Crane's place among realists and naturalists of the time. The novel is a tale of the savagery of New York City and the inability of residents to care for one another. Physical violence occurs throughout *Maggie: A Girl of the Streets,* and the brutal realism in the 19 vignettes in the novel stunned readers. The human savagery is evident when Jimmie hits Maggie, the father kicks Jimmie, and the mother fights with the father. The novel is full of descriptions of violence that employ animal images.

According to Michael Robertson, author of *Stephen Crane, Journalism, and the Making of Modern American Literature,* the connection between Crane's journalism and *Maggie* is worthy of careful analysis: "*Maggie* is indeed related to Crane's early journalism, but the relation is more complex than early reviewers suggested. The myth of the reporter-artist implies a simple progression from observation to journalism to fiction. In addition, the myth places fiction at the top of the immutable literary hierarchy, with journalism below, serving as a stepping-stone to higher things" (79). However, Robertson argues that the style of writing in Crane's journalism has similarities to his writing in *Maggie:*

> *Maggie* owes nothing directly to Crane's New York City newspaper sketches, which he wrote after drafting the novel. However, this is not to say that Crane's first novel has nothing in common with his journalism. *Maggie* reflects the same thematic and stylistic preoccupations evident in Crane's early newspaper writing about Sullivan County and the New Jersey shore. Just as Crane's *New-York Tribune* articles avoid the tongue clucking about overly daring bathing suits or backroom gambling that was common in resort news, *Maggie* lacks the condemnation of drink, violence, and sexual misconduct that were standard in slum literature. (78)

Stephen Crane, Journalism, and the Making of Modern American Literature is the most comprehensive study of Crane as a reporter to date. In it, Robertson discusses Crane's early journalism, his stories about New York, his travel journalism, and his war reporting. The final chapter addresses Crane's influence on Theodore Dreiser and Ernest Hemingway. Crane's contributions to journalism and literature ended when he died in 1900 of tuberculosis.

In "Stephen Crane's New York City Journalism and the Oft-Told Tale" that preceded Robertson's book about Crane, Robertson suggests that Crane's New York articles were based on actual events and followed the conventions of newspaper features:

> A study of those conventions undermines the view of Stephen Crane as creative artist hampered by journalistic insistence on "bare facts." The newspaper sketch was a flexible form that borrowed from the conventions of both news reporting and fiction. The sketch arose early in American journalism, but it became a widely popular form in the 1880s, with the development of Sunday newspaper feature sections. Sketches from the 1880s and 1890s are generally free of proper nouns specifying an exact location, specific persons, or a definite time. Both journalists and readers of the era were less concerned with verifiable facts than with essential verities of urban life that, they believed, could best be approached through a portrayal of the typical. ("Stephen Crane's New York City Journalism" 10)

Robertson undercuts what he describes as a "school-and-cemetery" story about the newspaper and the novel. He writes:

> There's an oft-told tale about the relationship between journalism and literature in the late-nineteenth and twentieth centuries that goes like this: Starting in the

1890s, metropolitan newspapers became a training ground for would-be novelists. On assignment in the city streets, ambitious young writers encountered a gritty and varied urban reality that served as a source of literary material, while in the newsroom crusty editors with green eyeshades and blue pencils taught writers to strip the fat off their style and write a crisp prose well-suited to the modern novel. However, the story continues, writers had to know when to get out of journalism. Too long a stint on a newspaper could destroy a writer's creativity, turn him into a hack unable to produce anything besides newspaper copy. The newspaper was a school for novelists, the story tells us, but it was also a cemetery for talent that stayed too long. ("Stephen Crane's New York City Journalism" 7)

In addition to the writers highlighted in this section and in Chapter 2 of *Settling the Borderland,* Robertson also lists Ambrose Bierce, James M. Cain, William Kennedy, Sinclair Lewis, Jack London, and Frank Norris as "important modern novelists who worked as reporters" ("Stephen Crane's New York City Journalism" 8). Unsurprisingly, one of those whom he also lists is Theodore Dreiser.

Theodore Dreiser

Like Crane, Theodore Dreiser was a naturalist and realist, a writer who believed that human behavior is predominantly determined by social forces, not free will. Born in poverty in Terre Haute, Indiana, in 1871, Dreiser struggled throughout his life to support his writing.

Dreiser worked for newspapers in Chicago (the *Chicago Daily Globe),* Pittsburgh (the *Pittsburgh Dispatch),* and St. Louis *(St. Louis Globe-Democrat).* He became a feature editor and the editor of a New York music magazine and a women's magazine. He was also a reporter for the *New York World. Theodore Dreiser's "Heard in the Corridors": Articles and Related Writings,* edited by T.D. Nostwich, is a compelling collection of his work during this time period.

Best known for his novels *Sister Carrie* and *An American Tragedy,* Dreiser focused on the cracks in the American dream. In both novels, Dreiser wrote about the sweat shops at the beginning of the Industrial Revolution. The robbery in *Sister Carrie* is based on a feature article Dreiser wrote; the point of view relies upon his interviews with real people; the chapter titles could be headlines in a daily newspaper. In fact, the entire novel reads as though it were a series of feature articles.

Sister Carrie is of particular interest to those invested in the connection between journalism and literature in Dreiser's work. During the time Dreiser spent in metropolitan centers, Chicago was growing by 50,000 per year and New York City struggled with an influx of immigrants and general overpopulation, both of which led to disease and unemployment. In *Sister Carrie,* Dreiser explores issues of class and the ways in which what one has predicts how one will be treated. He is also interested in how one's character is revealed by one's generosity or one's stinginess.

Having been a dishwasher, a busboy, a shipping clerk, a bill collector and a truck driver, Dreiser knew poverty. His autobiography, entitled *Newspaper Days,* relates his struggle to make enough money to write. Fishkin cites Dreiser's early and incorrect opinion about journalists of his time and his belief that they were famous and wealthy:

> I [thought of] reporters and newspaper men generally as receiving fabulous salaries, being sent on the most urgent and interesting missions. I think I confused, inextricably, reporters with ambassadors and prominent men generally. Their lives were laid among great people, the rich and famous, the powerful; and because of their position and facility of expression and mental force they were received everywhere as equals. Think of me, new, young, poor, being received in that way! (87; *Newspaper Days* 4)

Once again, the connection between a journalist's time in the newspaper industry and a novelist's reliance upon events of the day is obvious. Two critics are particularly astute in their commentary on Dreiser. Fishkin writes: "The seeds of his finest works of fiction were gathered during the twenty years Dreiser spent trafficking in the world of fact" (90). The other critic, Marilyn Ann Moss, provides a riveting first sentence in an essay about Dreiser: "Theodore Dreiser's journalistic writing was a configuration of factual data that ultimately coalesced into a personal mythos — a tale of how a young journalist might invent himself as a spokesman for American lives at the turn of the century" *(Sourcebook* 143).

Upton Sinclair

Like Crane and Dreiser, Upton Sinclair was an activist and former newspaper reporter. Born in Baltimore to an alcoholic father and a mother who came from a wealthy Southern family, Sinclair, too, would be obsessed with class differences in his life and work.

Sinclair published 90 books, pamphlets, and letters, although he is best known for *The Jungle.* Although *The Jungle* is fiction, it is based upon the weeks he spent working in a Chicago meatpacking plant and upon the interviews he conducted with immigrants while there.

Sinclair spoke out in favor of miners, he favored women's rights, he started the California branch of the American Civil Liberties Union, and he ran for governor of California in 1934 on the platform "End Poverty in California!" His importance in this study is due to his stories that appeared in *Appeal to Reason,* a Kansas weekly, and to his publication of *The Jungle.*

In 1900, there was no minimum wage, no maximum number of working hours, no employer liability, no food and drug laws, no votes for women, no education on birth control and venereal disease, few unions, no health insurance, no social security, and no unemployment compensation. Known as an ethnographer of the working poor, Sinclair challenged Americans to change the system and to address these wrongs.

Sinclair continues to draw readers. High school students remain enthusiastic about *The Jungle,* and historians, sociologists, and literary critics teach the novel in their college classes. The book has been called "literary journalism," a "journalistic novel," and other phrases familiar to those interested in the genre. Sinclair wrote the book when he was 26, and it was serialized in *Appeal to Reason.* The story he told was so graphic and so powerful that President Theodore Roosevelt invited Sinclair to the White House to verify his facts. Doubleday sent an attorney to confirm that conditions in the meatpacking plants were as bad as Sinclair described them, and, according to several critics, the attorney found the conditions to be worse. The publication of the novel about Jurgis Rudkus, a strong Lithuanian immigrant who could not break the cycle of poverty, led to the 1906 Pure Food and Drug Act, to the Meat Inspection Act, and to other social and economic reforms.

Recently, Christopher Phelps, associate professor of history at the Ohio State University at Mansfield, published a piece in *The Chronicle of Higher Education* entitled "How Should We Teach *The Jungle?*" His answer is that the novel is as much reportage as literature and that *The Jungle* should be taught as journalism: "It ought to be possible to consider *The Jungle* as both a transcription of social life and a work of literary imagination, as both reportage and social criticism" (B12). Arguing that *The Jungle* is "primarily a sympathetic sketch of the foreign born, those fabled 'masses yearning to breathe free' that Americans welcome in our poetry and disdain in the breach" (B10), Phelps writes:

> After all, *The Jungle* is as much reportage as literature. Sinclair's searing, graphic revelations were based on close observation. He spoke to workers and infiltrated the giant packinghouses, carrying a lunch pail in hand to make it seem he belonged there. Although a work of fiction, *The Jungle* is often classified as "muckraking," exposé journalism that blends revealed fact with moral indignation in the pursuit of social reform. (B10)

Phelps suggests that *The Jungle* can be considered allegory and that the tale of an immigrant family and the Chicago meatpacking industry can enhance discussion among students about the power of the corporation and the ways in which current meatpacking plants also rely upon people of color: "If, however, we consider Jurgis [Rudkus] a literary personification of the whole immigrant working class, then *The Jungle* illuminates social history" (B12). This argument, of course, foreshadows a discussion of the allegorical significance of literary journalism, which may be its strongest characteristic and may be what sets it apart most dramatically from everyday reporting and writing.

The Jungle covers the same time period as *Sister Carrie;* includes similar images of savagery and chaos; introduces characters who also are more symbolic than they are individualized; provides characters who are strong and who have a powerful survival instinct but who, like those in *Sister Carrie,* are nevertheless crushed by the social, political, and economic system; covers labor strikes like those in Dreiser's novel; and deals with child abuse, as does Dreiser.

Although Cather, Crane, Dreiser, and Sinclair shared muckraking, or the uncovering of social and political corruption, as the reason and focus for their writing, the next author, too, was concerned with similar issues that affected U.S. and international communities. One of the most famous and critically acclaimed former journalists who made his reputation writing fiction is Ernest Hemingway. A character in many of his novels, Hemingway was as colorful personally as he was talented professionally. Although he is mentioned in this study because of the literary giant he was and is, much has been written about his reliance upon journalism; therefore, the tribute that follows is brief and representative, not detailed and comprehensive.

Ernest Hemingway

Ernest Hemingway is one of the literary journalists who began his career in American newsrooms before becoming stifled by news styles and alienated by newsgathering practices. In spite of his concerns about newsgathering—concerns echoed by Cather, Crane, Dreiser, and others—Hemingway also respected what he learned during his time as a journalist. Two of the most important lessons include the bare-bones style that is so characteristic of his work and his obsession with contemporary issues of the day. In a 1935 article in *Esquire,* Hemingway argued vehemently for the importance of immediacy in writing:

> If it was reporting they would not remember it. When you describe something that has happened that day the timeliness makes people see it in their own imaginations. A month later that element of time is gone and your account would be flat and they would not see it in their minds or remember it. But if you make it up instead of describe it you can make it round and whole and solid and give it life. You create it, for good or bad. It is made; not described. It is just as true as the extent of your ability to make it and knowledge you put into it. (21)

Hemingway was the second of six children born into a doctor's family in Oak Park, Illinois, in an upper-middle class suburb. Exposed to literary classics from a young age, Hemingway was quick to express an interest in writing and in high school worked for the school newspaper and literary magazine. His foray into journalism is well known, both because of the wealth of critical material on his life and work and because of his own semi-autobiographical references in some of his best novels, including *The Sun Also Rises* and *For Whom the Bell Tolls.*

After Hemingway graduated from high school in 1916, he began his career as a reporter with the *Kansas City Star,* where he worked for five months. In 1918, he went overseas as a volunteer ambulance driver for the Red Cross during World War I. Of Hemingway, biographer Carlos Baker writes, "Melville called the sea his Harvard and his Yale. Hemingway's college . . . was the continent of Europe" (3). Severely wounded by mortar fragments, Hemingway endured a painful recovery and then in 1921 found work as a European correspondent for the *Toronto Star.*

It was then that Hemingway moved to Paris and became friends with Gertrude Stein, F. Scott Fitzgerald, Sherwood Anderson, and Ezra Pound. Having covered the Spanish Civil War in 1936 for the North American Newspaper Alliance, Hemingway used what he learned as the basis for his novel *For Whom the Bell Tolls*. (Paramount offered Hemingway $100,000 for the movie rights, and the film starred Gary Cooper as Robert Jordan and Ingrid Bergman as Maria.)

After the 1926 success of his first major novel, *The Sun Also Rises*, Hemingway focused on fiction, producing *Death in the Afternoon*, *The Green Hills of Africa*, *To Have and Have Not*, *Across the River and into the Trees*, *The Old Man and the Sea*, and other books. He won the Nobel Prize for Literature in 1954.

Despite his role in the development of the realistic American novel, Hemingway continued writing for magazines all his life, contributing both journalistic dispatches and articles to *Collier's, Cosmopolitan, Esquire, Look,* and other publications. He remains one of the shining examples of how effective journalism and an understanding of its role and purpose can inform one's fiction.

Hemingway believed that if death is the end of human life, then life takes on a sense of urgency and intensity. He believed in a code of honor, arguing that one's essential nature surfaces in a time of crisis. Hemingway's literary hero has a mission, is loyal to others, is skilled in his work, and is connected deeply and emotionally to others.

Since an important aspect of Hemingway's belief system is that heroism is defined by courage under pressure, it is no surprise that after a series of accidents and illnesses that began to debilitate him, he would kill himself in 1961. It is unlikely that Hemingway could imagine during his lifetime the impact his work would have on the future of American arts and letters.

Allegory and Literary Journalism

Hemingway and other giants of American literature believed in the power of writing to alter the world around them, they developed characters and themes that challenged the preconceptions of their readers, and they often struggled to make a living in order to pursue their art. One of the reasons literary journalism has become such a compelling and popular genre involves its headlong rush into phenomenological inquiry. Like those who chose to leave journalism and devote their lives to fiction, practitioners of literary journalism overwhelmingly consider their mission to be a search for meaning, for the deeper truth.

Even at the risk of being accused of didacticism, literary journalists often employ allegory, although it is doubtful that they sit at their computers and seek to employ symbols and allegorical systems as manipulative tools or as artifice. Two articles illustrate the importance of allegory in contemporary newsgathering; however, they are only the tip of the iceberg. Scholars of American literature expect writers of fiction to employ symbolism and metaphor liberally; less expected is a journalist's devotion to telling the stories of ordinary people who find themselves in extraordinary circumstances. Their lives take on a significance not unlike the lives of fictional characters in work by Cather, Crane, Dreiser, Sinclair, and Hemingway.

John Hellman argues that allegory is "a narrative made to develop some philosophical view" (10). While this may not always be the case, it is certainly true of literary journalists, who seek phenomenological significance and a higher truth and who devote themselves to conveying a kind of mythopoetic reality to readers. The language and techniques of literary journalism are those of literature, including narration, dialogue, description, stream of consciousness, and allegory.

The first article that illustrates the importance of an extended allegorical system in news writing is a 1994 article entitled "The Killer in the Next Tent" by Roger Rosenblatt. The article deals with what the author calls the "surreal horror of the Rwanda refugees," refugees who are Tutsis and Hutus and who are forced to reside in the same camps. At the time Rosenblatt wrote his story, the Tutsi guerrillas of the Rwandan Patriotic Front had been fighting the Hutu government of Rwanda since 1990. Since the fifteenth century, Hutu tribespeople were dominated by the Tutsis, their feudal rulers. When the League of Nations turned over the country to Belgium in 1919, the Tutsis were the favored class, in part because they more closely resembled Europeans. But in 1959, 100,000 Tutsis were killed and another 200,000 forced to flee. Soon after, Belgium turned the country over to the Hutus.

Rwanda gained independence in 1962, but by 1973 the country was taken over by a military coup. By 1990, Tutsi rebels and Ugandans moved into Rwanda to remove the government. Of the raw violence that ensured, Rosenblatt writes: "Under certain circumstances, not always predictable, people will do anything to one another. Going by the descriptions of events in Rwanda, it is doubtful that the Hutu killers felt any twinge of conscience as they went about their torturing and murdering. The same is true of Americans, Europeans and Asians when they have been caught up in their own spasms of depravity" (41).

Without announcing that he has moved into allegorical representation, Rosenblatt observes that one boy "saunters by wearing a San Francisco 49ers hat and a Nintendo T-shirt" (44). The symbol could refer to the political dominance of the United States, could testify to the importance of American popular culture abroad, could highlight children affected by the civil war, etc.

What Rosenblatt calls the "mixture of normal life and the presence of evil" (46) is most stunningly captured by a moment similar to a scene in George Orwell's journalistic short story "Shooting an Elephant." Rosenblatt writes compellingly (and horrifyingly) about the brutality of a crowd that encounters an African antelope that has been turned loose. The children "squeal with delight" and the women "begin to trill in a half-shriek" as they arm themselves with machetes:

> The waterbuck walks slowly at first in its normal dumb lope. Then, sensing danger, it quickens its pace to an awkward trot. A boy brings his machete down hard in its side. There is cheering. The animal bleats and runs uphill, its great body wobbling like a water bed, its horns thrust high in the air. Its eyes

show white and terror. It moves as fast as it can now. But the crowd engulfs it—50, 60 people—hacking again and again at its rump, its legs and back, until the accumulation of the blows cuts the animal in half. Then the crowd hacks at the two separate halves. They cut off the hooves, then the head. The trilling grows louder, then stops.

Now the pieces of the animal lie scattered on the road, wet with blood. Several hands grab hungrily at each piece, and there is nearly a fight. The people seem inches away from turning their machetes on one another but they do not. And no sooner has this moment occurred than it passes. The whole event, from the loosing of the waterbuck to the division of its body, has taken but half a minute. In a few more seconds, the pieces are gone and the people are back at their tasks. Only the bloodstains on the road testify to what happened here, and the rain will soon wash them away. (47)

This grisly event is Rosenblatt's parable about the mindless violence that lies at the root of the civil war and in the heart of men, women, and children. Killing a sensitive creature with such brutality becomes the symbol of war itself, and after the short narrative, Rosenblatt's tale ends. What else is there to say about inhumanity and cruelty?

The second story appeared in *Newsweek* April 15, 2002. On the cover of the magazine are two young women, Ayat al-Akhras and Rachel Levy, one a Palestinian suicide bomber and the other an Israeli casualty. The reader learns that Ayat al-Akhras, 18, secretly joined a martyr's brigade. Levy, 17, was apolitical and is said to have "shrugged off the risk of suicide bombings" (18). Relying upon symbolism, author Joshua Hammer writes the following introductory paragraph:

It was a typical Friday afternoon in the Kiryat Hayovel neighborhood of southern Jerusalem. At the Supersol market, the Sabbath rush was underway; shoppers pushed their carts past shelves stripped bare of bread and matzos for the weeklong Passover holiday. A line had formed at the delicatessen counter in the back, where Sivan Peretz wrapped chicken breasts and salmon steaks and made small talk with his customers. A middle-aged security guard stood poised inside the supermarket entrance, carefully searching bags. At 1:49 p.m., 17-year-old Rachel Levy—petite, with flowing hair and a girlish gap between her teeth—stepped off the bus from her nearby apartment block and strolled toward the market on a quick trip to buy red pepper and herbs for a fish dinner with her mother and two brothers. At the same moment, another girl—strikingly attractive with intense hazel eyes—walked toward the store's glass double doors. The teenagers met at the entrance, brushing past each other as the guard reached out to grab the hazel-eyed girl, whose outfit may have aroused suspicion. "Wait!" the guard cried. A split second later, a powerful explosion tore through the supermarket, gutting shelves and sending bodies flying. When the smoke cleared and the screaming stopped, the two teenage girls and the guard lay dead, three more victims of the madness of martyrdom. (18-20)

On the pages with this compressed narrative of senseless death are the photographs of suicide bombers and their victims. Editors included with an inset the following information: "Suicide bombings are now supported by 80 percent of the Palestinian population. At left, 20 of the 66 young Palestinian men and women who have blown themselves up since September 2000. At right, 150 of the 170 Israelis who died in the wave of bombings" (20). Staggering as the numbers might be, the story of al-Akhras and Levy is more powerful, more compelling, more focused, and infinitely more tragic than the numbers alone. By the end of the article, the readers know al-Akhras and Levy and their families and friends. Their tragedy is not soon to be forgotten.

Part of the reason the story of al-Akhras and Levy is so compelling is its reliance upon the two central, tragic figures as representative. Their role in this particular horrific story of war suggests the power of fable, parable, and allegorical tale. In *Settling the Borderland,* at least three women literary journalists—Joan Didion, Sara Davidson, and Susan Orlean—qualify for serious critical attention, not only as writers of nonfiction but as allegorists. Like literary journalism, allegory is in disrepute in some academic circles because, I would argue, it is misunderstood and often misdefined.

As noted in the introduction, literary journalists dance along the border between nonfiction and fiction, provide the context often missing in straight news stories, and highlight the role of perception, vantage point, and authorial voice in newsgathering. Literary journalists also acknowledge their humanity, their biases, and their concern about particular issues in their work. They immerse themselves in places they describe; they shadow the people they portray. In addition—perhaps as important as their challenge to the myth of objectivity—they remind us that the life of a "common" person engaged in an uncommon event can be the most compelling story of all. Finally, like the fictional figures in John Bunyan's allegory *Pilgrim's Progress,* a literary journalist's characters may be both flesh and blood and grounded in place and time and still be richly representative and suggestive. *Settling the Borderland: Other Voices in Literary Journalism* relies heavily upon the work of numerous literary critics and journalism scholars, none more than John C. Hartsock and Norman Sims, whose concept of the "borderlands between fact and fiction" (v) has fueled this and many other studies that followed *Literary Journalism in the Twentieth Century.* As noted earlier the study resists what Hartsock calls "critical closure" and relies upon a series of questions introduced by those who have just begun to ask the important questions about the definitions, characteristics, contributions, and future of studies in literary journalism.

Literary journalism is often allegorical in the sense that it makes tangible an extended symbolic system. In "The Politics of The New Journalism," John J. Pauly suggests that literary journalism helped to resurrect the "romantic vision of the writer" (119). Pauly argues that two of the strengths of literary journalism are its attack on establishment journalism's "fact-fetish" (121) and its revelation that the "truth of all writing is a matter for social negotiation" (122). Like poet William Carlos Williams—who wrote that "it is difficult/ to get the news from poems,/ yet men die miserably every day/ for lack/ of what is found there" *(Asphodel, That Greeny Flower and Other Love Poems* 19)—Pauly allows writers of nonfiction their place in a literary tradition that explores the depths and heights of human experience.

   What is found in poetry, as Pauly and Williams both understand, of course, is an acknowledgement of the complexity of life and human society and a vivid and lyrical language with which to communicate it. In an article entitled "Historical Perspective on the New Journalism," Joseph Webb employs the term "Romantic Reporter" in his discussion of literary journalists and their focus on "internal, rather than external, human processes" *(Sourcebook* 17), obviously suggesting that literary journalists aspire to a purpose higher than entertainment or even the dissemination of facts in their work; he also may be suggesting that the language used by literary journalists approaches poetry.

   In *Fables of Fact: The New Journalism as New Fiction,* Hellman introduces the concept of allegory. He argues that New Journalists and contemporary fiction writers share "an emphasis upon the perceiving consciousness as a transforming power, and a desire to avoid the distortion caused by an attempt to disguise that power" (13). To that end, according to Hellman, literary journalists frame narratives with forewords, afterwords, and other devices; employ a self-conscious, sometimes "highly obtrusive narrator" (13); create an episodic structure; emphasize allegorical and mythic patterns; employ parody and satire; and place philosophical and social concerns at the center of their work.

   In summary, news is not a collection of facts, no matter how finely arranged, and newsgathering is not merely the recording of a source's words or chronological events. As noted earlier, within human events are meanings, meanings that sometimes propel those involved in them toward other events, or toward a governing philosophy, or into relationship with others in a particular community. External events contain images and symbols that participants and observers may transform into interior reality—into a kind of allegory.

   Literary scholars usually agree that allegory is extended metaphor; that it equates persons and actions with meanings that lie outside the text; that characters often are personifications; that events and settings may be historical or fictitious. What may be lost, however, is that allegory operates as much through tension and concealment as through equations and correspondences. Allegory is born when one recognizes the limits of realism. When writers have set out on a metaphysical quest, when their meaning lies beyond the familiar, common, recognizable patterns of reality, they move into allegory.

   And finally, Hartsock, too, suggests that the result of what he calls "narrative journalism" was "social or cultural allegory, with potential meanings beyond the literal in the broadest sense of allegory's meaning. Largely, although not exclusively, that allegory is about embracing an understanding of the social or cultural Other" (22). Speaking broadly, Hartsock writes that classics of literary journalism such as *In Cold Blood* by Truman Capote and *Executioner's Song* by Norman Mailer might be considered "allegories about the dark side of the American experience" (78). He draws this conclusion because of "their attempts to understand the subjectivities of convicted murderers" (78) in a new and dramatic way.

   Allegory has been disparaged as a too-blatant system of correspondences that reduces the mysterious and profound to the concrete and simplistic. However, by studying the origin of allegory in American literature, one soon discovers that allegory is not reductive but expansive. Allegory does not provide tidy systems, although we may speak of an "allegorical system"; rather, it is the product of oppositions and tensions one must somehow hold in balance. By understanding this, we begin to confront the violence or conflict inherent in allegory.

Allegory has rich symbolic potential. When a writer such as Franz Kafka or Jorge Luis Borges changes men into insects or sets up hopelessly forking paths, respectively, he has stepped onto a plane that defies realism—has tapped into what the Transcendentalists knew as the unified world of Spirit behind the "thing." When one creates allegory—whether as a writer or reader—one moves into the realm of faith.

Yet one must not necessarily read for the moral or message within allegory—or even parable—for allegory points primarily to itself. Allegory builds upon contradiction and surprising reversals; through its employment of symbols, its significance approaches that of myth. As Angus Fletcher notes, allegories are not "dull systems" but "symbolic power struggles" (23). Allegories point both toward and away from themselves; they often point outside plot and character to a higher truth. To salvage allegory from the wastebin of second-rate fictional method, one must recognize that allegory can be nothing if not didactic. According to Fletcher, allegory "allows for instruction, for rationalizing, for categorizing and codifying, for casting spells. To conclude, allegories are the natural mirrors of ideology" (368).

Although critics have been loathe to discuss news as allegory—in part because such a discussion suggests that news has a fictive element—they have addressed in great depth the role of mythology in newsgathering and news reporting. In fact, at least one issue of *Journalism and Mass Communication Quarterly* has been devoted to the topic. In the special issue, Jack Lule, who has been chair of the department of journalism and communication at Lehigh University, summarizes the role of myth in American culture by saying that "myth has provided the stories that make sense of a society, for a society" (276) and that "myth is essential social narrative" (277). He also highlights the role of myth in news by connecting mythology with storytelling and alluding to the history of news ("with roots in drama, folktale, and myth") until it was reconceptualized in the late nineteenth century to be "objective and scientific" rather than "dramatic and mythic" (277).

Certainly, allegory and mythology are closely related, although allegory is more didactic and less universal. Both derive from a society's need for stories that explain the inexplicable; both rely upon symbols for their impact and cohesiveness; and both have a role in nonfiction, a genre that purports to be "true" while acknowledging its absolute reliance on the point of view of the storyteller.

At the center of many successful allegories is the quest. Hartsock discusses authors whose "mock heroic in the picaresque tradition" leads the readers on a long pilgrimage in which they identify with the hero or anti-hero. At the end of many examples of literary journalism that incorporate a journey, however, the "American dream is found to be empty" (163). In *The Orchid Thief,* Susan Orlean departs on a literal quest through the swamps of Florida in search of a ghost orchid; on a symbolic level, she and those who people her nonfiction novel are on a quest for something more ephemeral than even the rare orchid. In *Loose Change*, Sara Davidson writes a memoir of friendship, betrayal, and change at Berkeley in the 1960s, hoping, it would seem, to understand an entire generation by understanding herself and her two closest friends. In "Some Dreamers of the Golden Dream" and other essays in *Slouching Towards Bethlehem,* Joan Didion sets out on a journey to understand everything from middle-class America to the children of the 1960s. Like Rosenblatt's "The Killer in the Next Tent" and Joshua Hammer's tale of suicide bombers and their victims, these nonfiction novels and collections of essays depend upon extended symbolic systems for their impact.

Selected Classics of Literary Journalism

Although this section of Chapter 1 is essential because theory is nothing without examples, it merits a significant disclaimer. The classics of literary journalism listed by readers and critics inevitably and unsurprisingly differ widely. For example, Judith Paterson, who teaches literary journalism at the University of Maryland, published an article entitled "Literary Journalism's Twelve Best." In it, she lists (in order of publication date) *Homage to Catalonia* by George Orwell (1938), *Let Us Now Praise Famous Men* by James Agee (1941), *How to Cook a Wolf* by M.F.K. Fisher (1942), *In Cold Blood* by Truman Capote (1965), *Slouching Towards Bethlehem* by Joan Didion (1968), *Fame and Obscurity* by Gay Talese (1970), *Pilgrim at Tinker Creek* by Annie Dillard (1974), *Winners and Losers* by Gloria Emerson (1976), *The Right Stuff* by Tom Wolfe (1979), *Russian Journal* by Andrea Lee (1981), *House* by Tracy Kidder (1985), and *Maus: A Survivor's Tale* by Art Spiegelman (1986). Requesting course reading lists from David Abrahamson, Tom Connery, Norm Sims, and others would reveal, no doubt, wide discrepancies in the list of "best" works in literary journalism.

Settling the Borderland is devoted both to women literary journalists and to men who are less recognized as practitioners in the field. While it includes many of the works selected by Paterson and others, it focuses here on the works that illustrate ideas central to the thesis of *Settling the Borderland.* These works are representative of the genre, contain allegorical significance, illustrate the use of fictional techniques in describing actual events and real people, and provide enough range to illustrate the width and breadth of the field.

Chapter 3 will introduce the work of three women literary journalists, Joan Didion, Sara Davidson, and Susan Orlean. Although they have worked as journalists in the tradition of Cather, Crane, Dreiser, Sinclair, Twain, and others, they are known primarily as writers of nonfiction, although, certainly, Joan Didion has several novels to her credit. Because they perceive themselves as journalists and boast formidable interviewing and researching skills, their challenges differ from those who opted to move into a career writing fiction. These challenges lie at the heart of the controversies surrounding literary journalism.

One of the controversies involves the relationship of a journalist to his or her source. Given the personal nature of the extended relationships involved in literary journalism, this controversy is no small matter. *The Journalist and the Murderer* by Janet Malcolm raises important questions about the relationship between a journalist and her or his source; however, what is important about Malcolm's perspective in this chapter appears much later in her book when she explores the differences between literature and journalism, setting up a response to the question: "Why should the writer in one genre enjoy more privileges than the writer in the other?":

> The answer is: because the writer of fiction is entitled to more privileges. He is master of his own house and may do what he likes in it; he may even tear it down if he is so inclined . . . But the writer of nonfiction is only a renter, who must abide by the conditions of his lease, which stipulates that he leave the house—and its name is Actuality—as he found it. He may bring in his own furniture and arrange it as he likes (the so-called New Journalism is about the arrangement of furniture), and he may play his radio quietly. But he must not disturb the house's fundamental structure or tamper with any of its architectural features. The writer of nonfiction is under contract to the reader to limit himself to events that actually occurred and to characters who have counterparts in real life, and he may not embellish the truth about these events or these characters. (153)

Relationships between reporters and sources must be endlessly negotiated and renegotiated. Alexandra Fuller, author of the award-winning *Don't Let's Go to the Dogs Tonight*, writes in *Scribbling the Cat: Travels with an African Soldier* about the difficulty of maintaining one's perspective on a source, especially when that source is vulnerable and especially when immersion in the story requires travel and near-constant contact. After describing a journey into a soldier's personal heart of darkness, she writes:

> I had shaken loose the ghosts of K's past and he had allowed me into the deepest corners of his closet, not because I am a writer and I wanted to tell his story, but because he had believed himself in love with me and because he had believed that in some very specific way I belonged to him. And in return, I had listened to every word that K had spoken and watched the nuance of his every move, not because I was in love with him, but because I had believed that I wanted to write him into dry pages. It had been an idea based on a lie and on a hope neither of us could fulfill. It had been a broken contract from the start. (238)

Literary journalists who blend the event-oriented aspects of journalism with the techniques of fiction writers and with revolutionary progressivism have transformed nonfiction and blurred many of the lines Malcolm and Fuller delineate. In *Fables of Fact*, Hellman comments on the work of Michael Herr, Norman Mailer, Hunter S. Thompson, and Tom Wolfe. The beginning of the explosion of literary journalism in America, Hellman believes, was in 1965 with the publication of Tom Wolfe's *Kandy-Kolored Tangerine-Flake Streamline Baby* and Truman Capote's *In Cold Blood*. Before 1965, though, the American public also celebrated Norman Mailer, who wrote about John F. Kennedy and a Democratic Convention; Hunter S. Thompson, who published a piece on the Hell's Angels in *The Nation;* Jimmy Breslin, Joan Didion, and Gay Talese, who challenged the status quo in their reporting; and other "New Journalists."

This chapter briefly introduces four figures who are in their own ways larger than life and who have written books that are considered by many to be the best literary journalism has to offer. They are John Berendt, Truman Capote, Joan Didion, and Tom Wolfe. At the time of this study, Berendt, Didion, and Wolfe are alive and remain productive writers. Although Didion's work will be examined in detail in Chapter 3, it is here that we will introduce her most recent book *The Year of Magical Thinking,* which also became a Broadway play. *The Year of Magical Thinking* is testament to Didion's ability to write a memoir about grief that resonates powerfully with the American public. Because Hellman and others have emphasized work by men in literary journalism such as Norman Mailer and Hunter S. Thompson, their contribution to literary journalism is here acknowledged but not explicated. An exception is Truman Capote, who has received rich critical attention but who is essential to this study, having written what is often considered the first nonfiction novel.

What follows is, of course, to some extent an arbitrary list of writers. For example, how does one omit Jon Krakauer's *Into the Wild,* the provocative nonfiction novel about Chris McCandless ("Alexander Supertramp"); *Into Thin Air,* which deals with an ill-fated 1996 Mount Everest expedition; and *Under the Banner of Heaven,* which deals with the Church of Jesus Christ of Latter-Day Saints? Surely, there are not merely four classics of American literary journalism; as with the rest of this book, though, there are, in fact, representative texts that deserve particular attention and that serve as metaphors for equally notable works.

Truman Capote

One of the first generally acknowledged literary journalists who penned an American classic is Truman Capote. In spite of the diversity of selections in the "best" of literary journalism category, Capote is rarely omitted from anyone's list, partly because he believed *In Cold Blood* was the first novel in a new genre of nonfiction. The reasons for his popular appeal are as much a result of who he was as what he produced. In an obituary published in *Newsweek* in 1984, Jack Kroll writes of Capote:

> Most people who knew his name probably thought of him as some odd little gadfly among the glitterati, flitting from party to party, from talk show to talk show, telling faintly outrageous tales in that Little Lord Fauntleroy voice and forever feuding with Norman Mailer and Gore Vidal. It's doubtful that Capote ever prayed to be thought of in that way. If he prayed at all, it was certainly to be a true artist, a man who could move others with his vision of the world. And at his best that's what he was. In "Other Voices, Other Rooms," the book that made him famous at 23, in "Breakfast at Tiffany's" and in his best

stories and journalism, he produced a unique verbal music, a blend of shrewd-
ness and sentimentality that revealed human beings as hybrids both baroque
and banal. (69)

James Wolcott writes similarly of the young Capote in his *Vanity Fair* article
published in 1997. In the article "The Truman Show," he writes:

> Being the center of attention at least gave him a fixed position. When Ca-
> pote was in the second grade, he learned that he would be leaving Alabama to
> live up North with his mother. "He said he wanted to throw a party so grand
> that everybody would remember him," Jennings Faulk Carter, a cousin, recalls.
> He decided to host a Halloween costume party, and created elaborate games for
> the other children to play. The party was nearly stampeded by a visit from the
> Ku Klux Klan, who had heard tell that there might be Negroes present and set
> upon one scared (white) boy dressed as a robot, whose cardboard legs pre-
> vented him from fleeing. After Harper Lee's father and other powerful towns-
> folk gave the sheeted rednecks the big stare, the Klansmen slunk off to their
> cars. With its giddy buildup and unexpected drama, this going-away party was
> the forerunner to the masked Black and White Ball Capote would host for Kay
> Graham [the late owner and publisher of the *Washington Post*] in 1966, a night
> of operatic intrigue which was the Woodstock of the tuxedo brigade. (126).

Capote himself knew that as an adult he sought the attention that had been
denied to him when he was a child. In "Literature's Lost Boy," David Gates
cites Capote, who said of himself: "It's as if two different people were inside of
me. One is highly intelligent, imaginative and mature, and the other is a four-
teen-year-old" (62). Nothing in Capote's life illustrated how different he was
from many of those around him more than his time in the Midwest. When Capote traveled to Holcomb, Kansas, to conduct interviews for *In Cold Blood*,
residents were understandably taken aback by his demeanor and his accent: "If
Kansas was strange to Capote," writes Kenneth T. Reed, "Capote was just as
strange to Kansas . . . A Holcomb resident's recollection is typical: 'We did feel
pretty put off by Truman at first, with that funny little voice of his and the way
he dressed and all, but after we'd talked to him only for an hour, we just got so
we thoroughly enjoyed him'" (164).

Because of his extravagant nature, his genuine affection for others, and his
need for attention, what has become increasingly apparent is that Capote has
never lost his appeal. Accolades are being heaped upon the head of actor Philip
Seymour Hoffman, who plays the author in "Capote," a film based on Gerald
Clark's biography by the same name. In a film review entitled "Hoffman Gives
Soul to the Role of Capote" (Oct. 28, 2005), John DeFore of the *Austin American-Statesman* writes:

> In an early scene in small-town Kansas, we see the friction between the
> man and his image. Interviewing a friend of one of the murder victims who is
> reluctant to confide in this strange creature from New York, Capote unexpect-
> edly makes what feels like a confession, indirectly giving the girl permission to
> find him odd while offering her something to identify with. Within moments,

the interviewee has decided to share a piece of evidence she has previously kept hidden.

Is this interview a rare miracle of empathy, or an example of a journalist's genius for working his subject? That issue is the heart of the movie, as Capote meets and conducts marathon interviews with the killers, particularly the strangely magnetic Perry Smith. (1E/10E)

In the film Capote's relationship with Harper Lee, played by Catherine Keener, disintegrates as her book *To Kill a Mockingbird* becomes popular. Capote grows increasingly jealous of her success and wants his book to be published in order to gain the recognition he craves. According to DeFore, Capote is a "mess by the picture's end, praying for the killers' execution while pretending to be on their side" (10E). Later, DeFore writes, "[Director Bennett] Miller and screenwriter Dan Futterman, though, refuse to condemn the author, preferring to dig as deep as they can into the contradictory justifications for what he did and to portray him as a tragic figure whose masterpiece, *In Cold Blood,* came at the price of his soul" (10E).

"Capote" and "Infamous," another film about Capote's life, were in production simultaneously. The latter film stars Sandra Bullock, Gwyneth Paltrow, Sigourney Weaver, Jeff Daniels, Isabella Rossellini, Hope Davis, and Peter Bogdanovich. Toby Jones plays Capote. It is based on George Plimpton's *Truman Capote: In Which Various Friends, Enemies, Acquaintances and Detractors Recall His Turbulent Career.* Plimpton refers to the literary form he introduces as "oral narrative" or "oral biography" (62) in "Capote's Long Ride," an essay published in 1997 in *The New Yorker.*

It is clear from several biographies, news stories about Capote's life, obituaries that followed his tragic death in 1984, and the films about his life and work that Capote has withstood the test of time. For this study, it is *In Cold Blood* that is central to the discussion of the classics of literary journalism. *In Cold Blood* gives us Perry Smith, a cold-blooded murderer and an anti-hero akin to the protagonist in Albert Camus' *The Stranger.* A translation of the poem at the beginning of the novel suggests the way the reader is supposed to feel about Smith: "Human brothers who will live after us,/ Don't harden your hearts against us/ Because if you have pity on us poor ones,/ God will sooner have mercy on you" ("Ballad of the Hung," Francois Villon). Discussion of Capote's sympathy for Smith and the way his feelings for the killer might have distorted the truth of the novel continues; this study pays tribute to the powerful symbol Smith becomes while acknowledging that Capote's stream-of-consciousness interludes may or may not be journalistic in spite of Capote's claim that they capture the essence of his numerous interviews with Smith.

In 1959, Capote read a newspaper account about the murder of the Clutter family in Holcomb, Kansas, on Sunday, Nov. 15, of that year. Four members of the family, Herbert and Bonnie and two of their children, Nancy and Kenyon, were killed on their farm in a town with a population of approximately 1,100, a town in which residents did not lock their doors. Capote's title is drawn from the headline in the November 1959 issue of *Time* magazine about the murders, "In Cold Blood." Ultimately, the title can refer to the manner in which the murderers are put to death by the state, to the manner in which the family is killed, and/or to the manner in which Capote is thought by many to have exploited his sources.

In an interview in *Truman Capote: Conversations,* Capote said he didn't know immediately that the murder was what he had been looking for:

> But after reading the story it suddenly struck me that a crime, the study of one such, might provide the broad scope I needed to write the kind of book I wanted to write. Moreover, the human heart being what it is, murder was a theme not likely to darken and yellow with time.
>
> I thought about it all that November day, and part of the next; and then I said to myself: Well, why not this crime? The Clutter case. Why not pack up and go to Kansas and see what happens? (Inge, 51)

What followed Capote's fascination with the news story was 6,000 pages of notes, three years of research, and three more years of writing. Part of the reason for Capote's fascination with the murders was most likely how unusual such an event was in rural Kansas. Alvin A. Dewey, who conducted the investigation, said such murders are unusual today, and in 1959, "they were virtually unheard of" (2A). By the time the criminal investigation, trial, and execution were over, Capote had built relationships with each of the killers and had become especially fond of Smith. Whether that relationship was sexualized, as some have suggested, is unclear, but it was a powerful connection for both men. Capote described the relationship with the killers by saying: "Well, [Dick] Hickock and [Perry] Smith . . . who were very very good friends of mine (I mean became very close friends, very very close intimates in every conceivable way), would have gladly given me the things they wrote" (Inge, *Truman Capote: Conversations* 71).

Capote went to the execution of Hickock and Smith. Before he walked up the stairs to the gallows, Smith is said to have kissed him and said, "Adios, Amigo." Smith and Hickock were executed April 14 between midnight and 2 a.m. after their petition for a rehearing of their case was denied March 1, 1965. One of Plimpton's sources, Joe Fox, writes of Capote's trip back to New York after the execution:

> After the hanging, I sat next to Truman on the plane ride back to New York. He held my hand and cried most of the way. I remember thinking how odd it must have seemed to passengers sitting nearby—these two grown men apparently holding hands and one of them sobbing. It was a long trip. I couldn't read a copy of *Newsweek* or anything like that . . . not with Truman holding my hand. I stared straight ahead. (70)

In Cold Blood was serialized in *The New Yorker* before its publication in 1965. The allegorical nature of the novel was central to its popularity: In "The Truman Show," Wolcott writes, "The Clutters—mom, pop, son, daughter—are ready-made symbols: the model American family, America in microcosm, their murders a blow to the heartland and a desecration of the American dream" (130). In addition, what also captivated readers were the parallel narratives that allowed them to immerse themselves in the lives of the Clutters, the police and other investigators pursuing the fugitives, and the murderers themselves. What captivated literary scholars was Capote's use of stream of consciousness and other techniques and the book's place in the canon of naturalism: The idea of Perry Smith as a victim—with Capote's references to the "annihilating sky" (95)—suggest, of course, that Smith was destined to kill because of the trauma he had endured. Such a suggestion about the origins of criminal behavior was especially compelling during the 1960s, when so many previously entrenched attitudes and values were in flux.

When Flannery O'Connor discussed the reasons she used allegorical figures that were larger than life, she said that people had become so desensitized to evil and to their inhumanity toward one another that she had to draw "large and startling figures" (34) in order to remind them that what might be familiar might not be normal and might not deserve to be tolerated. Certainly, Perry Smith, a "large and startling figure," dominates Capote's nonfiction novel. *In Cold Blood* captivated America because of the portrayal of Smith, but it also became a bestseller for at least three other reasons: First, on one level the nonfiction novel is dreadfully realistic; on another level it is an allegory, a tale of innocence that leads to unwelcome experience for residents of rural Holcomb, Kansas, for the readers of the nonfiction novel, and for Capote. Second, *In Cold Blood* is an example of phenomenology, or the science of meaning, as Capote tries to make sense of four murders needlessly executed; in fact, *In Cold Blood* is subtitled *A True Account of a Multiple Murder and Its Consequences.* Finally, it is an example of naturalism, or the uneasy realization that many human events are random and that decisions such as those made by the tortured Perry Smith often seem fated.

Like Robert Frost's poem "Design"—in which Frost speculates about the cruelty that seems to "govern" even small events among insects—*In Cold Blood* raises questions about coincidence; about the actuality and motivation for evil unleashed in the world; about the existence of a benevolent, omniscient God; about goodness as accidental; and about the rationality of natural processes. The nonfiction novel raises important questions about the effects of seemingly random events such as car accidents, the genetics involved in mental illness, the violent home lives into which some people are born, etc. Frost's disturbing poem reads:

> I found a dimpled spider, fat and white,
> On a white heal-all, holding up a moth
> Like a white piece of rigid satin cloth—
> Assorted characters of death and blight
> Mixed ready to begin the morning right,
> Like the ingredients of a witches' broth—
> A snow-drop spider, a flower like a froth,
> And dead wings carried like a paper kite.
>
> What had that flower to do with being white,
> The wayside blue and innocent heal-all?
> What brought the kindred spider to that height,
> Then steered the white moth thither in the night?

What but design of darkness to appall?—
If design govern in a thing so small. (302)

Human beings need reasons for events, rely upon clear causes and effects, and experience "the blessed rage for order" (292) suggested in Wallace Stevens' poem "The Idea of Order at Key West." As Wes Chapman writes in "Human and Divine Design," Frost's poem is "a meditation on human attempts to see order in the universe—and human failures at perceiving the order that is actually present in nature" *(American Poetry* n.p.). *In Cold Blood* is an explanation—an inevitable ordering system—by Capote as he seeks answers to why he was obsessed by the *New York Times* story he read and why the events of 1959 had occurred. When teaching *In Cold Blood,* I heard a student tell another, "It's as though we complete ourselves through the people we're studying." I don't know if Capote completed himself, but he certainly learned more about his interests, his compassion, his philosophy about evil, and his role as interviewer.

One of the perils of literary journalism is an author's desire to create an invincible, unassailable conclusion, to have all narrative threads come together in the end. *In Cold Blood* suffers from this tendency. It has a rising action, a climax, a denouement, and a near-perfect conclusion. Did Capote ask the questions he asked in order to draw the conclusion he wanted to draw? Or as another student said to me, "Why did he tie it all together so perfectly in the cemetery?" It is true that Capote's role as a writer of fiction overtook his limited understanding of journalism and its higher purposes; it is also true that his moving from first-person to third-person narrative and back suggests a certain false authority, a kind of automatic filter.

What is most important, though, is to remember that Capote's phenomenological quest leads to more than an explanation of how people who have bad childhoods can hurt Christian families who live in idyllic communities. If that were all *In Cold Blood* were, readers would simply ask, "So what?" The nonfiction novel gained the readership and accolades it received because it—like stories about the murder of Jon Benet Ramsey in Boulder, Colorado, and Matthew Shepard in Laramie, Wyoming—captured the national imagination and suggested larger themes and larger questions.

Even the setting is significant: "Mr. Clutter seldom encountered trespassers on his property; a mile and a half from the highway, and arrived at by obscure roads, it was not a place that strangers came upon by chance" (23). The innocent life possible for residents of Holcomb was part of the American consciousness and would extend to the ruralcoms such as "The Andy Griffith Show" that grew increasingly more popular on American television. That evil could infiltrate such a God-fearing, trusting community terrified Americans in the 1960s and further disrupted the clear cause-effects on which they relied in a time of growing turbulence at home and abroad. In fact, in "American Gothic: What Rushes into the Newsless Void?" Jeffrey Toobin writes: "This kind of dialectic—the worthy clashing with the sinful, the high-minded with the debased—is a classic part of the Gothic tradition. We identify with its pulls and pushes because, of course, they're going on inside us all the time" (5).

The naturalism that pervades *In Cold Blood* links it to *Maggie: A Girl of the Streets* by Stephen Crane, *Sister Carrie* by Theodore Dreiser, and other nineteenth-century novels based on news events of the day. The existence of Fate is reflected in excerpts such as, "How as it possible that such effort, such plain virtue, could overnight be reduced to this—smoke, thinning as it rose and was received by the big, annihilating sky?" (95). The sky is not, of course, "annihilating," but such a personification suggests there is no escape from evil. Capote cites a local teacher: "Feeling wouldn't run half so high if this had happened to anyone *except* the Clutters. Anyone *less* admired. Prosperous. Secure. But that family represented everything people hereabouts really value and respect, and that such a thing could happen to them—well, it's like being told there is no God. It makes life seem pointless. I don't think people are so much frightened as they are deeply depressed" (105). One of the most powerful examples of naturalism in the nonfiction novel occurs after the investigators interview one of Smith's siblings. Capote writes:

> After the departure of the detectives, the composure . . . faltered; a familiar despair impended. She fought it, delayed its full impact until the party was done and the guests had gone, until she'd fed the children and bathed them and heard their prayers. Then the mood, like the evening ocean fog now clouding the street lamps, closed around her. She had said she was afraid of Perry, and she was, but was it simply Perry she feared, or was it a configuration of which he was part—the terrible destinies that seemed promised the four children of Florence Buckskin and Tex John Smith? The eldest, the brother she loved, had shot himself; Fern had fallen out of a window, or jumped; and Perry was committed to violence, a criminal. So, in a sense, she was the only survivor; and what tormented her was the thought that in time she, too, would be overwhelmed: go mad, or contract an incurable illness, or in a fire lose all she valued—home, husband, children. (209)

Alvin A. Dewey, former sheriff of Finney County and formerly a special agent of the Federal Bureau of Investigation, focuses on the illogical series of events that create the sense of dread present in *In Cold Blood.* "For it appeared to him 'ludicrously inconsistent' with the magnitude of the crime and the manifest cunning of the criminals, and 'inconceivable' that these men had entered a house expecting to find a money-filled safe, and then, not finding it, had thought it expedient to slaughter the family for perhaps a few dollars and a small portable radio" (215), he said. Later in the novel, Dewey observes that the murders were so odd as to be almost accidental. He thinks:

> The crime was a psychological accident, virtually an impersonal act; the victims might as well have been killed by lightning. Except for one thing: they had experienced prolonged terror, they had suffered. And Dewey could not forget their sufferings. Nonetheless, he found it possible to look at the man beside him without anger—with, rather, a measure of sympathy—for Perry Smith's life had been no bed of roses but pitiful, an ugly and lonely progress toward one mirage and then another. (277)

Certainly, Capote's portrayal of Smith suggests that he believed his anti-hero was almost preordained to commit the crimes he committed. At one point in the nonfiction novel, Smith says he sees himself and Dick as "'running a race without a finish line'—that was how it struck him" (230). Smith later tells Capote that during the murders he wasn't aware of hatred, rage, or other motivations for killing the family. His description of killing Herbert Clutter is the most startling: "I didn't want to harm the man. I thought he was a very nice gentleman. Soft-spoken. I thought so right up to the moment I cut his throat" (275). Capote also quotes Smith as saying, "They [the Clutters] never hurt me. Like other people. Like people have all my life. Maybe it's just that the Clutters were the ones who had to pay for it" (339).

Dick Hickock appears far more diabolical than Smith, although he is probably not the one who killed the family. Hickock's cruelty is nearly paralyzing and is better illustrated by Capote's account of the murder of a dog than by the murders of the Clutter family:

> The car was moving. A hundred feet ahead, a dog trotted along the side of the road. Dick swerved toward it. It was an old half-dead mongrel, brittle-boned and mangy, and the impact, as it met the car, was little more than what a bird might make. But Dick was satisfied. "Boy!" he said—and it was always what he said after running down a dog, which is something he did whenever the opportunity arose. "Boy! We sure splattered him!" (133)

In spite of the description of scenes such as this, Capote is unfaltering in his belief that criminals such as Hickock and Smith are the result of a lifetime of neglect and brutality. The heart of *In Cold Blood* is a compressed allegory similar to Joseph K's visit to the cathedral in Franz Kafka's *The Trial*. The pages that describe the crowd watching Smith and Hickock arrive at the courthouse are laden with symbolism, as Capote associates the killers with two starving alley cats. Capote writes:

> Among Garden City's animals are two gray tomcats who are always together—thin, dirty strays with strange and clever habits. The chief ceremony of their day is performed at twilight. First, they trot the length of Main Street, stopping to scrutinize the engine grilles of parked automobiles, particularly those stationed in front of the two hotels, the Windsor and Warren, for these cars, usually the property of travelers from afar, often yield what the bony, methodical creatures are hunting: slaughtered birds—crows, chickadees, and sparrows foolhardy enough to have flown into the path of oncoming motorists. Using their paws as though they are surgical instruments, the cats extract from the grilles every feathery particle. Having cruised Main Street, they invariably turn the corner at Main and Grant, then lope toward Courthouse Square, another of their hunting grounds—and a highly promising one on the afternoon of Wednesday, January 6, for the area swarmed with Finney County vehicles that had brought to town part of the crowd populating the square . . .
> No one lingered, neither the press corps nor any of the townspeople. Warm rooms and warm suppers beckoned them, and as they hurried away, leaving the cold square to the two gray cats, the miraculous autumn departed too; the year's first snow began to fall. (278, 280)

Although Capote may believe that at least Smith might have been redeemed had he been born into a loving community, his ability to understand the harrowing murder story is limited. Dewey promises to bring order to the bedlam, but he, like Capote, ultimately fails. "But even if I hadn't known the family, and liked them so well, I wouldn't feel any different," Dewey said. "Because I've seen some bad things, I sure as hell have. But nothing so vicious as this. However long it takes, it may be the rest of my life, I'm going to know what happened in that house: the why and the who" *(In Cold Blood* 96). Of course, neither Capote, nor Dewey, nor the reader will ever know entirely the who or the why.

Capote belongs in this study not only because he wrote a bestselling nonfiction novel but because of his admiration for journalists. In an article published in *Playboy* in 1968, Capote called journalism the "last great unexplored literary frontier" (Inge, *Truman Capote: Conversations* 122) and also called journalism "the most underestimated, the least explored of literary mediums" (Plimpton, *Truman Capote* 197). In fact, Reed writes in his biography *Truman Capote* that the author of *In Cold Blood* was an "inveterate devourer of newspapers" (102). Certainly, the newspaper story that inspired his greatest work suggests the power that real life held over Capote. Of the day in 1959 when he read the *New York Times* story, Capote writes:

> I found this very small headline that read "Eisenhower Appointee Murdered."
> The victim was a rancher in western Kansas, a wheat grower who had been an
> Eisenhower appointee to the Farm Credit Bureau. He, his wife, and two of their
> children had been murdered, and it was a complete mystery. They had no idea
> of who had done it or why, but the story struck me with tremendous force. I
> suddenly realized that perhaps a crime, after all, would be the ideal subject mat-
> ter for the massive job of reportage I wanted to do. I would have a wide range
> of characters, and, most importantly, it would be timeless. I knew it would take
> me five years, perhaps eight or ten years, to do this, and I couldn't work on
> some ephemeral, momentary thing. It had to be an event related to permanent
> emotions in people. (Reed, *Truman Capote* 102)

Criticism of *In Cold Blood* continues, partly because of techniques such as stream of consciousness employed in the nonfiction novel and partly because of Capote's questionable reportorial strategies. Hellman believes that, like conventional journalism, *In Cold Blood* employed the "illusion of objectivity" (20). For example, the reader is privy to the thoughts of the characters but is not told how the reporter knows those thoughts. For a journalist, however, this fact is more than troublesome. Capote's interviewing techniques—treated with suspicion by both journalists and literary scholars—are often attacked. Reed, one of Capote's defenders, writes:

> In earlier years Capote had trained himself not to write or use a tape re-
> corder during interviews, but instead to make notes from memory afterwards, a
> technique that provoked criticism from various reviewers when *In Cold Blood*
> was published. Some were never satisfied about the authenticity of the informa-
> tion and took the time to retrace all of Capote's steps to check the facts. There

were, however, many more defenders than detractors, and the subject provided a long and lively debate amongst the critics. (142)

Capote would win praise for other works—especially *Other Voices, Other Rooms*; *Tree of Night*; *The Grass Harp*; *Breakfast at Tiffany's*; *A Christmas Memory*; and *Music for Chameleons*—but it would be *In Cold Blood* that would guarantee him a place in American literary history. Much has been made of Capote's inability to produce more writing after *In Cold Blood,* but in all he wrote 25 plays, two novels, 60 short stories, more than 100 poems, and an autobiography. Surely, his literary legacy speaks for itself.

John Berendt

Murder is at the center of another magnum opus in American literary journalism. John Berendt once said he wanted to create something more permanent than a magazine article. There is no doubt he accomplished that goal—and much, much more—with the publication of *Midnight in the Garden of Good and Evil.* The critics who reviewed the book—and later the film by the same name—struggled to find a category into which the two texts would neatly fit. The book has been called a travelogue, a travel book, a tale of real-life murder, a diary, a character sketch, a cultural study, and an allegory. As a travel writer for *Sky,* Delta Airlines' travel magazine, put it: *"Midnight* is as much about a place as it is about a slaying" (53).

Some suggested that the inveterate Yankee author was drawn to Savannah because of the storytelling obsession Southerners possess. Some say Berendt lived in Savannah on weekends; some say he was there five years; other sources say seven years. Whatever the case, Berendt immersed himself in the Southern community for long enough to become part of the landscape. In this way, residents of Savannah felt safe enough in his presence to invest him with their secrets.

Ken Ringle writes in the Feb. 24, 1994, issue of the *Washington Post* that Berendt spent 30 years writing for magazines in New York, but he was lured to Savannah largely because of the love Southerners have for telling stories. Ringle claims Berendt moved to Savannah for five years and immersed himself in the community.

Opinions about how long Berendt lived in the South are nothing compared to the debate about the book itself. "Berendt acknowledges he changed some names for legal reasons and altered some sequences for readability, but that doesn't bother anyone here. They know he got things right," Ringle writes. He quotes Irma Harlan, director of Savannnah's regional library, who said, "In a strange way this book is a kind of celebration of Savannah. I believe he likes us." And Elizabeth Mercer Hammond, Johnny Mercer's niece, said, "I want you to know I've enjoyed your book. I'd never heard that story about my brother's drinking, but then it might be true. I'm not one to spoil a story when the truth might be less amusing" (Ringle C1).

Other critics and residents were not so lenient. Some were concerned that the book was neither fiction nor nonfiction. Others were concerned that Berendt treated some conversations and events as fact when they had simply been described to him by others. His "Author's Note" at the end of the novel reads:

> All the characters in this book are real, but it bears mentioning that I have used pseudonyms for a number of them in order to protect their privacy. Though this is a work of nonfiction, I have taken certain storytelling liberties, particularly having to do with the timing of events. Where the narrative strays from strict nonfiction, my intention has been to remain faithful to the characters and to the essential drift of events as they really happened. (n.p.)

The debate about the veracity of *Midnight in the Garden of Good and Evil* and its nearly unprecedented "Author's Note" continue, but whatever its mixture of fact and fiction, Berendt's book brings to life a city of mystery and beauty. In *US* (December 1997) appears an article entitled "After Midnight" by Justine Elias. The first paragraph reads:

> Welcome to the eternal party, located within a forest of 100-foot live-oak trees overhung with Spanish moss, where even the brightest sunlight seems like late-day shade. No visit to Savannah, Ga., is complete without a stop here at the Bonaventure Cemetery, a Victorian-era resting place for the city's most distinguished dead. In a region known for its hospitality, the Bonaventure is perversely inviting. The marble monuments, decorated with cherubs, sad-eyed angels, and Civil War veterans' crosses, were built on the site of a Colonial plantation that burned to the ground during a lavish dinner party. The host led everyone into the garden, where the revelry continued by the light of the raging fire. Legend has it that on quiet nights you can just about hear the laughter and the shattering of crystal glasses. What better place to spend eternity, locals say, than here, where the party never ends. The genteel and the grotesque, love and death, celebration and grief, the present and past, stood side by side—and still do. (89)

Elias calls Savannah a "place resolved to fight off the stultifying effects of modern living, to treasure its insularity, beauty and leisurely style," and he adds, *"Midnight's* Savannah is so Deep South you can't see out, and once you're there awhile, you don't want to" (89).

The themes in *Midnight in the Garden of Good and Evil* are representative of those included in articles by Berendt, such as "High-Heel Neil," which features a Republican businessman named Neil Cargile who enjoys cross-dressing. Cargile, a pilot, crashes a plane on an interstate, and reporters quickly arrive at the scene. In one introductory paragraph that follows a jovial understatement by Cargile ("I like being the center of attention"), Berendt writes:

> There was more than a grain of truth in Cargile's jest, as many of those who were watching the drama at home on television were well aware. Neil Cargile was a celebrated son of Nashville, a dashing figure of privilege and status who was never very far from the spotlight. He had played football at Vanderbilt, driven race cars, sailed yachts, and played polo. He was a man of

action and daring—of that there was no question. And yet when his friends saw his dapper image on television that night they were all seized by the same incongruous thought: Thank God he wasn't wearing a dress. (38).

Berendt's fascination with the characters in the Deep South—and the quirkiness of most human beings in whatever region they call home—is obvious. His celebration of those who dare to be different is also obvious:

> By the mid-nineteen-eighties, Nashville had become used to the sight of Neil Cargile in women's clothes. Out-of-towners were about the only people still taken aback by it. One evening, a woman who was visiting Nashville to see her grandparents suddenly leaned across the table at the 106 Club and told her grandfather, in an urgent but lowered voice, that a man had just come into the restaurant in a red dress. Her grandfather shrugged and went on eating. "That would be Neil Cargile," he said without bothering to turn around. (40)

Like his other work, *Midnight in the Garden of Good and Evil* celebrates those who march to a different drummer and who shun the ordinary. One of three finalists for the 1995 Pulitzer Prize for nonfiction, *Midnight in the Garden of Good and Evil* is a nonfiction novel—and an event. As Elias writes in "After Midnight":

> *Midnight* the book has become *Midnight* the phenomenon. This too is a strange tale: how a book's runaway success, and the fame, fortune and tourism boom it created, has changed the lives of its characters, its author and its place of origin. *Midnight in the Garden of Good and Evil* is Southern Gothic with a postmodern twist: It's interactive. People read the story, call their travel agent, see the town and meet the characters—or at least those who want to be met. (90)

A graduate of Harvard, Berendt has been an editor for *Esquire* and *New York Magazine,* and the fact that his bestseller about the Deep South was penned by a Yankee continues to intrigue his readers. Comparing *Midnight in the Garden of Good and Evil* to *In Cold Blood,* some critics focus on Berendt's description of his book as a nonfiction novel. But the book is also a "literary travelogue" (94), as Elias correctly notes, in the same genre as Peter Mayle's book about the South of France entitled *A Year in Provence.* Ultimately, discussions about the genres of literature pale in comparison to the experience of an evening in Bonaventure Cemetery with the possibility of seeing ghosts and hearing tales told at twilight.

Tom Wolfe

No study of literary journalism would be complete without praise for the man who is credited with the phrase "The New Journalism." In his work, Wolfe employed extended dialogue, personal point of view, and interior monologue.

He experimented with punctuation, including dots, dashes, exclamation points, etc. He mesmerized some critics and drove others crazy.

Calling Tom Wolfe an "American Jeremiah," Barbara Lounsberry celebrates the "strong social vision" of the man who coined the phrase "The New Journalism." Lounsberry argues that Wolfe is dominant in literary journalism because his work "illustrates the rhetorical strain in American literary nonfiction," because he sees "cultural movements in religious terms," and because he possesses an "evangelistic sensibility" (38, 64). Certainly, these characteristics suggest that Wolfe requires mention in a book about the passion, intensity, and didacticism of literary jornnalism.

In an article entitled "White Suit, Gray Eminence," Lawrence Biemiller remembers his first encounter with Tom Wolfe and writes, "The exclamation points—how could I have forgotten the exclamation points? Two in the first two sentences, 10 on the third page, seven in a mere five lines on page 11 . . .The fussy suits, the parties, the name-dropping, the exclamation points and italic interjections, the *O Destinys* and the one-word sentences, the ellipses and the em-dashes chasing one another across the pages—all so splendidly unmistakable, all so easily mocked. O peerless ego!—" (A56).

It is appropriate to begin this section both with a tongue-in-cheek tribute and with the first paragraph of a landmark article from *Time* magazine (Nov. 2, 1998) by Paul Gray:

> The megayield critical and commercial success of *The Bonfire of the Vanities* in 1987 made Tom Wolfe a rich and very gratified author indeed. That big, boisterous novel, his first, proved a point that he had been arguing, much to the annoyance of literary folks, for years: American fiction could still portray the hectic complexities of contemporary social life, could still capture the textures and rhythms of a seething modern city, if novelists would just leave their desks, maybe take a sabbatical from their professorships in creative writing and go out and report on the fabulous *stuff* taking place all around them. But, Wolfe complained, most post-'60s U.S. novelists had simply abandoned the passing scene in favor of introspection or self-conscious artifice. They had ceded public reality to journalists, of whom Wolfe was a notable example *(The Electric Kool-Aid Acid Test, The Right Stuff)* before he invaded the House of Fiction and noisily threw open the windows. (89)

Dapper, thin, and engaging, the figure of Tom Wolfe filled the white cover of *Time* magazine on Nov. 2, 1998. The headline tells it all: "Tom Wolfe Writes Again (The novelist with the white stuff is back with *A Man in Full.* More than a million copies, before anyone has read a word!)."

In an article entitled "Tom Wolfe's Revenge," former congressional reporter for the *Washington Times* Chris Harvey claims that "elements of the New Journalism that Wolfe so tirelessly promoted have become as commonplace as the pie chart in many newspapers, ranging from the *New York Times* to the *Oregonian* to the weekly *Washington City Paper"* (41). Harvey adds: "In his works, Wolfe chronicled subcultures—such as the hippie drug scene and the Black Panther movement—with the eye of a novelist. He toyed with extended dialogue, point of view and interior monologue. He even played with ellipses, dots, dashes and exclamation points—attempting, he wrote, to leave the illusion of people thinking" (42).

Best known for *The Electric Kool-Aid Acid Test, The Kandy-Kolored Tangerine-Flake Streamline Baby, The Bonfire of the Vanities,* and *A Man in Full,* Wolfe is at his representative best in *The Right Stuff,* a colossal bestseller that deals with myths of masculinity in America. *The Right Stuff,* one of Wolfe's more representative works, is a study of the legends that surround American astronauts, including John H. Glenn Jr., Virgil I. Grissom, and Alan B. Shepard Jr. In it, Wolfe focuses on mortality, something that affects astronauts and every person reading the nonfiction novel: "But somehow the unwritten protocol forbade discussions of this subject, which was the fear of death" (11). The drama in *The Right Stuff* emanates from the danger that permeates the training missions: "In time, the Navy would compile statistics showing that for a career Navy pilot, i.e., one who intended to keep flying for twenty years . . . there was a 23 percent probability that he would die in an aircraft accident" (15).

The title of Wolfe's novel is drawn from images of masculinity and heroism that pervade American popular culture. Real men are strong, courageous, invincible, patriotic, and fearless. The training Wolfe describes in his novel illustrates the fact that the men who submit to danger are the ultimate men, the stereotypical servants of the state: "And the idea was to prove at every foot of the way up that pyramid that you were one of the elected and anointed ones who had *the right stuff* and could move higher and higher and even—ultimately, God willing, one day—that you might be able to join that special few at the very top, that elite who had the capacity to bring tears to men's eyes, the very Brotherhood of the Right Stuff itself" (18). Tone in Wolfe's work is always rich and multi-faceted, but there is here and elsewhere in the novel an authorial detachment, a suggestion that masculinity may or may not be best proven by risking one's life: "*Manliness, manhood, manly courage . . .* there was something ancient, primordial, irresistible about the challenge of this stuff, no matter what a sophisticated and rational age one might think he lived in" (21).

Ultimately, Wolfe describes a world unknown to most Americans who supported the space race, who believed in the heroism of men who protected the nation. The American public and its fragmented and unrealistic sense of its warriors is obvious, as is the way in which their views have communicated themselves to the men who subject themselves to arduous service: "They looked upon themselves as men who lived by higher standards of behavior than civilians, as men who were the bearers and protectors of the most important values of American life, who maintained a sense of discipline while civilians abandoned themselves to hedonism, who maintained a sense of honor while civilians lived by opportunism and greed" (29). The commitment of these men is tied to national pride: "The panic became more and more apocalyptic. Nothing short of doom awaited the loser, now that the battle had begun . . . the House Select Committee on Astronautics, headed by House Speaker John McCormack, said that the United States faced the prospect of 'national extinction' if it did not catch up with the Soviet space program" (54-55).

Wolfe's skepticism about the value of human sacrifice is obvious as the narrative increases in intensity. On the day of a launch, Americans awaken without an understanding of what lies ahead for the men in whom they need to believe: "Now the sun was up, and all across the eastern half of the country people were doing the usual, turning on their radios and television sets, rolling the knobs in search of something to give the nerve endings a little tingle—and what suspense awaited them! An astronaut sat on the tip of a rocket, preparing to get himself blown to pieces" (189). The vacuous heroism that compels the public is obvious in descriptions of a man who became the image of a nation that could not be stopped: "That was what the sight of John Glenn did to Americans at that time. It primed them for the tears. And those tears ran like a river all over America. It was an extraordinary thing, being the sort of mortal who brought tears to other men's eyes" (279). Ultimately, of course, these heroes would be replaced by others. Names the public never imagined they would forget became part of history, part of the past:

> They would continue to be honored, and men would continue to be awed by their courage; but the day when an astronaut could parade up Broadway while traffic policemen wept in the intersections was no more. Never again would an astronaut be perceived as a protector of the people, risking his life to do battle in the heavens. Not even the first American to walk on the moon would ever know the outpouring of a people's most primal emotions that Shepard, Cooper, and above all, Glenn had known. The era of America's first single-combat warriors had come, and it had gone, perhaps never to be relived . . . It would have been still more impossible for his confreres to realize that the day might come when Americans would hear their names and say, "Oh, yes—now, which one was he?" (348)

Joan Didion

Settling the Borderland: Other Voices in Literary Journalism is partially devoted to an exploration of the primary texts and criticism—much of it written by men—that characterizes a complex and fascinating genre. It is primarily devoted to celebrating the women who are often overlooked in studies of literary journalism. One of the names that happily does *not* require resurrection is that of Joan Didion. Worthy of a lengthy study in Chapter 3, Didion is the author of the recent blockbuster entitled *The Year of Magical Thinking*, which deals with the death of Didion's husband of 40 years, John Gregory Dunne, in December 2003. Before Christmas their daughter Quintana became ill with pneumonia and septic shock and was put into an induced coma and on life support. Quintana later died. Appropriately, the dedication to *The Year of Magical Thinking* reads: "This book is for John and for Quintana."

In "Alone With Her Words," Cathleen McGuigan writes about *The Year of Magical Thinking,* a book that headline writers call Didion's "spare, stunning memoir of loss and grief" *(Newsweek,* Oct. 10, 2005):

Didion's intricate narrative moves forward, circles back, pauses to describe a memory with Dunne—a long-ago swim in a coastal cave, a rain-soaked walk in Paris—or to recall a fragment of a poem or a clue in a crossword puzzle. Then it dives down again to grasp a deeper meaning. There's something especially moving about her famously spare style here, how her elegant prose never threatens to spill over into the realm of the tell-all, even though she's telling us quite a lot. For us, her words, never squandered, are more than enough. (63)

Winner of a National Book Award, *The Year of Magical Thinking* has been adapted into a one-woman play, produced by Scott Rudin and directed by David Hare. Of the project, Didion said, "I think that the book is not a narrative; it's about a state of mind, and I think that will work well. And I had a strong sense that I really wanted to try a new form" (Associated Press, ABC News Internet Ventures). Hare likened the book to a "detective story in which the mystery is 'How the hell do I find a way to suffer less?'" (Associated Press, ABC News Internet Ventures). Didion writes about the almost unimaginable loss of her husband and daughter in a narrative that is therapeutic and cathartic but also devastatingly painful to relate:

Grief turns out to be a place none of us know until we reach it . . . Nor can we know ahead of the fact (and here lies the heart of the difference between grief as we imagine it and grief as it is) the unending absence that follows, the void, the very opposite of meaning, the relentless succession of moments during which we will confront the experience of meaninglessness itself. *(The Year* 188-89)

Her love for her husband, who was also her confidant, her writing companion, and her best friend, is palpable: "For forty years I saw myself through John's eyes. I did not age . . . We are imperfect mortal beings, aware of that mortality even as we push it away, failed by our very complication, so wired that when we mourn our losses we also mourn, for better or for worse, ourselves. As we were. As were are no longer. As we will one day not be at all" (197-98).

The eulogy to mortality itself continues with lines such as, "Leis go brown, tectonic plates shift, deep currents move, islands vanish, rooms get forgotten" (227). Like Didion's other work, *The Year of Magical Thinking* is intensely personal at the same time that it is starkly universal. Her grief is our grief; her realizations, ours:

This is my attempt to make sense of the period that followed, weeks and then months that cut loose any fixed idea I had ever had about death, about illness, about probability and luck, about good fortune and bad, about marriage and children and memory, about grief, about the ways in which people do and do not deal with the fact that life ends, about the shallowness of sanity, about life itself. I have been a writer my entire life. As a writer, even as a child, long before what I wrote began to be published, I developed a sense that meaning itself was resident in the rhythms of words and sentences and paragraphs, a technique for withholding whatever it was I thought or believed behind an increasingly impenetrable polish. The way I write is who I am, or have become, yet this is a case in which I wish I had instead of words and their rhythms, a cutting room, equipped with an Avid, a digital editing system on which I could touch a key and collapse the sequence of time, show you simultaneously all the frames of memory that come to me now, let you pick the takes, the marginally different expressions, the variant readings of the same lines. This is a case in which I need more than words to find the meaning. This is a case in which I need whatever it is I think or believe to be penetrable, if only for myself. (7-8)

Although *The Year of Magical Thinking* is Didion's most recent contribution to literary journalism, no list of classics in the genre is complete without reference to Didion's book about terror and international politics, *Salvador*. The book provides the perfect balance between personal point of view and an analysis of issues of universal significance. Making appropriate and provocative reference to Joseph Conrad's *Heart of Darkness* at the beginning of *Salvador*, Didion describes traveling with her husband to El Salvador in 1982 during the height of civil war. During her two weeks there, she gazes upon the country's "ghost resorts on the empty Pacific beaches" (13). The thesis of the book is that "terror is the given of the place" and that American foreign policy is flawed: "The dead and pieces of the dead turn up in El Salvador everywhere, every day, as taken for granted as in a nightmare, or a horror movie" (19). The juxtaposition of images (tourism and war, music and a deserted mall, etc.) is central to the book, providing a haunting sense of dislocation. Didion writes:

> The Sheraton always seems brighter and more mildly festive than either the Camino Real or the Presidente, with children in the pool and flowers and pretty women in pastel dresses, but there are usually several bulletproofed Cherokee Chiefs in the parking area, and the men drinking in the lobby often carry the little zippered purses that in San Salvador suggest not passports or credit cards but Browning 9-mm. pistols. (23)

As is often true in Didion's best work, she admits her own disillusionment and her emotional connection to place and event. In a section about "Central America's Largest Shopping Mall," she writes:

> This was a shopping center that embodied the future for which El Salvador was presumably being saved, and I wrote it down dutifully, this being the kind of "color" I knew how to interpret, the kind of inductive irony, the detail that was supposed to illuminate the story. As I wrote it down I realized that I was no longer much interested in this kind of irony, that this was a story that would not be illuminated by such details, that this was a story that would perhaps not be illuminated at all, that this was perhaps even less a "story" than a true *noche obscura*. As I waited to cross back over the Boulevard de los Heroes to the Camino Real I noticed soldiers herding a young civilian into a van, their guns at the boy's back, and I walked straight ahead, not wanting to see anything at all. (34-35)

In this country smaller than various counties in California, Didion confronts terror and "elusive shadows" (67) and "the official American delusion, the illusion of plausibility, the sense that the American undertaking in El Salvador might turn out to be, from the right angle, in the right light, just another difficult but possible mission in another troubled but possible country" (87-88). As is often true in Didion's work, there is no critical closure, no sense of thematic resolution in *Salvador*. In fact, if there were, this classic of literary journalism might fall prey to the too-simple conclusions provided by government officials and mainstream media.

In Chapter 3, we will revisit the contributions of Joan Didion, one of the founders of American literary journalism. Here, it is important simply to high-light the fact that Didion continues to write, continues to draw readers, and continues to talk about her own personal struggles and moments of epiphany in a way that is inclusive, representative, and rich. Readers identify with her and are challenged by her life and the questions she asks herself. Most significantly, Didion continues to succeed as a social spokesperson, as someone who sees even the smallest events in their cosmic context.

In *The Art of Fact: Contemporary Artists of Nonfiction*, Lounsberry compares Didion to F. Scott Fitzgerald because of their "similar interests in wealth and illusion, the beautiful and the damned, the lost Eden of the American Dream and the dark night of the American soul" (107). She later writes:

> Didion's artistic gift has been to enrich the autobiographical strain in American literary nonfiction. She uses herself as both a probe and a model of American society. Her confessions of personal illusions both encourage reader sympathy and identification with her views, and demonstrate how prone Americans are to illusion. (136)

As noted earlier, the classics of American literary journalism and the well-known authors included in this chapter are merely representative of the border-land in which literary journalists work. Those included here are examples of writers who choose to employ literary techniques in the interest of retelling ac-tual events and who struggle to maintain ethical relationships with sources while entertaining the reading public; those who devote themselves to a faithful repre-sentation of actual occurrences while acknowledging the importance of rising action, climax, and denouement; and those who recognize that becoming a part of the action forever alters the text.

Before we revisit literary journalists such as Didion, however, we will turn to more in-depth analysis of work by those who drew from their experience in journalism but who opted—for the most part—to devote their careers to fiction. All are well known for their contributions in American literary history, but they have not received the critical attention they deserve for their reliance on journal-ism. The study begins with an examination of short stories and poetry by Edgar Allan Poe and Walt Whitman. Both nineteenth-century writers, they knew one another and relied on current events for some of their best work.

Chapter 2.
From Straight News
To Literary Journalism and Fiction

The second section of *Settling the Borderland: Other Voices in Literary Journalism* celebrates five authors in American literary history who, although they have won numerous accolades for their fiction, are not generally recognized as literary journalists. Critics too often overlook Edgar Allan Poe, Katherine Anne Porter, John Steinbeck, Eudora Welty, and Walt Whitman as writers who borrowed from their journalistic training and who remained interested throughout their careers in events that were rooted in time and in people who actually lived. Representing both the nineteenth and twentieth centuries, these authors also are symbolic of particular regions and intellectual traditions.

Although *Settling the Borderland* focuses primarily on women literary journalists who have failed to gain their just due, Poe, Steinbeck, and Whitman are worthy of note because they, too, are often overlooked in studies of the tenets and historical significance of one category of literary journalism.

Edgar Allan Poe and Walt Whitman

The influence of journalism on Edgar Allan Poe's work is undeniable. In "The Mystery of Marie Roget," Poe writes, "We gave the Future to the winds, and slumbered tranquilly in the Present, weaving the dull world around us into dreams" (198). There is no clearer description of how an artist transforms mundane human events into poetry, and the purpose of this section of *Settling the Borderland: Other Voices in Literary Journalism* is to illustrate the ways in which both Edgar Allan Poe (1809-1849) and Walt Whitman (1819-1892)—contemporaries who knew one another—used what they learned as journalists to create art. This section of Chapter 2 is important because less scholarly work about the reliance of Poe and Whitman on journalism exists and because these authors left journalism to write fiction, much like the women whose work is central to this chapter.

Drawn from the social philosophies that Walt Whitman developed while walking the streets of New York as a reporter and editor, *Leaves of Grass* celebrates the individual and praises the American landscape. Similarly, mirroring events described in New York newspapers, two of Edgar Allan Poe's detective stories, "The Murders in the Rue Morgue" and "The Mystery of Marie Roget," are persuasive examples of how his art, too, borrowed from life.

From the time Poe and Whitman were in their early twenties, they were editors as well as writers of prose and poetry. They knew and respected one another. Although these facts are familiar to those in literary circles, few print media critics address the influence of journalism on their fiction. Publication of *The Collected Writings of Walt Whitman: The Journalism* has helped to fill the critical void. Edited by Herbert Bergman—with Douglas A. Noverr and Edward J. Recchia as associate editors—*The Journalism* provides detailed biographical information and extensive critique of Whitman's dependence upon his experiences in journalism. Volume One (1998) deals with Whitman's journalism from 1834-1846; Volume Two (2003), with 1846-1848. Together, the collections provide more than 1,000 pages of Whitman's essays, travel pieces, editorials, and news stories from his journalism career.

The teeming life that Whitman encountered daily on the streets of New York was the foundation for his best poetry. In fact, Shelley Fisher Fishkin argues in *From Fact to Fiction: Journalism and Imaginative Writing in America* that it was during his early newspaper work that he "first stumbled upon subjects, styles, stances, and strategies to which he would later return" (15) in his poetry. Determined to "evoke the scene before him in all its color and solidity" in a newspaper article, Whitman recorded the "specific concrete details" (17) that would later form the core of his poetry, Fishkin writes.

Certainly, the practice of journalism during the nineteenth century served the same purpose as it did for Tom Wolfe and his brigade of "New Journalists" in the twentieth: It paid the bills while they crafted the fiction that would make them famous. However, Poe and Whitman are part of a stream of writers—including Willa Cather, Stephen Crane, Theodore Dreiser, Ernest Hemingway, Katherine Anne Porter, Upton Sinclair, John Steinbeck, Mark Twain, and Eudora Welty—who gleaned both subject matter and perspective from their experience as journalists and their careful reading of newspapers.

Described by critic Michael Allen as "an intense young poet, forced by necessity to direct his limited energies into journalism" (101), Poe worked as a freelance writer from 1831 to 1835 and as a journalist from 1835 to 1849. Although he worked primarily for magazines and literary publications, his assessment of newspapers is echoed in the words of C. August Dupin, his precise detective, in "The Mystery of Marie Roget": "We should bear in mind that, in general, it is the object of our newspapers rather to create a sensation—to make a point—than to further the cause of truth," Dupin said. "The latter end is only pursued when it seems coincident with the former" (206).

Walt Whitman and Journalism

Ezra Greenspan suggests in *Walt Whitman and the American Reader* that Whitman joined others who pursued journalism and wrote poetry and prose during their spare moments:

> If he was forced at times into a hand-to-mouth existence and to scramble from job to job, he was only doing what more talented and experienced magazinists, such as Poe, were also doing in adapting themselves to the helter-skelter, as yet unsystematized ways of the new literary culture, in which positions were often tenuous and ventures frequently failed. Such was to be the pattern of Whitman's activity throughout his journalism career. (51-52)

Whitman, like Poe, was drawn into journalism early in his life. Ultimately, he wrote profiles, travel pieces, editorials, news stories, features, and literary reviews. In fact, as late as 1862, Whitman was still earning money as a freelance writer and journalist. A printer's apprentice at 13, Whitman founded and edited the *Long-Islander,* a weekly in Huntington, N.Y., when he was 19 and then worked as a compositor on the *Long Island Democrat* at the age of 20. He later was a reporter and editor at a series of newspapers, beginning in 1840 with the *Aurora,* the *Evening Tattler,* and the *New York Democrat.* Whitman then worked as an editor, reporter, and critic on the *Long Island Star* (1845-46), the *Brooklyn Eagle* (1846-48), the *New Orleans Crescent* (1848), the *Brooklyn Freeman* (1848-49), and the *Brooklyn Daily Times* (1857-59). He also wrote sketches for the *New York Evening Post* and the *Brooklyn Daily Advertiser* from 1850-51.

With the ongoing, tumultuous transition between the Party and the Penny Press eras, the 1840s were a particularly exciting period for Whitman. The number of newspapers was skyrocketing in New York City. In 1841, there were two major newspapers, one of which was Horace Greeley's *New York Tribune.* By 1845, there were 20. As Whitman biographer Gay Wilson Allen writes, "Vituperative editorials [during this period] were nothing new, but this was organized warfare, the result of rapid changes taking place in city journalism. The establishment of the 'penny press' in the previous decade had greatly enlarged the newspaper-reading public, and thereby encouraged the starting of new papers" *(Solitary* 41).

Although literary critics too often overlook the impact of Whitman's early career on his work, a few find it essential. In his article "The Influence of Whitman's Journalism on *Leaves of Grass,"* Bergman said that journalism is an "important part of the background of the *Leaves of Grass.* It is impossible to understand the growth, the scope, and the bloodstream of the *Leaves [of Grass]* without understanding how much editorial experience lay behind it . . . Walt must be regarded as very definitely a product of American journalism" ("Influence" 399). Bergman writes:

> Whitman's journalistic experience on the *Times, Aurora, Eagle,* and other newspapers not only helped him to acquire courage in dealing with all topics; it also helped him to rid himself of his provincialism, to acquire his historical and social sense, and to achieve a cosmic quality in his themes, as he had to generalize in his editorials. His absorption of the phenomena of America helped him to become the representative, all-embracing man of *Leaves of Grass,* the all-inclusive "I." As a journalist, Whitman came to know, and react to, America in close detail; as a journalistic social critic, he saw America's deficiencies. To remedy these deficiencies and to enable America to realize its potential, in his poetry he presented himself as representative of all selves, as a new, or re-created image of America; and he continued his social criticism, though it is more prevalent in the prose. ("Influence" 400)

Bergman adds that "the man in *Leaves of Grass* is strongly the journalistic Whitman: Whitman was a journalist and editor while *Leaves of Grass* was 'simmering' and when he was revising and expanding it" ("Influence" 401).

Thomas L. Brasher, author of *Whitman as Editor of the Brooklyn Daily Eagle,* agrees, claiming that Whitman "plainly showed a journalistic zest and expansiveness for anything from manifest destiny to swill milk" (13). He writes:

> It is true enough that the prosody of the *Leaves* was not foreshadowed in the *Eagle:* but that is scarcely sufficient reason for dismissing the ideas formulated in that paper as irrelevant to the ideas later expressed in the poetry. The child was father of the man just as surely for Whitman as for any other person. (14-15)

Brasher believes that journalism taught Whitman to use life experiences (the "varied kind of life which reporters are likely to know"—15) as raw material.

Brasher is correct in his assessment, for if *Leaves of Grass* is anything, it is a celebration of the individual embodying and finding connection with the sprawling nation. As Whitman writes in "Song of Myself," "I am not an earth nor am adjunct of an earth,/ I am the mate and companion of people, all just as immortal and fathomless as myself,/ (They do not know how immortal, but I know") *(Leaves of Grass: The Deathbed Edition* 26). Similarly, in another explosion of enthusiasm, Whitman writes:

> I am of old and young, of the foolish as much as the wise,
> Regardless of others, ever regardful of others,
> Maternal as well as paternal, a child as well as a man,
> Stuff'd with the stuff that is coarse and stuff'd with the stuff that is fine,
> One of the Nation of many nations, the smallest the same and the largest the
>   same . . .
> Of every hue and caste am I, of every rank and religion,
> A farmer, mechanic, artist, gentleman, sailor, quaker,

Prisoner, fancy-man, rowdy, lawyer, physician, priest.
I resist any thing better than my own diversity,
Breathe the air but leave plenty after me,
And am not stuck up, and am in my place. *(Leaves of Grass: The Deathbed Edition* 33-34)

Joseph Jay Rubin and Charles H. Brown, editors of *Walt Whitman of the New York Aurora: Editor at Twenty-Two,* suggest that Whitman's social concerns during his time at the *Aurora* led to his writing "To a Common Prostitute" and "Song of Myself." Like Stephen Crane, Whitman cared especially about the "oppression of the poor, the innocent, or the helpless" (Allen, *Solitary* 51). During his time at the *Aurora,* he was deeply affected by the arrest of 50 prostitutes on Broadway, writing an article that called the occurrence "villainous" (Allen, *Solitary* 51-52). In addition to writing the affirming poem "To a Common Prostitute," Whitman also included the following lines in "Song of Myself":

The prostitute draggles her shawl, her bonnet bobs on her tipsy and pimpled
     neck,
The crowd laugh at her blackguard oaths, the men jeer and wink to each other,
(Miserable! I do not laugh at your oaths nor jeer you). *(Leaves of Grass: The Deathbed Edition* 32)

The next few years of Whitman's journalistic career were no more stable than the earlier ones, but they were filled with the zest for social issues that would become his journalistic trademark and would fuel his later fiction. Fired in May 1842 from his position at the *Aurora,* Whitman took over as editor of the *New York Evening Tattler.* Then in September 1845, Whitman began writing about social issues, including education reform, at the *Long Island Star,* a small daily owned by a Whig, Alden J. Spooner. He also was a theater and music reviewer at the *Star.* Whitman, a Democrat, was not trusted to cover politics, so he was assigned the Brooklyn education beat.

For one of his most controversial columns, Whitman drew on personal belief and on a fictional event described in his first short story, which appeared in August 1841 in the *Democratic Review.* The story, "Death in a Schoolroom," dealt with a boy who was killed by his teacher. Whitman transferred his protest of corporal punishment in the classroom to a newspaper column, and he received numerous negative responses. Having covered a lecture in Brooklyn by educator Horace Mann that opposed physical discipline by teachers, Whitman wrote, "Are not some of our Brooklyn teachers a little too profuse of this satanic power?" (Gay Wilson Allen, *Walt Whitman* 47)

In addition to stories by Whitman, the *Democratic Review* had published Poe, William Cullen Bryant, Nathaniel Hawthorne, James Russell Lowell, John Greenleaf Whittier, and others. Five of Whitman's stories ran between January and September 1842. Whitman also published for the *American Review* during the 1840s. *(The American Review* was already famous for having published Poe's "The Raven.")

In 1846, when Whitman became the editor of the *Brooklyn Daily Eagle* at the age of 27, he continued both his work as a social activist and his commitment to gaining exposure for literary figures. On June 1, 1846, Whitman wrote a column entitled "Ourselves and the 'Eagle.'" Its thesis follows:

> We really feel a desire to talk on many subjects, to *all* the people of Brooklyn; and it *ain't* their ninepences we want so much either. There is a curious kind of sympathy (haven't you ever thought of it before?) that arises in the mind of a newspaper conductor with the public he serves . . . Daily communion creates a sort of brotherhood and sisterhood between the two parties. *(Uncollected Poetry and Prose,* I, 115)

During this time, Whitman set up a literary department at the *Eagle*. He published work by William Cullen Bryant, Nathaniel Hawthorne, Oliver Wendell Holmes, Washington Irving, Henry Wadsworth Longfellow, Poe ("A Tale of the Ragged Mountains"), and John Greenleaf Whittier.

Whitman's tenure at the *Eagle* ended in January 1848 because he disagreed with the editor, Isaac Van Anden, about the "Free Soil" bill that prohibited slavery in annexed territories. Having been fired again, Whitman then traveled to Louisiana to write for a paper begun by J.W. McClure, the *New Orleans Crescent,* but he resigned three months later.

Whitman's next newspaper job was at the *Brooklyn Freeman,* a "Free Soil" paper, from 1848 to 1849. He then wrote and edited for the *Brooklyn Daily Times* from 1857 to 1859, contributing editorials dealing with social issues and civic improvement. In her book about literary journalists, Fishkin summarizes Whitman's numerous social concerns:

> He deplored in his editorials the evils of the slave trade, of capital punishment, of police brutality toward prostitutes and children of the poor, the low wages of garment workers, the flogging of children in the public schools, the long hours of store clerks, prison conditions, and the hostility of many Americans toward foreigners. His compassion for the poor, the forgotten, the outcast, the suffering, and the oppressed resonated with greater force with each new instance of injustice and oppression he exposed. (26)

Eventually, however, Whitman abandoned journalism as a full-time career, and the number of freelance submissions dwindled. Allen describes this period of Whitman's life by saying:

> It seems very unlikely that a man with Whitman's journalistic experience and wide acquaintance with editors could not obtain another newspaper position. [Horace] Greeley accepted these poems for the *Tribune,* and [William Cullen] Bryant, the editor of the *New York Post,* was a good friend of his, with whom he had often taken long walks. Surely they could have helped him to obtain another position. One must conclude that Walt Whitman did not want another newspaper position. He did not want to risk further betrayal by political compromisers. He was sick of the profession of journalism precisely because he believed so strongly in freedom and justice for all humanity. *(Walt Whitman* 54)

Bergman concludes that Whitman had "outgrown his journalism" ("Influence" 403) by the late 1850s.

It was not lack of talent or conviction that edged Whitman out of journalism. Greenspan notes that in the Nov. 9, 1842, issue of the *New York Herald,* Whitman is listed among the top 52 New York newspaper editors. He adds that appearing on the list was a "compliment Whitman would have particularly appreciated since it was given in the context of statements about the rising glory of journalism in harmony with his own ideological convictions" (51).

Whitman's appreciation of the individual and the American artist created a natural predisposition for a relationship with his journalistic colleague Edgar Allan Poe. The two respected each other and paid tribute to one another's fiction. In 1845, Whitman submitted a short essay entitled "Art-Music and Heart-Music" to the *Broadway Journal,* of which Poe was the editor. Poe published it Nov. 29, 1845, with an editorial endorsement. According to critic Philip Callow, Whitman was "charmed" by his encounter with Poe: "He was won over at once by Poe in the flesh, shaking hands with a quiet, cordial man who may or may not have been sober. Always swayed by courtesy and kindness, Whitman was charmed" (93). Allen describes the encounter with Poe, inserting Whitman's words: "Some time later Whitman called on Poe—probably to collect for the article—and found the poet 'very cordial, in a quiet way . . . I have a distinct and pleasing remembrance of his looks, voice, manner and matter; very kindly and human, but subdued, perhaps a little jaded" *(Solitary* 71).

Although most critics think the men had contact only on rare occasions, Joseph Jay Rubin believes that Whitman and Poe saw each other regularly: "Whitman saw his colleague often, since Poe attended to his duties [at the *Mirror]* faithfully at a corner desk, and both frequented the oyster cellar conducted in the heart of the Ann Street printing district by a Washingtonian famous for terrapin stew" *(Historic* 111).

The year after Poe published the younger poet's essay, Whitman edited a tragic news item about Poe that appeared in the Brooklyn *Eagle.* It read: "It is stated that Mr. Poe, the poet and author, now lies dangerously ill with brain fever, and that his wife is in the last stages of consumption. They are said to be without money and without friends, actually suffering from disease and destitution in New York" (Callow 93).

Although Whitman respected Poe and his work, the two men could not have been more different in sensibility and perspective. Whitman was engaged in local and national politics; he was an optimist; he was social and unusually outspoken. Poe, on the other hand, was pessimistic, often lonely, and locked into a relentlessly dark vision.

In *Specimen Days* (1882), Whitman evaluated the work of his colleague by saying: "Poe's verses illustrate an intense faculty for technical and abstract beauty . . . an incorrigible propensity towards nocturnal themes, a demoniac undertone behind every page—and by final judgment, probably belong among the electric lights of imaginative literature, brilliant and dazzling, but with no heart" (Callow 95). Whitman once described a dream in which he saw a "slender, slight, beautiful figure, a dim man, apparently enjoying all the terror, the murk and the dislocation of which he was the center and the victim. That figure of my lurid dream might stand for Edgar Poe, his spirit, his fortunes, and his poems, themselves all lurid dreams" (Callow 95).

Poe died in 1849. In November 1875, Whitman traveled to Baltimore for the reburial of Poe's remains and the dedication of a monument in Poe's honor. He was one of few who made the journey to bid another farewell to his professional acquaintance and fellow artist.

Edgar Allan Poe and Journalism

Poe worked as a journalist from 1835 until he died, and according to Robert D. Jacobs in *Poe: Journalist and Critic,* those who study Poe's life usually fail to consider the "often intolerable pressures of a journalistic career" (vii). Further, he argues that critics overlook the polemic that sets journalists such as Whitman and Poe apart from their literary fellows. According to Jacobs, during Poe's time as assistant editor of the *Broadway Journal,* his reviews were "marked by a growing insistence that a literary work avoid obscurity and profundity" (356). Quite simply, he said, Poe believed that "neither insight nor feeling had value unless they could be transmitted to others" (121).

Certainly, both Whitman and Poe opposed the characterization of a true artist as alienated and self-absorbed. In fact, in the "Preface to the 1855 Edition of *Leaves of Grass,"* Whitman wrote: "The art of art, the glory of expression and the sunshine of the light of letters is simplicity. Nothing is better than simplicity . . . nothing can make up for excess or for the lack of definiteness" (895). Whitman also argued for the timeliness of journalism: "The direct trial of him who would be the greatest poet is today. If he does not flood himself with the immediate age as with vast oceanic tides . . . let him merge in the general run and wait his development" (903).

Similarly, in a book about Poe and his devotion to British magazines, Michael Allen argues that "a serious writer who is also a journalist is likely to be particularly preoccupied with things like popularity, the nature of the audience, the building of reputations, the extent to which good writing can be widely successful. This is certainly the case with Poe" (3). It was, of course, also the case with Whitman, who wanted *Leaves of Grass* to appeal to the masses, as well as to the literary elite.

Whatever the case, journalism had as direct an impact on Poe as it did on Whitman, and in some ways, it was an impact that is more clearly documentable. In fact, two ideas for Poe's mystery stories—upon which modern detective fiction is founded—were drawn from newspaper articles.

"The Murders in the Rue Morgue" and "The Mystery of Marie Roget," two of three detective tales featuring Dupin, contain numerous details taken from newspaper stories Poe read and perhaps clipped. Lesser-known stories, including "Diddling Considered as One of the Exact Sciences" and the "Oblong Box," also were based on real events.

Poe's first five short stories were published by the *Philadelphia Saturday Courier* in 1832, and in 1833, "Ms. Found in a Bottle" appeared in the *Balti-*

more *Saturday Visitor* and won a literary prize. The prize led to an assistant editorship on the Richmond *Southern Literary Messenger* from 1835 to 1837. After a few months in New York, Poe moved to Philadelphia and worked for *Burton's Gentleman's Magazine, Graham's Magazine, The Saturday Museum* and other publications from 1838 to 1844. "The Gold Bug" won a literary prize in 1843 and was published by the *Philadelphia Dollar Newspaper.* In 1844, Poe moved to New York and worked sporadically at the *Evening Mirror* and the *Broadway Journal.* "The Raven" was published in the *Mirror* in 1945.

Subtitled "A Sequel to 'The Murders in the Rue Morgue,'" "The Mystery of Marie Roget" prompted John Walsh, himself a former journalist, to write *Poe the Detective: The Curious Circumstances Behind the Mystery of Marie Roget.* "The Mystery of Marie Roget" is distinct because it is based upon a true event and because Poe claimed that in spite of the police department's failure to solve the case, he had succeeded in doing so. In fact, Poe's solution was incorrect, and Walsh delights in showing the lengths to which Poe went to edit away his blame. Poe made a series of changes in "The Mystery of Marie Roget" in order to cover himself when installments of the story appeared in the *Ladies Companion* magazine.

The case attracted tremendous attention in New York. The body of Mary Cecilia Rogers, a "cigar girl" who worked in a New York tobacco shop, was found floating in the Hudson River in July 1841. New York newspapers covered the investigation from September through October. One of the reasons editors were so interested in the case was that Rogers' house was at 126 Nassau St. in the heart of the newspaper district. According to Walsh, who systematically reconstructed the New York neighborhood during the 1840s, there were 20 newspaper and periodical offices on Nassau Street and another 20 nearby. Walsh writes, "Horace Greeley's New York *Tribune* and James Gordon Bennett's New York *Herald* were both just around the corner on Ann Street; murder on the doorstep, whether of a cat or a king, can scarcely be overlooked" (8). Walsh also reveals that Poe lived for a time within 15 minutes from the shop where Rogers worked and may have known her.

Rogers' name had been in print years before, when, on Oct. 5, 1838, she ran away from home, allegedly to commit suicide. The New York papers *Journal of Commerce,* the *Sun, Times and Commercial Intelligencer,* and *Weekly Herald* ran the story. Soon after this event in 1839, Rogers quit her job at the tobacco store. She and her mother then opened a boardinghouse on Nassau Street.

On Sunday, July 25, 1841, Rogers vanished. Her body was found with her head and forehead severely battered. On Aug. 1, 1841, both the *New York Herald* and the *Mercury* ran stories about the murder on page one. Thorough coverage lasted six weeks. Claiming that Rogers had been raped by at least three men and strangled, the *New York Tribune* reported on Aug. 6, 1841: "The terrible Murder of Miss Rogers excites daily a deeper and wider interest in our city. Well may it do so . . ."

Poe supported the original speculation that the "cigar girl" was killed by several men. In his tale based on the crime, he writes, "The general impression, so far as we were enabled to glean it from the newspapers, seemed to be, that

Marie had been the victim of a *gang* of desperadoes—that by these she had been borne across the river, maltreated and murdered" (203).

The story was not complete until 1842, when, after more than a year of silence, the New York newspapers returned to the murder. Frederica Loss, owner of the Weehawken inn where Rogers was last seen, said on her deathbed that Rogers died on her property following an abortion. According to Justice Gilbert Merritt, who issued a ruling Nov. 14, Loss and her three sons were guilty of murder and disposal of the body.

Most journalists, as Walsh points out, are interested in crime, and Poe was, "despite his known preference for a poetical career, for practical reasons a magazinist" (2). Others, too, were obsessed with the murder, as evidenced by a poem by "E.S." in the Sept. 27, 1841, issue of the *New York Herald.* Entitled "Lines on the death of M.R.," the poem reads: "Hark! heard ye not that note of fear/ Burst wildly on the palsied ear,/ Far in the tangled wood?" (5).

In Poe's short story, the name "Rogers" is changed to "Roget," the setting is not New York but Paris, the murdered woman is 22, and she works in a "parfumerie," not a tobacco shop. Further, Frederica Loss is renamed "Madame Deluc," and Roget's lover commits suicide after her murder. The names of New York's prominent newspapers are changed as well. However, the human interest inherent in the case remains. Poe writes:

> The atrocity of this murder (for it was at once evident that murder had been committed), the youth and beauty of the victim, and, above all, her previous notoriety, conspired to produce intense excitement in the minds of the sensitive Parisians. I can call to mind no similar occurrence producing so general and so intense an effect. For several weeks, in the discussion of this one absorbing theme, even the momentous political topics of the day were forgotten. (199)

Dupin solves the crime by a semiological analysis of the stories published in the local newspapers and the reports filed by Parisian police.

The real-life inspiration for "The Mystery of Marie Roget" is only part of the story, however. Richard Kopley argues that Poe took ideas from news stories published in the *Philadelphia Saturday News* for another well-known piece, "The Murders in the Rue Morgue." The pieces Poe came to "refashion" (7) for "The Murders in the Rue Morgue" appeared in mid and late 1838, Kopley writes, and others formed the basis for his creation of Dupin, who also appears in "The Purloined Letter."

"The Murders in the Rue Morgue" is both one of Poe's most provocative and least believable tales. In it, an orangutan kills Madame L'Espanaye and her daughter, Mademoiselle Camille L'Espanaye, after climbing into their home through a window. The daughter's body is jammed upside down into the chimney. The orangutan slits the mother's throat and flings her body from the window.

Dupin solves the crime because of its *"outre"* nature. Unlike "The Mystery of Marie Roget," where clues are buried, the facts of "The Murders in the Rue Morgue" are obvious but point to a conclusion so unfathomable that no one surmises it. Speaking of an unsuccessful Parisian detective working on the case,

Dupin says: "He impaired his vision by holding the object too close. He might see, perhaps, one or two points with unusual clearness, but in doing so he, necessarily, lost sight of the matter as a whole. Thus there is such a thing as being too profound. Truth is not always in a well" (186). Later, he adds: "It appears to me that this mystery is considered insoluble, for the very reason which should cause it to be regarded as easy of solution—I mean for the *outre* character of its features. The police are confounded by the seeming absence of motive—not for the murder itself—but for the atrocity of the murder" (187).

One news article to which Kopley alludes is entitled "Orang Outang," published May 26, 1838. According to the reporter, the orangutan in the London Zoo was extremely powerful and often tried to break out of its cage. The similarity to Poe's murderous beast is obvious.

Another important detail for the story appeared in an article entitled "Deliberate Murder in Broadway, at Midday" (Aug. 4, 1838). In that story, Edward Coleman, who suspected his wife of infidelity, had slit her throat with a razor on the street in broad daylight July 28. Kopley writes:

> The important correspondences between the *Saturday News* piece on Coleman's murder of his wife and Poe's tale of an orangoutang's murder of two women involve distinctly similar language. The newspaper story characterizes Coleman's act as an "atrocious murder"; Poe's story refers to the ourangoutang's act as a "murder [that was] singularly atrocious" . . . The news story states that Coleman murdered his wife by "nearly severing her head from her body with a razor," and later reasserts that Coleman's razor "nearly severed her head from her body." Poe's work states of the razor-flourishing orangoutang, "With one determined sweep of its muscular arm it nearly severed her head from her body . . . The *Saturday News* piece refers to Coleman's then "dropping her [his dead wife] upon the pavement"; Poe's tale relates that the orangoutang "hurled [the body of Madame L'Espanaye] through the window headlong" to "the stone pavement." Finally, the *Saturday News* piece asserts that, feigning insanity in prison (on the advice of his counsel, it is implied), Coleman responded to questions with answers "of the most *outre* kind"; Poe's story remarks on the "excessively *outre*" manner in which the younger L'Espanaye's body was disposed of. On Aug. 18, 1838, the *Saturday News* included an untitled piece about a French woman whose former servant had robbed her. The story refers to "the thief's likely object, 'the iron box containing her jewelry,' suggestive of the 'small iron safe,' 'the iron chest' of the L'Espanayes which contained 'some papers' and had probably contained Madame L'Espanaye's two bags of gold francs, and other valuables." (9)

Another clue to Poe's mysterious tale appeared Sept. 22, 1838, and is entitled "A Mischievous Ape." The ape, according to Kopley's research, escaped from a "stable"; Dupin says late in "The Murders in the Rue Morgue" that the orangutan was at a "livery stable" (11). Both animals opened a window to enter the house. Kopley writes that "once chased out of the house, the ape in this news story 'seized hold of the hair of a child' and 'nearly took his scalp off'; Poe's orangoutang 'seized Madame L'Espanaye by the hair' and tore her hair out 'by the roots,' revealing 'the flesh of the scalp'" (11).

Whether or not it was the basis for Poe's macabre tales of horror or for Whitman's celebration of energy and hope, journalism lured numerous young American writers to its ranks. According to some critics, their work as editors at least paid their bills and kept them in contact with the literary elite. According to others, the time Whitman, Poe, and others worked in newspaper and magazine offices was utterly wasted. Fortunately, a few argue that the time Whitman and Poe spent building careers in journalism was adroitly and creatively reclaimed in some of the best fiction of the nineteenth century.

The tradition established by Crane, Dreiser, Hemingway, Poe, and Whitman is formidable indeed. Like Virginia Woolf in *A Room of One's Own,* though, one must wonder how many female contemporaries of these giants of American literature have been overlooked. How many of their stories were lost? How many of their careers were squelched? Just as Woolf wonders if William Shakespeare had a sister—and what she might have written—this study both celebrates the contributions of men in American letters and seeks to suggest that there might be others whose work has been made peripheral. While lauding Crane and Dreiser for what they overcame in order to write and praising them for their realistic portrayals of women, it is also important to remember the absent voices of women writers themselves and of women who—with training and encouragement—might have written works that could have rivaled novels such as *Maggie: A Girl of the Streets, Sister Carrie,* and *The Sun Also Rises.*

Fortunately, two women writers were both prolific and received significant critical acclaim. They knew one another, attended some of the same writers workshops, and read one another's work. They are often included in collections of essays about Southern women writers, although their time in journalism is usually overlooked or treated superficially. The women are Katherine Anne Porter, a Texas native who wrote short stories and novels, and Eudora Welty, who spent her life in Jackson, Mississippi, and who gave readers some of the most distinctive fictional characters in American literature.

Katherine Anne Porter wrote for a Fort Worth tabloid, *The Critic,* and for Denver's *Rocky Mountain News* (1918-1919), and Eudora Welty freelanced for Mississippi newspapers, wrote copy for radio station WJDX in Jackson, wrote a Sunday column about Jackson society for the *Memphis Commercial Appeal,* and photographed rural Mississippians for a federal agency, the Works Progress Administration. The women's short, aborted careers in media affected their development as writers of fiction. A study of their work reveals the importance of place and the supremacy of the moment and (with some exceptions that will be noted) indicates a desire to stand outside the action as observers instead of interpreters, an important journalistic device.

Settling the Borderland: Other Voices in Literary Journalism analyzes the style, structure, and intent of *Pale Horse, Pale Rider;* "The Grave"; and *The Never-Ending Wrong* by Porter and "A Piece of News," "Why I Live at the P.O.," "Death of a Traveling Salesman," "A Worn Path," and *Photographs* by Welty. An examination of their work reveals the importance of newspaper work in the fictional references to editors and newsrooms in Porter's prose; the significance of perception as reality and the devotion to detail in Porter's work; the effect of Welty's experience as a photographer on her ability to isolate and contain the moment; and the influence of writing society news on Welty's ability to portray with realism and humor the fictional inhabitants of Mississippi.

Porter and Welty saw into the life of things and found what Welty called "my real subject: human relationships" *(One Writer's Beginnings* 87). Having worked in media and having been captivated by real people in real situations, both used what they had learned as observers of human nature and as news and feature writers. The pathway between journalism and fiction for Porter and Welty cannot be said to be clearly definable, but it can be said to be significant. Their frequent use of fly-on-the-wall point of view, their attention to detail, their references to newspapers (in works such as *Pale Horse, Pale Rider* and "A Piece of News"), their devotion to description and place, their concern with chronology and narrative, and their passion for capturing the moment may be said to have been born in their early experiences in journalism, whether journalism meant a traditional newspaper or a tabloid with a feature bent such as *The Critic* (Porter) or photography (Welty).

Katherine Anne Porter

Katherine Anne Porter is one of the women whose work will be discussed at length in this study, although the pathway between her work as an "objective" reporter and her recognition as a fiction writer are rarely acknowledged. A study of Porter's work reveals the importance of place and the supremacy of the moment and—with the exception of the extended essay *The Never-Ending Wrong*—indicates a desire to observe without passing judgment on the events she describes.

It is true that Porter broke the bounds of conventional journalism and turned to a genre that better utilized her talents. However, it is also true that having been relegated to "women's" news by the editors of her day, Porter may have left journalism to avoid the rampant sexism present there. Certainly, Porter was not the only woman to be shuffled to the women's pages or sent to cover theater or fashion simply because of her gender. Porter's friend Eudora Welty, for example, once wrote that the only reason she was designated a "junior publicity agent" during her work for the Works Progress Administration was that the title "senior publicity agent" was reserved for men. While working as a publicity agent for a government office in Mississippi, Welty worked with Louis Johnson, a professional newsman. She writes, "I worked directly under another publicity agent who knew a lot more than I did. He was a professional newsman, named Louis Johnson. He's dead now. He was a senior publicity agent. I was a junior publicity agent—which also indicated I was a *girl*. We sometimes traveled together, and he did the news work and I did feature stories, interviews, and took some pictures" *(Photographs* xxv).

Furthermore, it is difficult to separate the harsh words of a Cather or Porter about journalism as a profession from the treatment they received at the hands of male editors. In her article "Katherine Anne Porter, Journalist," biographer Joan Givner acknowledges Porter's rejection of her own work as a journalist and calls it "unfortunate" because it "deflected attention from material which is crucial to the understanding of Porter's life and art" (69). Late in her career, Porter said:

> I forgive [one] critic here and now, and forever, for calling me a "newspaper woman" in the public prints. I consider it an actionable libel, but, as is too often the case in these incidents, he has a small patch of solid ground under him . . .
>
> Fifty-odd years ago, for eight short months of my ever-lengthening (or shortening?) life, I did have a kind of a job on a newspaper, *The Rocky Mountain News.* (Givner, "Journalist" 69)

In spite of her feelings about journalism, Porter was a dedicated newspaperwoman during the short time she spent in the field. Instinctively, she understood the importance of careful observation and utilized her skill in both her newspaper stories and her fiction. A strong journalistic influence—not an obvious part of her memoirs or the published conversations with her—emerges in an analysis of three selected works, a short novel, *Pale Horse, Pale Rider;* an extended essay, *The Never-Ending Wrong;* and a short story, "The Grave."

Porter's journalism career had begun several years before her often-chronicled time at the *Rocky Mountain News,* however. Porter moved to Chicago when she was 21 and, according to one biographical account, worked as a reporter for a short time (until she was distracted by watching a film in production, went back to the newspaper five days later, was paid $18 and summarily fired). She also worked for the *The Critic,* a friend's newspaper in Fort Worth, before moving from Texas to Colorado in 1917 with fellow journalist Kitty Barry Crawford. The women rented a cabin on Cheyenne Mountain near Colorado Springs.

Porter later moved to Denver, rented a room in a boardinghouse at 1510 York St., and became a reporter for the *Rocky Mountain News,* then at 1720 Welton St., earning approximately $20 per week. She reviewed books, plays and concerts; interviewed celebrities; and rewrote crime stories. According to Enrique Hank Lopez, Porter's "incorruptible tell-it-like-it-is attitude"—presumably developed during this time at the *Rocky Mountain News*—was later adopted by Miranda in *Pale Horse, Pale Rider* (46).

This study explores Porter's use of style and point of view and takes seriously the autobiographical allusions to her early media career. It also reveals her desperate longing to believe in a personal, individual truth. Such a commitment to truth puts Porter in the company of the journalists who make a living relaying the truth of everyday events—filtered though it may be through their experience and beliefs.

Media critic Roger Rosenblatt understands the separate function of the reporter and the writer of fiction, as does Porter, although both underestimate the power of news communicated artistically. In his essay "Journalism and the Larger Truth," Rosenblatt writes:

If one asks, then, where the larger truth is to be sought, the answer is where it has always been: in history, poetry, art, nature, education, conversation; in the tunnels of one's own mind. People may have come to expect too much of journalism . . . The trouble is that people have also come to expect too much of journalism at its best, because they have invested too much power in it, and in so doing have neglected or forfeited other sources of power in their lives. Journalists appear to give answers, but essentially they ask a question: What shall we make of this? A culture that would rely on the news for truth could not answer that question because it already would have lost the qualities of mind that make the news worth knowing. (133)

Rosenblatt does not suggest the supremacy of fiction over journalism. He argues instead that the two cannot be compared, for they provide two different truths for the reader.

Before journalists and media scholars began to address the fact that truth is often a matter of perspective or vantage point, reporters were asked to be objective and to cover both sides of the story (as though only two existed). While Porter worked for newspapers in Illinois, Texas, and Colorado, the prevailing philosophy was that newspapers printed the truth (or ought to). A recurring theme in Porter's novels and short stories is the longing for personal truth; for example, in *Old Mortality,* Miranda dismisses "other people's memory of the past" and establishes her independence. Miranda thinks:

Ah, but there is my own life to come yet, she thought, my own life now and beyond. I don't want any promises. I won't have false hopes, I won't be romantic about myself. I can't live in their world any longer, she told herself, listening to the voices back of her. Let them tell their stories to each other. Let them go on explaining how things happened. I don't care. At least I can know the truth about what happens to me, she assured herself silently, making a promise to herself, in her hopefulness, her ignorance. (Porter, *Stories* 221)

Although Porter knows that Miranda is destined to fail, she is sympathetic to the longings of her heroine, whom many critics have understood to be the young Porter herself. Even in Miranda's moment of self-deception, Porter supports her desire to be the authority over her own life and over the fiction she writes about herself.

Pale Horse, Pale Rider

In *Pale Horse, Pale Rider* Miranda seeks assurance that she can discern truth, but that desire is consistently undercut. Her colleague Mary Towney, the society editor, says with sarcasm, "I read it in a New York newspaper, so it's bound to be true" (Porter, *Stories* 284). As a journalist familiar with the William Randolph Hearst-Joseph Pulitzer-Adolph Ochs newspaper wars from the early 1880s to the early 1900s, the fictional Towney would understand the irony of her words even as she reveals a desire for a newspaper's account to be reliable. Instead, yellow journalists (a term derived from the fact that Hearst and Pulitzer fought over ownership of Richard Outcault's cartoon strip "Hogan's Alley," which featured a character known as the "Yellow Kid") often told the truth only when it was sensational enough to sell newspapers. Only Ochs, editor of the *New York Times,* succeeded in providing reliable information because he promised to provide "all the news that's fit to print," now the newspaper's page one slogan, and then followed through.

The pathway between journalism and fiction for Porter is significant. As with Welty, her frequent use of fly-on-the-wall point of view; her attention to detail; her description of newspaper culture; her devotion to description and place; her concern with chronology, event and narrative; and her passion for capturing the moment may be said to have been born during her early experiences in newsrooms. Some of these literary tendencies may also have derived from the storytelling tradition of the South and the folklore of Texas, her home state.

In spite of her disdain for everyday journalism, Porter's short career in media most certainly affected her development as a writer of fiction. The importance of newspaper work in the fictional references to editors and newsrooms is obvious; less perceptible is the influence of journalism on Porter's understanding of the significance of perception as reality, on her interest in historical event, and on her devotion to detail. Furthermore, Porter exhibited the single most important trait for any successful journalist: an obsession with the people around her. She once said of herself: "I have a personal and instant interest in every human being that comes within ten feet of me, and I have never seen any two alike, but I discover the most marvelous differences" (Kunitz, *Authors* 539).

Porter describes her own journalistic experiences in *Pale Horse, Pale Rider,* a short novel. The title comes from a spiritual quoted by Miranda, the heroine: "Pale horse, pale rider, done taken my lover away" (Porter, *Stories* 303). In the novel, Miranda and her friend Towney are banished to routine jobs at a newspaper—one to a theater beat, the other to a society beat. In *Pale Horse, Pale Rider,* Porter deals fictionally with two events in her own life: her work as a reporter for the *Rocky Mountain News* from 1918-1919 (she wrote 81 stories with bylines between Feb. 8, 1919, and Aug. 17, 1919) and her near-fatal illness during an epidemic that struck Denver in the fall of 1918. Kathryn Adams Sexton chronicles Porter's years as a reporter in her 1961 unpublished thesis "Katherine Anne Porter's Years in Denver." In it she organizes the 81 bylined stories by Porter and interviews many who knew Porter during 1918-19 in Denver. The articles are broken down into reviews of dramatic productions, reviews of operas and concerts, profile interviews, and light special-assignment stories. Either Porter was not capable of writing hard news, or her editors underestimated her ability. Of course, the case may also be made that the writing of reviews and features—often considered by editors the domain of women reporters for women readers—may need to be taken more seriously as being of interest for readers of both genders.

As we will learn, the fictional episodes included in *Pale Horse, Pale Rider* are often autobiographical. One of those is particularly important in understanding where Porter found herself as she struggled to carve out a career in a male-dominated newsroom. In it, Mary Townsend, the society editor, and Miranda (Porter's acknowledged personal voice) fail to please their male editors when they are assigned to cover an elopement. Their punishment is to be assigned to cover news considered important only to women. Although they may have failed to cover the human interest story well, young reporters of any gender are susceptible to the errors the two young women made. Clearly, Porter's point is that the punishment for poor judgment should not be to be put on the fashion or theater beat.

The novel chronicles the flu epidemic that hit Denver during Porter's time at the *Rocky Mountain News*. Porter's new love (named Adam in the novel) died, and she became seriously ill herself. Some critics believe Porter met a lieutenant at the Tabor Grand Opera House in Denver, although that fact has not been documented with solid evidence. In the late fall of 1918, both of them contracted the flu, and he later died.

Articles in the *Rocky Mountain News* attest to the seriousness of the flu epidemic in Denver. According to Sexton, the epidemic raged in the Army camps in late September, and by October 6 public places in Denver were closed to help contain the virus. By November 12 the "flu ban was lifted, and theaters and places of amusement were again opened" (Sexton 103).

The pale rider of the text is Death, and during her illness Porter believed she was dying; her hair turned white and she became crippled when one leg swelled from phlebitis. Quoted in an article in the *Denver Post* on March 22, 1956 (an interview precipitated by a planned television adaptation of *Pale Horse, Pale Rider*), she remembered the epidemic: "I was taken ill with the flu. They gave me up. The paper had my obit set in type" (Hendrick, *Katherine Anne Porter* 76). Asked about her lover, Porter—fighting back tears—said, "It's in the story. He died. The last I remember seeing him . . . It's a true story . . . It seems to me true that I died then, I died once, and I have never feared death since" (Lopez 223). Porter also wrote of that period of her life: "My mood for several years thereafter was that it was not a world worth living in" (Lopez 48). She treats the experience fictionally by describing Miranda's "lost rapture":

> There was no escape. Dr. Hildesheim, Miss Tanner, the nurses in the diet kitchen, the chemist, the surgeon, the precise machine of the hospital, the whole humane conviction and custom of society, conspired to pull her inseparable rack of bones and wasted flesh to its feet, to put in order her disordered mind, and to set her once more safely in the road that would lead her again to death. (Porter, *Stories* 314)

In the novel, Miranda's experiences and salary certainly reflect accounts of Porter's early days as a reporter. Asked for money to support the war effort, Miranda says in *Pale Horse, Pale Rider*, "I have eighteen dollars a week and not another cent in the world. I simply cannot buy anything" (Porter, *Stories* 273). She also describes the exhaustion and recurring deadlines of newspaper work. Porter writes: "After working for three years on a morning newspaper she had an illusion of maturity and experience; but it was fatigue merely, she decided, from keeping what she had been brought up to believe were unnatural hours, eating casually at dirty little restaurants, drinking bad coffee all night, and smoking too much" (Porter, *Stories* 280).

With humor and obvious first-hand knowledge, Porter describes Miranda's conflicts with irate readers and impatient editors. The descriptions of the newsroom (where people sat on her desk and where she heard the incessant "rattle of typewriters" and the "steady rumble of presses") are realistic, as are Porter's memories of rigid stylistic principles:

> They lolled away, past the Society Editor's desk, past Bill the City Editor's desk, past the long copydesk where old man Gibbons sat all night shouting at intervals, "Jarge! Jarge!" and the copyboy would come flying. "Never say *people* when you mean *persons,*" old man Gibbons had instructed Miranda, "and never say *practically,* say *virtually*, and don't for God's sake ever so long as I am at this desk use the barbarism *inasmuch* under any circumstances whatsoever. Now you're educated, you may go." (Porter, *Stories* 274)

In her 1961 thesis at the University of Colorado at Boulder, Sexton documents her interviews with those who worked with Porter at the *Rocky Mountain News* in 1918. She says that Bill, the city editor, is William C. Shanklin; Old Man Gibbons is Frank McClelland; Jarge is George Day, the copy boy (later the Rev. George T. Day); Mary Townsend is Porter's friend Eva Chappell; and Charles E. Lounsbury is Chuck Rouncivale, sports editor (89). One of Sexton's sources also remembers Adam as a "tall, blonde, debonair, and young lieutenant who called for Miss Porter at the *News* office during their short acquaintance" (95).

After her experiences in Chicago, Fort Worth, and Denver, Porter moved to New York (1919), Mexico (1920), and back to Fort Worth (1921) to write for a trade magazine. And in a 1963 interview for the *Paris Review,* Porter "indicated that it was better for a writer to work as a waitress than as a newspaperwoman; it was better to take dull jobs that would not take all her mind or time" (Hendrick, *Katherine Anne Porter* 22). Porter's career as a journalist may have been prompted by a need to support herself, and she left journalism—not primarily because of its low salaries and long days—but because she valued the writing of fiction more than the writing of news and features.

In addition to the long hours and poor pay of the working journalist, Porter struggled with the sexism implicit in the newsrooms of the early 1900s. She often was given stories considered the domain of women. One biographer says of Porter's earliest newspaper assignments:

> It was a huge brawling city, seething with surface excitements, particularly so for a young convent girl . . . But the articles she wrote had nothing to do with that aspect of Chicago; her assignments were those generally given to female reporters—wedding notices, obituaries and cultural activities, plus filling in as a coffee-maker and sandwich-getter for the editorial staff. Crime stories and political scandals were the exclusive province of male reporters. (Lopez 39)

During her brief stint at *The Critic* in Fort Worth in 1917, Porter wrote society columns, fashion news, and drama reviews for the weekly newspaper that was devoted to politics, drama, and local events. The woman who would one day win a Pulitzer Prize and the National Book Award was assigned to stories about music clubs. One critic includes a particularly poor excerpt from one of Porter's *Rocky Mountain News* stories: "The music club is organizing Sing Songs, where our soldier boys may harmonize together quite chummily" (Lopez 44).

When Porter applied for the job at the *Rocky Mountain News,* the editor cited her lack of experience (a fair claim) and was "shocked to find that the applicant, K. Porter, was a woman" (117), records Joan Givner in her biography *Katherine Anne Porter: A Life.* Porter took her experience with the *Rocky Mountain News* and created the *Blue Mountain News* of *Pale Horse, Pale Rider.* In the novel Miranda strikes up a friendship with Townsend, the society editor, at the *News.* Porter writes of the two women reporters with compassion born of experience:

> [Mary Townsend's] column was called Ye Towne Gossyp, so of course everybody called her Towney. Miranda and Towney had a great deal in common, and liked each other. They had both been real reporters once, and had been sent together to "cover" a scandalous elopement in which no marriage had taken place, after all, and the recaptured girl, her face swollen, had sat with her mother who was moaning steadily under a mound of blankets. They had both wept painfully and implored the young reporters to suppress the worst of the story. They had suppressed it, and the rival newspaper printed it all the next day. Miranda and Towney had then taken their punishment together, and had been degraded publicly to routine female jobs, one to the theaters, the other to society. (Porter, *Stories* 274-75)

Porter implies that concern for the objects of the news story was seen as weakness by the male editors and disdained as "female" failure or poor judgment. Their "punishment" was to be relegated to female news beats—often considered frivolous and undemanding.

Porter's belief in the equality of women is clear. In a May 4, 1919, column in the *Rocky Mountain News,* Porter writes of the stereotypically virtuous and insipid women in dramatic productions of the day: "We are deadly weary of the women who kneel, in song and story, at the feet of the world asking forgiveness for problematical errors. Why don't they stand on their feet and say: 'Yes, I did it. What are you going to do about it, my friends?'" (Sexton 33). Porter believed in the equality of professional women, and she challenged herself never to "kneel . . . at the feet of the world."

Considering Porter's experience as a newspaperwoman, I find it unsurprising that she deals in her fiction with the restrictive social order awaiting female children. In "The Grave," Porter tells of nine-year-old Miranda's exploring an old family graveyard with her brother. Not fond of dolls, Miranda wears overalls and reaps the scorn of the community:

> Ordinarily, Miranda preferred her overalls to any other dress, though it was making rather a scandal in the countryside, for the year was 1903, and in the back country the law of female decorum had teeth in it. Her father had been

criticized for letting his girls dress like boys and go careening around astride barebacked horses. Big sister Maria, the really independent and fearless one, in spite of her rather affected ways, rode at a dead run with only a rope knotted around her horse's nose. (Porter, *Stories* 364)

Older women in the community snarled at Miranda: "Ain't you ashamed of yo-self, Missy? It's against the Scriptures to dress like that. Whut yo Pappy thinkin about?" (Porter, *Stories* 365).

Porter created strong, independent women (such as Miranda and Ellen Weatherall of "The Jilting of Granny Weatherall") and treasured the things of the heart. A cutline beneath a photo of Porter in *The Critic* after she was hired in 1917 is ironic in noting that Porter's interests ran counter to established society: "She has come to Fort Worth to devote her young life to *The Critic*. Miss Porter likes things which many people consider frivolous and of no consequence—Society and the many small factors which go toward making life pleasant and interesting" (Givner, *A Life* 118).

What made life "pleasant and interesting" for Porter were human relation-ships and the wonder and intricacy of human growth and change, but as Givner notes, "Porter herself never acknowledged and probably never realized how much she gained at this time from her journalistic experience" (Givner, *A Life* 137). What she gained was in part an awareness that no event is isolated or un-important and that events are part of a web affecting many people profoundly. The simplest occurrence covered by a newspaper reporter or a short-story writer may reverberate through time.

"The Grave"

William L. Nance writes in *Katherine Anne Porter and the Art of Rejection* that Porter's characters lived lives of deep desperation and that their progression was, at best, linear. He writes: "For all [of her characters], life begins in bitter-ness and corruption, proceeds in pain and lovelessness through successively deeper disillusions, and ends in nothingness, the foreknowledge of which casts a gradually thickening pall of despair over all of it" (245). However, in his bleak summary Nance fails to understand two of Porter's themes: the value of self-discovery and the ultimate cost of acquiring one's own truth. Surely in *Pale Horse, Pale Rider,* "The Grave" and other works, the quest for self-awareness is not without reward. In "The Grave," a young Miranda and her twelve-year-old brother Paul take their Winchester rifles into the woods to shoot small game. They explore a graveyard in which the coffins have been dug up and moved, and in the course of the day discover treasures: a gold ring and tiny silver dove (laden with symbolism, as numerous critics have noted).

The two shoot a pregnant rabbit, and when Paul cuts it open, the children discover unborn baby rabbits. The description of the dead rabbit marks Porter as a master of detail and precise observation, a gift that had served her well during her days as a reporter:

Very carefully he slit the thin flesh from the center ribs to the flanks, and a scarlet bag appeared. He slit again and pulled the bag open, and there lay a bundle of tiny rabbits, each wrapped in a thin scarlet veil. The brother pulled these off and there they were, dark gray, their sleek wet down lying in minute even ripples, like a baby's head just washed, their unbelievably small delicate ears folded close, their little blind faces almost featureless. (Porter, *Stories* 366)

What is important about the central event in "The Grave" is that Porter never explains it; she recreates the moment and—in Ernest Hemingway fashion— allows the reader to bring it to life. The reader may then deal with the rich possibilities that range from horror at the grotesque sight of dead baby rabbits to wonder at the fragility of life and appreciation for the initiation experience of the two children. The story ends with Miranda walking down a city street 20 years later: "One day she was picking her path among the puddles and crushed refuse of a market street in a strange city of a strange country, when without warning, plain and clear in its true colors as if she looked through a frame upon a scene that had not stirred or changed since the moment it happened, the episode of that far-off day leaped from its burial place before her mind's eye" (Porter, *Stories* 367). She passes a vendor carrying dyed sugar sweets, reminding her of the tiny unborn rabbits, and that memory reminds her of her brother:

It was a very hot day and the smell in the market, with its piles of raw flesh and wilting flowers, was like the mingled sweetness and corruption she had smelled that other day in the empty cemetery at home: the day she had remembered always until now vaguely as the time she and her brother had found treasure in the opened graves. Instantly upon this thought the dreadful vision faded, and she saw clearly her brother, whose childhood face she had forgotten, standing again in the blazing sunshine, again twelve years old, a pleased sober smile in his eyes, turning the silver dove over and over in his hands. (Porter, *Stories* 367-68)

A slogan that editors utter often in newsrooms is "Show; don't tell." "The Grave" is one of the finest expressions in American literature of a writer's doing just that. Porter invites the reader to construct his or her own understanding of the "sweetness and corruption" of the described experience. Her reliance on detail links her to the literary journalism of Ernest Hemingway, Joan Didion, and Tom Wolfe. Cutting open the dead rabbit—a graphic and intense moment— takes on a significance of its own. Porter practices well her journalistic obligation to accuracy, detail, and stark observation. Often, Porter explores techniques of fiction-writing, including stream-of-consciousness, but she is never more persuasive than when she relates a narrative from the detached perspective of an observer (reporter). In "The Grave," the memory of the day in the graveyard with Paul evokes specific thoughts (longing for childhood, desire to see her brother, a sense of isolation in a strange city, etc.), but the meaning is created by the reader as he or she interacts with the rich sign system in the story, with its silver doves, gold rings, hollowed-out graves, and unborn babies.

Miranda, whose name is from the Spanish "mirar," which means "to watch," longs to see, to understand. "Oh, I want to *see*" (59), she cries. Porter writes, "Yet she wanted most deeply to see and to know. Having seen, she felt at once as if she had known all along. The very memory of her former ignorance faded, she had always known just this" (60). In spite of the reader's identification with Miranda, the events of the story are left intact and are relayed with careful attention to time and description.

The former newspaperwoman remained devoted to truth throughout her career in fiction, although even when writing the simplest of news stories she never mistook accuracy and factual relation of event for "truth" in its purest form. Having called Miranda her "witness, observer, or sharer," Porter herself attests to the fact that it is Miranda who best captures her own quiet quest: "All stories of any sort with Miranda in it are based on some particularly personal experience of my own and Miranda is not intended to be a self-portrait—she is my representative, the witness, observer, or sharer, sometimes all three in the stories where she figures" (Sexton 3, 142). In "Old Mortality," Porter clarifies the connection between herself and her fictional creation when she writes:

> What is the truth, she asked herself as intently as if the question had never been asked, the truth, even about the smallest, the least important of all the things I must find out? and where shall I begin to look for it? Her mind closed stubbornly against remembering, not the past but the legend of the past, other people's memory of the past, at which she had spent her life peering in wonder like a child at a magic-lantern show. (Porter, *Stories* 221)

Porter's work, which is often based on actual events, illustrates, interprets, and persuades. Even in their dedication to chronology and fact, her narratives appeal to the part of the reader that longs to order, to understand, and—as Miranda would say—to see. Miranda's thoughts recorded at the end of "Old Mortality" are a dramatic monologue, of course, for Porter knows well that Miranda—like her ancestors—inevitably will deceive herself and that she will retell history as she needs to remember it. Nonetheless, the author of news stories and Pulitzer Prize-winning fiction never seems to have despaired of one day being in possession of "the truth about what happens" (Porter, *Stories* 221).

The Never-Ending Wrong

Radically different from "The Grave" in theme and intent is the extended, didactic essay *The Never-Ending Wrong,* an example of Porter's personal investment in event and of her longing to believe in society and the judicial system. The essay is too biased to be reputable journalism, but it remains a testament to Porter's courage. In the foreword, Porter writes:

> This book is not for the popular or best-selling list for a few weeks or months. It is a plain, full record of a crime that belongs to history.
> When a reporter from a newspaper here in Maryland asked to talk to me, he said he had heard that I was writing another book . . . what about? . . . I gave him the title and the names of Sacco and Vanzetti. There was a wavering pause

. . . then: "Well, I don't really know anything about them . . . for me it's just history."

It is my conviction that when events are forgotten, buried in the cellar of the page—they are no longer even history. *(Wrong* vii)

Ironically, by compromising the focus and style of *The Never-Ending Wrong*—by denying it placement in the "popular or best-selling list for a few weeks or months"—Porter relegated the arrest, trial, and execution of Nicola Sacco and Bartolomeo Vanzetti to the very place she dreaded—the unpopular and unread "cellar of the page."

Porter became interested in the trial of the shoemaker and the fisherman, both accused of a violent robbery and murder on April 15, 1920, in South Braintree, Massachusetts. The Italians were political activists, and Porter and her group, which boasted literary notables like John Dos Passos and Edna St. Vincent Millay, suspected the motives of those who arrested and sentenced the two. Those who opposed the verdict believed that Sacco and Vanzetti had been found guilty primarily because they had been called "foreigners" and "anarchists" throughout the trial. The period after the end of World War I was characterized by heavy pressure toward ethnic unification, Americanization and forced culturalization. It also was the end of a massive immigration period and was a time of economic turmoil. Documenting the hatred the public felt toward Sacco and Vanzetti, Porter writes in *The Never-Ending Wrong:*

> Judge Webster Thayer, during the Sacco-Vanzetti episode, was heard to boast while playing golf, "Did you see what I did to those anarchistic bastards?" and the grim little person named Rosa Baron . . . who was head of my particular group during the Sacco-Vanzetti demonstrations in Boston snapped at me when I expressed the wish that we might save the lives of Sacco and Vanzetti: "Alive—what for? They are no earthly good to us alive." *(Wrong* 5-6)

Although modern reporters have abandoned the notion that objectivity is possible in news coverage, Porter became overly involved in the case, making her especially suspect as a reliable witness. The same accusations leveled against Capote (as he both describes and creates the character Perry Smith in *In Cold Blood)* can be leveled against Porter and her treatment of Sacco and Vanzetti. She writes:

> They were put to death in the electric chair at Charlestown Prison at midnight on the 23rd of August, 1927, a desolate dark midnight, a night for perpetual remembrance and mourning. I was one of the many hundreds who stood in anxious vigil watching the light in the prison tower, which we had been told would fail at the moment of death; it was a moment of strange heartbreak. (Porter, *Wrong* 8)

The melodrama in the passage is unlike Porter's carefully crafted tales of a young female reporter in Denver and her description of the two children exploring a graveyard in "The Grave." The narrative becomes an essay, personal and occasionally compelling, but is not straight news, a feature, an editorial, or even an example of commentary. Read as if it were a journal, *The Never-Ending Wrong* chronicles Porter's own political development more effectively than it ever addresses the charges against Sacco and Vanzetti. Explaining her disillusionment with communism, for example, Porter writes:

> I flew off Lenin's locomotive and his vision of history in a wide arc in Boston, Massachusetts, on August 21, 1927; it was two days before the putting to death of Sacco and Vanzetti, to the great ideological satisfaction of the Communist-headed group with which I had gone up to Boston. It was exactly what they had hoped for and predicted from the first: another injustice of the iniquitous capitalistic system against the working class. *(Wrong* 20)

When Porter marched in protest against the impending executions, she was arrested, released on bail and re-arrested in a recurring, ritualistic manner. As she said, "My elbow was always taken quietly by the same mild little blond officer, day after day; he was very Irish, very patient, very damned bored with the whole incomprehensible show" (*Wrong* 25).

Porter includes dialogue between "her policeman" and herself, lending even more support to the sense that *The Never-Ending Wrong* is a personal memoir of a public controversy and not a news story designed to inform or persuade. Her disdain for those appointed to the latter task is apparent in the piece when she describes "several of the more enterprising young reporters . . . swarming over the scene like crows to a freshly planted cornfield" (*Wrong* 36). Porter calls the execution a "terrible wrong" that was perpetrated "not only against the two men" but "against all of us, against our common humanity and our shared will to avert what we believed to be not merely a failure in the use of the instrument of the law, an injustice committed through mere human weakness and misunderstanding, but a blindly arrogant, self-righteous determination not to be moved by any arguments, the obstinate assumption of the infallibility of a handful of men intoxicated with the vanity of power and gone mad with wounded self-importance" (*Wrong* 43). From her post outside the prison, Porter recalls her horror at the execution: "Life felt very grubby and mean, as if we were all of us soiled and disgraced and would never in this world live it down" (*Wrong* 45). That sense led her to the title, which she bases on the "anguish that human beings inflict on each other—the never-ending wrong, forever incurable" (*Wrong* 62).

The Never-Ending Wrong cannot compete with the remainder of Porter's canon. "The Grave," for example, demonstrates mastery of the short-story genre and of language itself. But the extended essay does provide another glimpse into Porter's connection with historical event and her desire to record and understand it. Ironically, in this case her rejection of the formulas she learned while writing for newspapers may be said to have hampered her.

Porter boasted a relatively small canon when she died on Sept. 18, 1980, at the Carriage Hill Nursing Home in Silver Spring, Maryland. Her works include *Flowering Judas and Other Stories; Pale Horse, Pale Rider; The Leaning Tower and Other Stories; The Days Before;* and *Ship of Fools.* However, she won great literary acclaim for the short stories and novellas she wrote primarily between 1922 and 1940, and her novel, *The Ship of Fools* (1962), won her popular and financial success. *The Collected Stories of Katherine Anne Porter* (1965) won her both the Pulitzer Prize and the National Book Award for Fiction in 1966. In 1967 she received the Gold Medal for Fiction of the National Institute of Arts and Letters. (The award is given only once every five years and had previously gone to William Faulkner.) Following awards at other institutions, Howard Payne University in Brownwood, Texas, bestowed an honorary doctorate on Porter during the first symposium on her works in 1976.

Porter never acknowledged the debt she owed to her training and experience as a journalist, and most critics have avoided assessing it. In one newspaper article, published in *The Denver Post* on Jan. 31, 1937, an unnamed newspaper reporter ventures:

> After cultivating an unusual gift for word arrangements, which captivated a large reading public when she was a Denver newspaper reporter, Katherine Anne Porter has been designated to receive one of the four $2500 fellowship awards by the Book of the Month Club to "writers whose works are insufficiently read." (Sexton 71)

Perhaps much of her work was and is "insufficiently read." However, Katherine Anne Porter stands as an example of a woman who began her career in the newsroom and developed a broad repertoire of writing—newspaper stories, essays, short stories, and novels—for which she is now receiving praise. It is left to contemporary scholars to pay tribute to her contributions to literature and to continue to critique her newspaper stories, her fiction, and her extended nonfiction.

Eudora Welty

Eudora Welty had a more varied media career than Porter. She began her college education as a sixteen-year-old freshman at the Mississippi State College for Women in Columbus, Mississippi. As she says in the chapter "Finding a Voice" in *One Writer's Beginnings,* Welty began her writing career as a reporter for the college newspaper: "I was lucky enough to have found for myself, at the very beginning, an outside shell, that of freshman reporter on our college newspaper, *The Spectator.* I became a wit and humorist of the parochial kind, and the amount I was able to show off in print must have been a great comfort to me" (79).

Welty then transferred to the University of Wisconsin, from where she graduated with a bachelor's degree in 1929. She entered the School of Business at Columbia University to study advertising. Welty also freelanced for local newspapers and wrote the society column for Jackson, Mississippi, printed Sundays in the *Memphis Commercial Appeal.* She spent a year with the Mississippi Advertising Commission writing copy and taking photos for state tourism publications.

Finally, in 1938 Welty accepted a job with the Works Progress Administration as a junior publicity agent. More than her work with newspapers (which contributed significantly to her ability to reproduce the dialect and capture the regional humor in her short stories), the time Welty spent with WPA altered her perspective on art forever. Welty herself says that her "first full-time job was rewarding to me in a way I could never have foreseen in those early days of my writing" *(One Writer's Beginnings* 84). Established to combat the Great Depression, the WPA needed photographers to travel across the state, write articles for county newspapers, and take photos. Welty writes dramatically about the contributions photography made to her way of seeing and to her method of recording human experience in prose:

> With the accretion of years, the hundreds of photographs—life as I found it, all unposed—constitute a record of that desolate period; but most of what I learned for myself came right at the time and directly out of the *taking* of the pictures. The camera was a hand-held auxiliary of wanting-to-know.
> It had more than information and accuracy to teach me. I learned in the doing how *ready* I had to be. Life doesn't hold still. A good snapshot stopped a moment from running away. Photography taught me that to be able to capture transience, by being ready to click the shutter at the crucial moment, was the greatest need I had. Making pictures of people in all sorts of situations, I learned that every feeling waits upon its gesture; and I had to be prepared to recognize this moment when I saw it. There were things a story writer needed to know. And I felt the need to hold transient life in *words*—there's so much more of life that only words can convey—strongly enough to last me as long as I lived. *(One Writer's Beginnings* 84-85)

As Louise Westling says in her book *Eudora Welty*, photography "trained Welty's vision, by focusing and fixing information in precise images, teaching her to see human emotion as it is expressed in movement, and helping her understand how to capture the transient moment" (15).

Welty took 1,200 photos throughout the 82 counties of Mississippi. She captured on film the cotton pickers, schoolteachers, Baptist deacons, nurses, weavers, storekeepers, farmers, Confederate veterans, children, washerwomen, and others who peopled the state. As Westling correctly notes, Welty did not see people as "sociological data or political victims" but instead approached them "with a sense of kinship and admiration for the spirit with which they lived their difficult lives" *(Eudora Welty* 55). Welty said when interviewed for a collection of her photographs that her "pictures were made in sympathy, not exploitation" *(Photographs* xxvi):

> I was never questioned, or avoided. There was no self-consciousness on either side. I just spoke to persons on the street and said, "Do you mind if I take this picture?" And they didn't care. There was no sense of violation of anything on either side. I don't think it existed; I know it didn't in my attitude, or in theirs. All of that unself-consciousness is gone now. There is no such relationship between a photographer and a subject possible any longer. *(Photography* xiv)

Whatever motivated Welty to become an experienced photographer, little question exists concerning her true vocation. In *Photographs,* a 1989 collection of her photography that followed *One Time, One Place* in 1970, Welty says that although she continued taking pictures, she never lost her literary direction: "The new jobs I had all had to do with journalism, not pictures. And fiction writing was my real work all along. That never let up" (xviii).

The Short Stories

Welty's journalistic experience also contributed to her short stories in innumerable ways. From the importance of a newspaper article in attesting to the significance of a person's life ("A Piece of News"), to the importance of the society columns Welty wrote in depicting Southern families with humor and insight ("Why I Live at the P.O."), to the importance of newswriting experience in creating a sustained and detailed narrative ("Death of a Traveling Salesman"), to the importance of photography in Welty's portraits of the Mississippi poor ("A Worn Path"), journalism remained a central influence in Welty's literary talents. Her very determination to remain at a distance, as an observer of event, may be traced to Welty's early journalistic training: "I wished to be, not effaced, but invisible—actually a powerful position. Perspective, the line of vision, the frame of vision—these set a distance" (87), writes Welty in *One Writer's Beginnings.*

In "A Piece of News," Welty creates Ruby Fisher, a lonely woman whose husband beats her each time she commits adultery, a rather regular occurrence: "When Clyde would make her blue, she would go out onto the road, some car would slow down, and if it had a Tennessee license, the lucky kind, the chances were that she would spend the afternoon in the shed of the empty gin" (*Stories* 14), writes Welty. Isolated and escaping more and more often into fantasy, Ruby one day brings home a bag of coffee wrapped in a newspaper. Lying in front of the fire, she opens the paper, which takes on a kind of sacred importance: "Presently she stirred and reached under her back for the newspaper. Then she squatted there, touching the printed page as if it were fragile. She did not merely look at it—she watched it, as if it were unpredictable, like a young girl watching a baby" (Welty, *Stories* 12-13).

In horrible and startling irony, the newspaper contains a short news story that reads: "Mrs. Ruby Fisher had the misfortune to be shot in the leg by her husband this week." For a few moments, Ruby imagines that the woman described is she herself, and she fantasizes that she is "beautiful, desirable, and dead" (Welty, *Stories* 14). The woman who has no real place and no real significance in her world now seems important: "She kept looking out the window, suffused with the warmth from the fire and with the pity and beauty and power of her death" (Welty, *Stories* 15). Ruby, of course, realizes that the article is either false or about someone else, but when her husband tells her that "it's a lie" (Welty, *Stories* 16), Ruby exclaims, "That's what's in the newspaper about me" (Welty, *Stories* 16).

Welty the journalist understands the woman's desire to believe the "truth," the facts as printed in the newspaper. Welty the fiction writer realizes the dramatic potential of a woman's psychological need to create her own fantasy to protect her from reality. And Welty the observer of humanity understands longing for identity and wholeness. With precision, Welty describes Ruby after her husband explains that the Ruby Fisher mentioned in the newspaper lives in another state:

> Ruby folded her still trembling hands into her skirt. She stood stooping by the window until everything, outside and in, was quieted before she went to her supper.
> It was dark and vague outside. The storm had rolled away to faintness like a wagon crossing a bridge. (Welty, *Stories* 16)

The newspaper, a reliable record of truth, has tricked Ruby Fisher. Once again, she is unimportant, "dark," "vague," and drifting away to "faintness."

"Why I Live at the P.O." is as different from "A Piece of News" in tone and style as it could possibly be. When reading the humorous short story—full of exaggeration and dramatic monologue—one must recognize the effect of Welty's having written society news in Jackson. The family saga of Mama, Papa-Daddy, Uncle Rondo, Stella-Rondo, Shirley T., and Sister begins and ends explosively. Sister, the postmistress of the smallest post office in Mississippi, is overwhelmed by her own sense of importance and jealous of her sister's arrival (reminiscent, of course, of the parable of the prodigal son in the New Testament). Humor derives from the speaker's inability to see herself clearly, as is obvious from the first paragraph:

> I was getting along fine with Mama, Papa-Daddy and Uncle Rondo until my sister Stella-Rondo just separated from her husband and came back home again. Mr. Whitaker! Of course I went with Mr. Whitaker first, when he first appeared here in China Grove, taking "Pose Yourself" photos, and Stella-Rondo broke us up. Told him I was one-sided. Bigger on one side than the other, which is a deliberate, calculated falsehood: I'm the same. Stella-Rondo is exactly twelve months to the day younger than I am and for that reason she's spoiled. (Welty, *Stories* 46).

Welty plays throughout "Why I Live at the P.O." with stereotypes of hierarchy in the South, with the real or imagined competitiveness between Southern women, with systems of manners, and with societal conventions. Shirley T., for example, is passed off as Stella-Rondo's "little adopted girl" (Welty, *Stories* 50), but Sister not only believes she is her sister's biological child by the cad Joe Whitaker, but she suggests the child may be mentally retarded: "'Mama,' I says, 'can that child talk?' I simply had to whisper! 'Mama, I wonder if that child can be—you know—in any way? Do you realize,' I says, 'that she hasn't spoken one single, solitary word to a human being up to this minute? This is the way she looks,' I says, and I looked like this" (Welty, *Stories* 51). Certainly vicious, Sister is also funny, partly because she is part of a family full of eccentrics. Mama initially believes something may be wrong with Shirley T. because

"Joe Whitaker frequently drank like a fish . . . I believed to my soul he drank *chemicals*" (Welty, *Stories* 51). Of course, in saying this, Mama gives away the fact that she, too, thinks Shirley T. is Stella-Rondo's biological child.

Other social conventions are ridiculed in "Why I Live at the P.O." Simply growing up in Mississippi and observing her community critically would provide Welty with plenty of subject matter, but writing society news and realizing how seriously it is taken could also explain Welty's finely honed humor. Southerners are stereotyped as willfully ignorant of family skeletons, for example, and Welty lets Sister challenge that taboo:

> "Why, Sister," said Mama. "Here I thought we were going to have a pleasant Fourth of July, and you start right out not believing a word your own baby sister tells you!"
> "Just like Cousin Annie Flo. Went to her grave denying the facts of life," I remind Mama.
> "I told you if you ever mentioned Annie Flo's name I'd slap your face," says Mama, and slaps my face. (Welty, *Stories* 50)

Welty makes playful fun of Southern double names ("Annie Flo," etc.), and she pokes even more fun at Southern notions of masculinity by letting Uncle Rondo parade privately around in a pink kimono. When Sister ridicules him, Uncle Rondo retaliates: "But at 6:30 a.m. the next morning, he threw a whole five-cent package of some unsold one-inch firecrackers from the store as hard as he could into my bedroom and they every one went off. Not one bad one in the string. Anybody else, there'd be one that wouldn't go off" (Welty, *Stories* 53).

Even Southern pride comes under fire, for in the end Sister is forced to live at the post office. Her family members refuse to check their mail anymore. Sister, righteously indignant, stays true to her character to the bitter end:

> And that's the last I've laid eyes on any of my family or my family laid eyes on me for five solid days and nights. Stella-Rondo may be telling the most horrible tales in the world about Mr. Whitaker, but I haven't heard them. As I tell everybody, I draw my own conclusions . . . But oh, I like it here. It's ideal, as I've been saying . . .
> Some of the folks here in town are taking up for me and some turned against me. I know which is which. There are always people who will quit buying stamps just to get on the right side of Papa-Daddy.
> But here I am, and here I'll stay. I want the world to know I'm happy. (Welty, *Stories* 56)

Of course, Sister is miserable, and the family is distressed about Stella-Rondo's baby and her separation from Mr. Whitaker, an unmentionable event in conservative Southern society. No one understood the sanctity of Southern tradition better than Welty herself, and yet her wit is playful and steady, not vengeful or explosive like the wit of writers such as H.L. Mencken. Welty loved the South and portrayed her fellow Southerners with fondness and easy grace.

Welty's first published story, "Death of a Traveling Salesman," testifies to her ability to sustain narrative and suggests an attachment to realism found often in news stories characterized by tragedy. In the story, R.J. Bowman, who for 14 years had sold shoes in Mississippi, suffers a heart attack and dies. Although the facts are simple, Welty explores his death and seems to conclude that Bowman died because he was lonely and lost and had abandoned his will to live. Bowman literally becomes lost while driving his Ford across the state one afternoon; Welty makes good use of symbols and says Bowman "distrusted the road without signposts" (Welty, *Stories* 119).

Bowman's life has been marked by nothing but steady work, as the "stares of . . . distant people had followed him solidly like a wall, impenetrable" (Welty, *Stories* 120). After wrecking his car, Bowman is taken in and cared for by a couple expecting a baby and obviously very much in love. Their life together reminds Bowman of the emptiness of his own life:

> But he wanted to leap up, to say to [the woman], I have been sick and I found out then, only then, how lonely I am. Is it too late? My heart puts up a struggle inside me, and you may have heard it, protesting against emptiness. . . It should be flooded with love . . .
>
> But he moved a trembling hand across his eyes, and looked at the placid crouching woman across the room . . . He felt ashamed and exhausted by the thought that he might, in one more moment, have tried by simple words and embraces to communicate some strange thing—something which seemed always to have just escaped him. (Welty, *Stories* 125)

Before running, terrified in his lostness, to his car, Bowman thinks, "A marriage, a fruitful marriage. That simple thing. Anyone could have had that" (Welty, *Stories* 129). A simple news story item is thereby transformed by an artist into a universal tale with which all who have lost a dream can identify.

Welty the photographer depicted characters such as Bowman with finesse and insight, never missing a detail. Her portrait of Phoenix Jackson in "A Worn Path" is perhaps her finest characterization. Named for the bird who rises from the ashes and for Welty's hometown, Phoenix Jackson makes an annual pilgrimage to town to buy a gift for her grandson. The old black woman must have reminded Welty of many such figures photographed during her work for the WPA:

> She wore a dark striped dress reaching down to her shoe tops, and an equally long apron of bleached sugar sacks, with a full pocket: all neat and tidy, but every time she took a step she might have fallen over her shoelaces, which dragged from her unlaced shoes. She looked straight ahead. Her eyes were blue with age. Her skin had a pattern all its own of numberless branching wrinkles and as though a whole little tree stood in the middle of her forehead, but a golden color ran underneath, and the two knobs of her cheeks were illuminated by a yellow burning under the dark. Under the red rag her hair came down on her neck in the frailest of ringlets, still black, and with an odor like copper. (Welty, *Stories* 142)

Welty celebrates Phoenix Jackson's courage and strength, as Phoenix picks her way with a thin cane through treacherous country rife with objects to deceive an elderly traveler: "Thorns, you doing your appointed work. Never want to let folks pass, no sir. Old eyes thought you was a pretty little *green* bush" (Welty, *Stories* 143). Phoenix accomplishes her mission and returns to her cabin slowly and deliberately, having come to life for the reader.

Photography and Other Media

Capturing a moment in fiction or in photography was one of Welty's highest callings. She also marveled at the courage of those she met during the Depression years and tried to portray them as the heroic people she believed they were. As Welty writes in the introduction to *Photographs*, poverty in Mississippi, "white and black, really didn't have too much to do with the Depression. It was ongoing. Mississippi was long since poor, long devastated" (xvii). In one photo entitled "Woman of the 'Thirties," Welty describes the black woman from Hinds County (1935) standing strong and stark against a sterile background:

She has a very sensitive face, as you can see; she was well aware of her predicament in poverty, and had good reasons for hopelessness. Well, she *wasn't* hopeless. That was the point. She was courageous. She thought it was a hopeless situation, but she was tackling it. (xxvii)

Here, of course, Welty could be describing Phoenix Jackson herself.

When Eudora Welty's book *Photographs* was published, newsman Robert MacNeil called her photos "acts of love." In a speech in 1990 at the State Historical Museum in Jackson, Mississippi, the former co-anchor of the "MacNeil/Lehrer NewsHour" praised Welty's respect and affection for the subjects of her photographs: "The person who took these pictures is not indifferent: she is curious but affectionate. I think her pictures are acts of love. I don't mean personal love but the kind of encompassing love that some few people feel for their fellow humanity; a loving sensibility that is not blind to human folly, greed, cruelty—but witnesses it all compassionately" (10).

Rarely if ever are phrases such as "encompassing love" or a "loving sensibility" used to describe media professionals—whether they are reporters, editors, advertising executives, or public relations practitioners—even though some of these professionals might exhibit compassion toward the people who play a role in their stories, ads, and campaigns. MacNeil addresses the way goals of media professionals affect news products when he writes:

The news industry gambles on futures in the commodity of human suffering and spends lavishly to record it. Over land and ocean without rest thousands speed at the bidding of networks or newsmagazines to track down the most bloody, the most tragic, the most touching, most sentimental, most patriotic images they can find. And those images become our news, and increasingly our national memory and our history . . . The person taking the pictures cares only to get an effective picture. He may be totally indifferent to the human condition he witnesses. Indeed if he is a professional he had better be indifferent, or he would be sick with the accumulated suffering he has witnessed. (9-10)

Media professionals consider their work a public service and, as MacNeil suggests, practice detachment as a way to avoid bias and promote fairness and balance. The success of fiction writers, however, often depends instead on their intimate connection with their subjects and surroundings, something Welty in particular understood. Although her photographs might not appear on the cover of *Life* magazine, they are infused with the same empathy and tenderness that drive her descriptions of character and theme.

In spite of the fact that she worked in advertising, radio, newspapers, public relations, and photography, Welty's compassion for others and her desire to portray people in all their complexity drew the Pulitzer Prize-winning novelist and short-story writer away from a life in media. MacNeil observes that Welty's photographs "are not judgments and they are not editorials or propaganda, they are not studies in sociology. Hers is an objective lens" (8). By juxtaposing Welty's work with that of journalists, MacNeil is not glorifying Welty at the expense of those in his own chosen field; he is, however, suggesting a distinction between using a source as a metaphor or media artifact and making a source an art object.

Understandably distracted by her novels and short-story collections, literary critics rarely refer to Welty's media experience, except to make connections between her photography and her fiction. Few attribute much significance to the fact that Welty designed and wrote copy for ads, freelanced for Mississippi newspapers, and worked as a copywriter for WJDX radio in Jackson. They often do not draw conclusions about the fact that she wrote a Sunday column about Jackson society for the *Memphis Commercial Appeal,* served as a publicity agent for the WPA, and produced several volumes of photographs.

This study argues that omitting references to Welty's academic training and early media employment is, in fact, a costly oversight, for she—like Tom Wolfe, Joan Didion and others—often drew from her experiences with media. As we have seen, because of its reliance on an understanding of Southern society and the comedic value of gossip, the short story "Why I Live at the P.O." is more rich when one realizes that Welty once wrote society news for a Memphis newspaper. Similarly, the vivid description of Phoenix Jackson in "A Worn Path" is more startling when one knows that Welty was an enthusiastic photographer. In addition to references to often-cited secondary sources, this study draws predominantly upon primary materials (interviews, autobiographical documents, letters, brochures, newsletters and unpublished photographs) collected by the Mississippi Department of Archives and History in Jackson. It is these sources that best illustrate Welty's understanding of the impact of her media work on her fiction.

Contributing to a lack of critical attention to Welty's training and experience in media are two quite understandable factors: First, in spite of her willingness to be interviewed, Welty rarely spoke about her interest in journalism, advertising, and public relations. Second, Welty is better understood alongside Carson McCullers, Flannery O'Connor, Katherine Anne Porter, and other

Southern women fiction writers than she is alongside writers of jingles, radio copy, features, or society news. For these reasons and others, Welty's media training is often neglected.

In one interview with Charlotte Capers during which Welty addressed media careers, she said that she was never tempted to pursue journalism as her life's work: "I never did take journalism. And I instinctively shied away from it, although later on I took some jobs in it, but I think my instinct was right, and I still say that to people who invite my opinion, students, that I think you should take a job, if you want to be a writer, a serious writer, you should take a job that does not use words in a way that is not imaginative" (n.p.). Although it is tempting to hear Welty's words and place her in the company of Willa Cather, Stephen Crane, and others who disparaged journalism as hack writing, Welty never denied the value of newspapers to relay information; instead, she simply believed that editorials and news stories should persuade and inform, respectively, and that she should employ her talents in another genre with other objectives.

In a rare comparison between literature and journalism, Welty said in a 1973 interview with Don Lee Keith that "fiction is one thing: journalism's another. The distinguishing factor is that in the novel, there is the possibility that both writer and reader may share an act of imagination" (Prenshaw, *Conversations* 151). Welty longed to use her imagination—not to transmit real events in writing—but to recreate them. As she said, "Whatever our theme in writing, it is old and tried. Whatever our place, it has been visited by the stranger, it will never be new again. Some day it may not even be. It is only the vision that can be new, but this is enough" *(Three Papers on Fiction* 15). Welty made another comparison in 1986 in an interview with Albert J. Devlin and Peggy Whitman Prenshaw, this time between literature and didactic forms of journalism:

> I don't think literature—I'm talking about fiction now—I don't think it can exhort . . . I think it speaks to what is more deeply within, that is, the personal, and conveys its meaning that way . . . I wouldn't like to read a work of fiction that I thought had an ulterior motive, to persuade me politically . . . I think things should be written to persuade, but openly as a column or an editorial or a speech . . . This is not to say that I condescend to such writing or think of it as less important. *(Welty: A Life in Literature* 25-26)

Because Welty's statements about the differences between journalism and fiction are few and brief, critics are left to speculate about why Welty turned her back on a career in media. Elizabeth A. Meese, for example, wrote that journalism "was not easily done in conjunction with fiction writing. Doubtless she felt a diffusion rather than a concentration of her energies in simultaneously pursuing varieties of self-expression" (Prenshaw, *Eudora Welty: Critical Essays* 409). Other critics simply make their own connections without Welty's confirmation or denial. For example, Peter Schmidt links a piece Welty called "a witty piece of journalism" for the *Junior League Magazine* ("Women!! Make Turban in Own Home!") with the humor in her short story "Why I Live at the P.O." (109).

One may argue that Welty's short career in media affected her development as a writer of fiction. For example, a study of her work reveals the importance of place and the supremacy of the moment and indicates a desire to stand outside the action as an observer instead of an interpreter. Further, Welty demonstrates an awareness of the ambiguity of life that can be traced to the sense of realism journalists possess. While a fiction writer may manipulate characters in order to make their reactions reasonable or to frame a narrative, Welty resists that impulse. She understood that unmediated life is rarely well ordered, and in her fiction she celebrates those who live exuberantly in spite of their unanswered questions.

For Welty, fictional events could be more true than real ones, but she believed places in her fiction must communicate "actuality" to the reader in much the same manner that journalists rely on clear and accurate description of place to recreate the event for a reader. She writes:

> This makes it the business of writing, and the responsibility of the writer, to disentangle the significant—in character, incident, setting, mood, everything—from the random and meaningless and irrelevant that in real life surround and beset it . . . Actuality, it's true, is an even bigger risk to the novel than fancy writing is, being frequently even more confusing, irrelevant, diluted, and generally far-fetched than ill-chosen words can make it. Yet somehow, the world of appearance in the novel has got to *seem* actuality. *(Three Papers on Fiction* 5)

Suzanne Marrs, a professor and friend of Welty's, testifies to Welty's success in recreating place when she writes that readers believe in Phoenix Jackson, the central character in "A Worn Path," because they "recognize and believe in the world that she inhabits" ("Eudora Welty's Photography" 288). Even details such as Welty's choice of names are tied to real life and, occasionally, to actual news coverage:

> When I first began writing I didn't realize the importance of names. I would just name characters anything. And then I realized how much it mattered, for cadence . . . The other day I was reading in the *Jackson Daily News* the list of people arrested for drunk driving. There was this man whose name was Quovadis something. "Quovadis, whither goest thou." It's just wonderful. *(Welty: A Life in Literature* 11)

An examination of Welty's fiction reveals the effect of her experience as a photographer on her ability to isolate and contain the moment, the influence that writing society news had on her ability to portray with realism and humor the fictional inhabitants of Mississippi, and numerous other connections. Welty's interest in journalism emerged early, and her experience in newspapers was brief but significant to her. She worked on the newspaper staff at Jackson Central High School and at the Mississippi State College for Women. In addition to personal style, Welty developed other skills during her time in print media, claiming in an interview with Charlotte Capers that because of newspapers she "learned to try to organize my thoughts" (n.p.) and in an interview with Jean Todd Freeman that she had developed a desire "to want to see something on the page, objective, in type" (Prenshaw, *Conversations* 185).

Later, when Welty took a job at WJDX, a radio station her father had established in Jackson, Mississippi, she found herself in charge of a newsletter. The January 1932 issue of "Lamar Life Radio News" includes a news story Welty wrote about a flood in the studio. In it, readers will immediately recognize the humor that infuses short stories such as "Why I Live at the P.O." The editorialized news story follows:

> Flood times came to WJDX not long ago with a tide of water right through the studio. When the eleventh floor of a Jackson skyscraper floods, you know it . . .
>
> The torrents of rain that had flooded Jackson that morning had come in good portion to rest on the Lamar roof, and then, having nothing better to do, went on in to the studio . . .
>
> But don't think that if you live on the eleventh floor you can't have a flood. Anything can happen in a radio station. (n.p.)

In addition to her writing at the station, Welty also worked briefly for a newspaper begun by friend Ralph Hilton, who later worked for the Associated Press and edited a county newspaper in Hilton Head, S.C. "He got hold of some space up over a store—and under that flat hot tin roof it was like working inside a popcorn popper," Welty said. "But we survived briefly, even if we never put Fred Sullens and the *Daily News* out of business" (Prenshaw, *Conversations* 204).

From 1933 to 1936, Welty took pictures for the Works Progress Administration, but in spite of the publication of her photos, she considered herself primarily a journalist. "I was doing a newspaper job, really—interviewing" (Prenshaw, *Conversations* 155), she said. Meese wrote that Welty "traveled and spoke with people by day; at night she wrote up what she saw for use as filler in county newspapers" ("Constructing" 402). Welty talked about the impact of her interviews with Mississippians in post-Depression America in books such as *Losing Battles*: "I have traveled all over the state . . . I have known what poor families live like . . . The battles being lost seem so much more important when there is so little left to lose" (Prenshaw, *Conversations* 28). Taking pictures for the WPA, Welty told Charles T. Bunting, led her to write *Losing Battles,* a novel in which "indomitability" is the central theme. "I don't feel it's a novel of despair at all," she said. "I feel it's more a novel of admiration for the human being who can cope with any condition, even ignorance, and keep a courage, a joy of life, even, that's unquenchable" (Prenshaw, *Conversations* 48).

Other work in print media was more abbreviated but no less colorful than Welty's time writing for school newspapers and radio stations. In 1944, for example, Welty was part of the *New York Times Book Review* staff, using the name "Michael Ravenna" in order to make reviews about the accounts of battles in Europe, North Africa, and the South Pacific seem more credible. According to interviewer Walter Clemons, "Michael Ravenna's sage judgments came to be quoted prominently in publishers' ads, and invitations from radio networks for Mr. Ravenna to appear on their programs had to be politely declined on grounds that he had been called away to the battlefronts" (Prenshaw, *Conversations* 33).

As Welty writes in her series of autobiographical essays, her "first paid work was in communications" *(One Writer's Beginnings* 84) at WJDX radio, where she earned $65 a month for writing scripts and "cleaning the bird cage" *(Eudora Welty* 16), according to biographer Ruth M. Vande Kieft. In a column entitled "A Salute from One of the Family," Welty honored her father, Christian Webb Welty, on the fiftieth anniversary of his company, Lamar Life Insurance, for his foresight in having established the radio station. She also stated how much she enjoyed one of her first jobs in media: "I must say it was the sort of job a young girl considers ideal: it was part-time, and it was vague. I edited, as one of my duties, a little newsletter . . . It was the nicest job I ever had" ("A Salute" 5).

One of Welty's tasks from 1931-33 was to print the radio station's schedules, because—as newspaper editors began to perceive radio as a strong competitor—they began to refuse to print them. Welty talks in several interviews about the rift that grew between WJDX and the local newspaper in her hometown: "Fred Sullens [editor of the *Jackson Daily News]* fought us from the start, called us traitors, said we were trying to take away their advertising and their news" (Prenshaw, *Conversations* 203). As one of her other responsibilities, Welty also wrote letters for the station. Asked by one interviewer to whom she wrote the letters, she responded with characteristic wit, "To ourselves. 'Dear WJDX, I *love* getting the opera on Saturday. Don't *ever* take it away!' We wrote all the letters and mailed them in. It was a good cause" (Prenshaw, *Conversations* 203).

Although Welty gained less acclaim for her work in broadcasting, advertising, and public relations than she did for her contributions to print media and photography, it is important to note that she was trained in and worked in numerous and diverse areas of communications. As noted earlier, after two years at the Mississippi State College for Women (1925-27), Welty transferred to the University of Wisconsin, from which she graduated with a bachelor's degree in English in 1929. She then attended the School of Business at Columbia University, studying advertising and writing and selling advertising on the side (1930-31).

To some extent, her decision to study advertising was a direct result of her father's desire for her to be able to support herself with a concrete skill. However, post-Depression America was struggling to rebound economically, and Welty discovered that her options in business were severely limited.

Still, Welty spent a year with the Mississippi Advertising Commission writing copy and taking photos for state tourism publications. Asked if she would have called herself a "public relations person," Welty told Capers, "I suppose so, and I don't know how well I did it at all. It was not anything I knew much about" (n.p.). Welty was quite clear about her reasons for leaving advertising, saying, "I quit advertising because it was too much like sticking pins into people to make them buy things that they didn't need or really much want. And then, too, advertising is so filled with taboos—you are scared to say this thing and that thing; scared to use this page and that kind of type, and so on. What's the use of learning fears?" (Prenshaw, *Conversations* 5).

Much more important than advertising and public relations to Welty was her experience as a photographer. Although her father was an avid photographer who introduced Welty to the field, most of her photography experience was a direct result of the three years she spent as a junior publicity agent for the WPA.

Meese and other critics are fascinated by the fact that Welty took pictures of individuals and rarely photographed WPA projects. Meese argues that Welty's interviews and essays are "examples of how visual images trigger her narrative impulse" (Prenshaw, *Eudora Welty: Critical Essays* 407) but are not examples of the social documents actually requested by the WPA. Certainly, more than her work with newspapers (which contributed significantly to her ability to reproduce the dialect and capture the regional humor in her short stories), the time Welty spent with the WPA helped to teach her what is significant about art and its ability to capture a moment and elevate the human spirit.

Albert J. Devlin states in *Eudora Welty's Chronicle* that "every writer who considers the importance of place in Welty's fiction dutifully begins by quoting her descriptions of this fruitful gathering time" (ix). In an interview with Gayle Graham Yates, Welty summarizes the years she spent working for the WPA in her typically humble way: "The photography itself was not anything because I was uneducated in that, too, but I think the pictures grew to be valuable because they are a very accurate picture of the time I took them in, which is gone. You know. Back in the Depression. And so time made them, gave them a value. I loved—I love photography, and it taught me a lot, too" ("An Interview" 104).

What makes Welty's photos notable is what MacNeil attributes to her unthreatening demeanor. Of the subjects of her photos, MacNeil writes: "They are not defensive with her; they remain in unguarded positions, like the languid woman in the cover photograph, 'Saturday Off.' They do not sense in her anything to make them strike attitudes, to strut or conceal. She puts their vanity at ease, she does not arouse their shame. She is someone who is permitted in moment after moment to share their humanity on their level, without pretenses" (6). Unlike what MacNeil considers the sensationalistic bent of contemporary photography, Welty's photographs "reveal a mind drunk with curiosity about the mundane" (13), he writes.

Welty would no doubt agree with MacNeil's assessment, although her humility would prompt her to call her photos "snapshots" taken with outdated photographic equipment. However, she understood the impact of her work and revealed it in the following excerpt from the preface to her first collection of photos, *One Time, One Place: Mississippi in the Depression*. There she wrote:

> A better and less ignorant photographer would certainly have come up with better pictures, but not these pictures; for he could hardly have been as well positioned as I was, moving through the scene openly and yet invisibly because I was a part of it, born into it, taken for granted.
> Neither would a social-worker photographer have taken these same pictures. The book is offered, I should explain, not as a social document but as a family album—which is something both less and more, but unadorned. ("One Time, One Place" 351)

This statement reflects Welty's understanding that her photos are intimate portraits of those for whom she cared. They were not social statements as much as they were personal photos of people Welty herself wanted to remember.

In *Photographs,* one picture, entitled "Baptist deacon, Jackson" (1930s), features a dignified African-American man who embodies the Southern definition of "gentleman." Standing tall, he holds his walking cane and looks directly at the photographer. The trust between the races reflected in the photograph, Welty said later, has disappeared: "In taking all these pictures, I was attended, I now know, by an angel—a presence of trust. In particular, the photographs of black persons by a white person may not testify soon again to such intimacy. It is trust that dates the pictures now, more than the vanished years" ("One Time, One Place" 352).

Also evident in the photos is Welty's reluctance to make of a photographic subject a metaphor. Just as she creates individuals in her short stories, rejecting allegory and symbolism in favor of the realistic characters who people her fiction, Welty argued that the focus of her photos was—as it was with a woman she photographed—"not the Depression, not the Black, not the South, not even the perennially sorry state of the whole world, but the story of her life in her face" ("One Time, One Place" 354). She added:

> And though I did not take these pictures to prove anything, I think they most assuredly do show something—which is to make a far better claim for them. Her face to me is full of meaning more truthful and more terrible and, I think, more noble than any generalization about people could have prepared me for or could describe for me now. I learned from my own pictures, one by one, and had to; for I think we are the breakers of our own hearts. ("One Time, One Place" 354)

Welty took pictures for 20 years, did her own developing, and was featured in two shows in New York City. On at least two occasions, Welty submitted photos that accompanied her writing to publishers, although the photos were rejected. In one interview, Welty said, "I don't know why I thought it would be a good idea to have the pictures illustrate my stories. Oh well, none of the publishers ever thought so either" (Prenshaw, *Conversations* 146).

A snapshot, Welty argued, "is a moment's glimpse" ("One Time, One Place" 354). Welty's photos are not invasive or manipulative. They are not sensationalistic. They are not a misery index, nor are they a historical document to be filed so that we can remember a former time or specific cultural artifacts. The faces are those of real human beings to whom Welty was drawn. Those pictured are courageous, determined and—on film—eternal.

Whatever motivated Welty to became an experienced photographer, little question exists concerning her true vocation. As noted earlier, in *Photographs,* Welty said that although she took pictures for many years, she never lost her literary direction: "The new jobs I had all had to do with journalism, not pictures. And fiction writing was my real work all along. That never let up" (xviii). Similarly, in an interview with schoolchildren at Davis School in Jackson, Welty said, "I took those pictures for myself because I was interested at the time. I liked it, but that was not my end in view. I wanted to be a writer. I like using words. But it taught me a lot—photography" (n.p.).

Her very determination to remain at a distance, as an observer of event, may be traced to Welty's early journalism. However, Welty's seeming objectivity should not be confused with unconcern. In every interview about her photos, Welty expressed great admiration for her subjects. For example, in a story by the Associated Press in 1989, she is quoted as saying that her favorite photo is of a middle-aged woman standing with her hands at her side and wearing a tattered sweater: "It shows such a marvelous character. These were taken in the Depression when everybody had absolutely nothing. And she looked so valiant and courageous, dignified and completely self-possessed while she was poor—and in an old sweater full of holes" ("Welty Photos" 1E).

Although critics have been slow to deal with most of Welty's media experience, they have been quick to note her reliance upon photography and the visual in her construction of character and place in her fiction. In "Eudora Welty's Photography: Images into Fiction," Marrs relates three ways in which Welty's photographs impact her art: "Her photographs of encounters prefigure her fictional concern with human relationships, with love and separateness; her increasing emphasis upon locale prefigures her increasingly detailed and emblematic use of setting in her stories and novels; and her photographs of cemeteries and parades prefigure the central role of these images in the symbolic structure of her fiction" (294). Ultimately, Marrs writes, Welty's photographs parallel the description of the Natchez Trace and other locations in books such as *The Robber Bridegroom* and *The Wide Net and Other Stories*. "Welty's creation of setting directly parallels her framing vision as a photographer," writes Marrs, and "this metaphoric stress upon setting does not vanish from Welty's fiction when she ceases to write about the Trace" (290).

Critics such as Barbara McKenzie, Louise Westling, Peggy Whitman Prenshaw, and Suzanne Marrs have argued persuasively for Welty's reliance upon photography as she wrote short stories such as "Livvie" and "A Worn Path." McKenzie discusses the role of light and nostalgia in photography and fiction and the manner in which the act of taking a picture or recording an event in a narrative implies one's desire to capture time. McKenzie cites an interview with Welty during which she said, "I see things in pictures . . . I love painting. I have no talent for it. The only talent I have—for writing, I was blessed with it—is quite visual" (Prenshaw, *Eudora Welty: Critical Essays* 389).

Westling, who views much photography as an intrusive act, said that after Welty's WPA job, she put away her camera: "For the rest of her life, she would explore the human comedy with the more discursive and narrative medium of language. All her fiction, however, would be affected by the visual lessons she had learned from photography and would manifest the same sympathy for its subjects that characterizes the photographs" (Westling, "The Loving Observer of *One Time, One Place*" 184). Not surprisingly, it is Welty herself who attests to the importance of photography in her understanding of themes in literature: "In the most unpretentious snapshot lies the wish to clasp fleeting life. Framing a few square inches of space of the fraction of a second, the photographer may capture—rescue from oblivion—fellow human beings caught in the act of living. He is devoted to the human quality of transcience" (Welty, "A Word on the Photographs" n.p.).

Partly because of the desire to avoid didacticism, partly because of a reluctance to objectify people, and partly because of a longing to connect with others instead of simply describing them, Welty rejected the idea of a career in media. Welty's goal in portraying her subjects in photos, short stories, or novels was to reveal them in their wholeness. She never wanted to instruct or startle the viewer or reader: "[My] wish, indeed my continuing passion, would be not to point the finger in judgment but to part a curtain, that invisible shadow that falls between people, the veil of indifference to each other's presence, each other's wonder, each other's human plight" ("One Time, One Place" 355).

As MacNeil argues, each of Welty's photographs is most certainly an act of love, but so, too, is her fiction. Nobel laureate Toni Morrison is quoted in a July 23, 2001, *New York Times* article about Welty's death as saying: "She was exceptional, a beautiful writer, very knowing, measured. There was a profound kind of intimacy in her writing . . . She just understood people and revealed things about them very economically" (n.p.).

Welty's canon suggests someone whose work should be as central to American literature survey courses as that of Hemingway. Welty won the Pulitzer in 1973 for *The Optimist's Daughter*. Other works include *The Robber Bridegroom, Delta Wedding, The Wide Net and Other Stories, The Golden Apples, The Ponder Heart,* and *Losing Battles*. Her short-story collection *A Curtain of Green* included some of her most beloved work, including "A Worn Path" and "Why I Live at the P.O." (It contained an introduction by Katherine Anne Porter.) Because of his devotion to the short story "Why I Live at the P.O.," Steven Dorner, the developer of the e-mail program Eudora, named it after her. Two books, *One Time, One Place: Mississippi in the Depression* and *Eudora Welty Photographs*, feature more than 300 of her photos. *One Writer's Beginnings* was a memoir based on lectures she presented at Harvard University.

Willa Cather, Edna Ferber, Katherine Anne Porter, and Eudora Welty are a few of the women who moved from newspaper writing to fiction. All deserve far more critical attention than they have received in order for readers to understand more about the pathways between journalism and fiction. Certainly, what is truthful may be different from what is factual, and it is through a study of literary journalism that the gray area—the borderland that lies between fiction and nonfiction—may be best explored.

It would be remiss to move into Chapter 3 and the other category of literary journalism—what Tom Wolfe called "The New Journalism"—without paying tribute to another giant in American letters, John Steinbeck. More space will be devoted to him than to Stephen Crane, Theodore Dreiser, Ernest Hemingway, Edgar Allan Poe, Upton Sinclair, and Walt Whitman, not because he dwarfs any one of them in talent but because too little has been written about Steinbeck and his nonfiction. Steinbeck's coverage of World War II and Vietnam and his news stories, nonfiction essays, and memoir entitled *Travels with Charley in Search of America* deserve serious attention.

John Steinbeck

John Steinbeck based much of his fiction on actual events and experimented with several genres of nonfiction, including personal essays, travel writing, and political and social commentary. In spite of this fact, his interest in journalism often is treated as ancillary to his writing of fiction, which is regarded as his real work and true calling. Steinbeck scholars allude to journalism when discussing Steinbeck's development as a writer or when chronicling and categorizing his work, but to date they have not investigated Steinbeck's role as a literary journalist with the same analytical zeal they bring to the study of his fiction. "The truth is that Steinbeck was really a journalist at heart," Gore Vidal said in a 1993 interview with Steinbeck biographer Jay Parini. "All of his best work was journalism in that it was inspired by daily events, by current circumstances. He didn't 'invent' things. He 'found' them" (*Steinbeck* 274).

Although important and often quoted, Vidal's statement refers primarily to Steinbeck's fiction that is "inspired by daily events," or, in other words, fiction that is drawn from the same reservoir as traditional journalism. This study, on the other hand, identifies Steinbeck as a literary journalist, pays tribute to the journalism that led to *The Grapes of Wrath*, and explores the importance of *Travels with Charley in Search of America* as an example of Steinbeck's skill as a writer of extended nonfiction. The study is divided into three parts: 1) The first section consists of an overview of the tenets of literary journalism most applicable to Steinbeck's work, a chronicle of Steinbeck's time as a journalist, and a list of several publications that suggest his ability to move comfortably across the arguably indistinct lines between fiction and nonfiction; 2) the second section is a discussion of *Travels with Charley* as an undervalued example of literary journalism; and 3) the third section is a tribute to the artistry exhibited by Steinbeck in *The Grapes of Wrath* as he transforms historical figures and events into their mythical representations.

Because *Travels with Charley* is understood to be nonfiction and illustrates clearly several accepted tenets of literary journalism, I will introduce it first, even though it was published more than 20 years after *The Grapes of Wrath*. In doing so, I am not suggesting that *Travels with Charley* deserves more critical acclaim than *The Grapes of Wrath*; in fact, blurring the lines between fiction and nonfiction, *The Grapes of Wrath* remains a notable example of Steinbeck's ability to write a celebrated fictional work that depends upon people he knew and events he lived.

Since Steinbeck's biographers and critics are often trained in literary criticism and not professional journalism, much of their scholarship tends to focus upon the historical distinctions between news and feature writing, upon traditional notions of truth-telling in American journalism practice, and upon Steinbeck's reliance on realism as a kind of reconstructed journalism. In the introduction to *America and Americans and Selected Nonfiction,* for example, editors Susan Shillinglaw and Jackson J. Benson write, "Steinbeck's journalism is the record of a man who wanted to get it right, who wanted to see clearly and accurately, without superciliousness—and without ever claiming that his was the definitive, or even a fully accurate, view. He always tried for the human perspective, as much as possible without prejudice" (xvii).

While the themes introduced by scholars such as Shillinglaw, Benson, and others and the recently published collections of Steinbeck's nonfiction are essential, it remains imperative to examine Steinbeck's contribution to literary journalism as well. To that end, this study relies upon *Travels with Charley* and *The Grapes of Wrath* to illustrate several tenets of literary journalism, including an unapologetic first-person point of view, advocacy for the deeper truth that underlies events, immersion in the lives of subjects, and the use of actual sources with (admittedly) recreated dialogue.

It is important to remember that Steinbeck did not simply experiment with journalistic techniques; he also worked as a serious and committed journalist at several times in his career. Most notably, Steinbeck covered World War II and wrote insightfully about international politics. In a July 5, 1943, article, a *Newsweek* reporter praised Steinbeck's coverage of the war, saying that Steinbeck's "cold grey eyes didn't miss a trick, that with scarcely any note-taking he soaked up information like a sponge, wrote very fast on a portable typewriter, and became haywire if interrupted" (Parini, *Steinbeck* 275). Although Steinbeck did not describe himself as a journalist, he understood the complexity of journalism as a field and celebrated its influence at the same time that he warned of its dangers. Steinbeck writes:

> What can I say about journalism? It has the greatest virtue and the greatest evil. It is the first thing the dictator controls. It is the mother of literature and the perpetrator of crap. In many cases it is the only history we have and yet it is the tool of the worst men. But over a long period of time and because it is the product of so many men, it is perhaps the purest thing we have. Honesty has a way of creeping in even when it was not intended. (Parini, *Steinbeck* 391)

In addition to his belief that journalism is the "only history we have," Steinbeck shared with journalists a reliance upon actual events and told compelling stories that advocated social and political change. While traditional news reporters retell chronological events, quote sources directly, and allow readers to draw conclusions from the facts, Steinbeck said in a letter to one of his sources for *The Grapes of Wrath* that his purpose in writing about his experiences was "to do some good and no harm" (Parini, *Steinbeck* 180). His fiction and nonfiction had a purpose: He wanted to increase people's awareness and lead them to action on behalf of others while causing as little damage as possible.

Critics who have addressed Steinbeck's nonfiction and discussed whether or not he should be considered a journalist do not necessarily deal with the discrete genres within journalism itself. In addition to straight news, news-features, features, commentary, personal essays, editorials, and other journalistic forms, literary journalism is of particular importance in understanding Steinbeck's nonfiction. Literary journalism, also known as "creative nonfiction," "The New Journalism," "art-journalism," "essay fiction," "factual fiction," "historical fiction," and "parajournalism," is generally understood to be two-pronged: It encompasses writers such as Willa Cather, Stephen Crane, Theodore Dreiser, Ernest Hemingway, Katherine Anne Porter, Upton Sinclair, and others who spent time working as journalists and who subsequently gained their reputations as writers of fiction; it also embraces those described as "The New Journalists," such as Sara Davidson, Joan Didion, Norman Mailer, and Tom Wolfe, who employ narration, description, and dialogue in writing about actual events and who remained in journalism and transformed it.

Like Steinbeck, literary journalists rely upon daily events, focus on the contributions of average people, immerse themselves in the lives of those they cover, and interview sources with a deep commitment to the underlying truth of their statements. They sometimes employ composites, rearrange conversations, and experiment with chronology. At the heart of all their work is a profound curiosity about the world and about those who people it: "I have never passed an unshaded window without looking in, have never closed my ears to a conversation that was none of my business," Steinbeck wrote in *Travels with Charley.* "I can justify or even dignify this by protesting that in my trade I must know about people, but I suspect that I am simply curious" (90). Finally, literary journalists organize their work around a dominant theme or message, as Steinbeck most assuredly did.

Literary journalism often is treated as secondary by scholars of both literature and media. For some, writing exclusively from the imagination (if such ever occurs) is privileged over borrowing from social and political history or becoming too invested in everyday events. For others, following breaking news, transcribing statements on the scene, and writing hard-hitting, "just-the-facts-ma'am" journalism is more challenging than working in solitude while inventing characters and plots. However true these categorizations may be, it is important not to overstate the positions of literary critics and media studies scholars. Certainly, academics who study literature often do justice to disciplines such as creative writing, nonfiction, and journalism—often housed within their own departments—and consider them worthy genres in the field of literary inquiry. Conversely, those who consider themselves specialists in media often pay tribute to fiction and its central role in American intellectual life.

However, scholars in literature and media do sometimes view one another with suspicion, and it is this interpretive gap that interests those committed to a study of literary journalism. At the heart of the debate is the theoretical orientation and artistic development of those who practiced "The New Journalism"—a phrase, as noted in Chapter 1, that was coined by Tom Wolfe and that originally described literary experimentation by working journalists in the 1960s and 1970s. These reporters contributed their time to print media with the express desire of eventually writing the great American (fiction) novel. As practicing journalists, they themselves privileged fiction writing as a life pursuit. Imagine their surprise, as Wolfe notes repeatedly in *The New Journalism,* when it became evident that nonfiction eventually would eclipse fiction as the most compelling narrative for American readers. John Berendt's *Midnight in the Garden of Good and Evil,* Steven Gaines's *Philistines at the Hedgerow: Passion and*

Property in the Hamptons, and Ted Conover's *Newjack: Guarding Sing Sing* remind us that the nonfiction novel continues to draw readers and critics. Finally, experimentation by notables such as Joan Didion—who moves easily between political essays in *After Henry* and extended fiction in *The Last Thing He Wanted*—remains a sign that important challenges lie in the exploration of the assumed boundaries between "fact" and "fiction."

In spite of Steinbeck's skill in writing nonfiction, Parini acknowledges that "much less attention has been paid" to Steinbeck's nonfiction than his fiction *(Travels* vii). In his 1995 biography of Steinbeck, Parini writes that Steinbeck's "dramatic work and nonfiction have usually been ignored" *(Steinbeck* xvi). Although scholars such as Warren G. French and William Howarth address Steinbeck's nonfiction extensively, they do so as a way to shed light upon Steinbeck's fiction and/or to argue (correctly) for Steinbeck's versatility as a writer. Certainly, the richness of a study of *The Grapes of Wrath* for journalists, sociologists, historians, folklorists, and scholars in religious studies is well established. (Agnes McNeill Donohue even divides her collection entitled *A Casebook on The Grapes of Wrath* into essays about the novel as a social document and essays about it as literature.)

Since Steinbeck's biographers and critics are often trained in literary criticism and not professional journalism, however, their scholarship tends to focus upon the historical distinctions between news and feature writing, upon traditional notions of truth-telling in American journalism practice, and upon Steinbeck's reliance on realism as a kind of reconstructed journalism. While these themes are helpful, it remains imperative to examine Steinbeck's contribution to literary journalism as well. This study relies upon two works, *The Harvest Gypsies* (republished with another essay as *Their Blood Is Strong)* and *Travels with Charley in Search of America,* as evidence of Steinbeck's particular contributions to literary journalism. As noted, it centers upon several tenets of literary journalism, including an unapologetic first-person point of view; advocacy for the deeper truth that underlies events; immersion in the lives of subjects; and the use of actual sources with recreated dialogue.

Before a discussion of the texts central to this study, it is important to remember that works such as *The Grapes of Wrath* are not unique in Steinbeck's canon: Steinbeck often relied upon daily events as fodder for his work. A description of life in a Mexican town became *The Forgotten Village* in 1941; this narrative would later become part of *The Pearl* (1947). A voyage down the coastline of California into Mexico similarly would become the *Sea of Cortez* (1941). In 1942, Steinbeck traveled with a photographer through Texas, Arizona, California, Florida, and Illinois to study how bomber crews are selected and trained. His journey took him to 20 airfields. In the tradition of immersion in literary journalism, Steinbeck lived the life of the pilots on whom he reported. "Steinbeck managed to fly on virtually every kind of plane the armed forces had in their command," writes Parini. "He attended classes with the men, ate dinner with them, slept in their barracks" *(Steinbeck* 268). The result was *Bombs Away: The Story of a Bomber Team* (1942). Hollywood bought rights to the story for $250,000, and Steinbeck gave the money to the Air Force Aid Society Trust

Fund. *Bombs Away*, called war propaganda by critics, is better described as an example of literary journalism.

Because of his interest in the war effort, Steinbeck longed to become a war correspondent, but the Associated Press and Reuters turned him down. In 1943, he began covering World War II for the *New York Herald Tribune*, writing 85 bylined dispatches that were syndicated nationally. His European dispatches from World War II were collected in 1959 into *Once There Was a War*. His war column was syndicated in every state but Oklahoma, and newspapers in Argentina, Chile, and Bolivia published some of his columns in translation. During this time, Steinbeck said he was treated badly by journalists: "I arrived as a Johnny-come-lately, a sacred cow, a kind of tourist." However, when the journalists realized he was serious about his writing and would not compete with them by trying to write straight news, they were then "very kind" to him, he said (*Steinbeck* 271). He spent five months in England, North Africa, and Italy. According to Parini, Steinbeck "came, increasingly, to see himself as a journalist, and he took pride in these dispatches, a few of which . . . aspire to the condition of art" *(Steinbeck* 274).

Steinbeck's flirtation with journalism continued. In 1953, Steinbeck contributed a final article to *Collier's* and published a travel report on an Italian resort in *Harper's Bazaar*. A visit into the Soviet Union with photographer Robert Capa became *A Russian Journal* (1948). He wrote about cars for *Ford Times* and about travel for *Holiday*. His 1954 Paris articles were translated for publication in the weekend edition of *Le Figaro,* a French morning newspaper. In 1957, *Esquire* published Steinbeck's defense of playwright Arthur Miller, who was being charged with contempt of Congress. From 1955-60, he was an editor-at-large for the *Saturday Review*. In 1956, Steinbeck attended both major political parties' presidential nominating conventions for the *Louisville Courier-Journal*. Editor Mark Ethridge hired him and syndicated his work. Charles Whitaker, then a member of the Syndicated Newspaper Editors, said in 1992 that Steinbeck "was like a cub reporter: enthusiastic, tentative, eager to please us" at the Democratic National Convention. "He threw himself into this reporting in a way that surprised everyone," Whitaker said (*Steinbeck* 394).

As Steinbeck continued to gather material from real life, he could not know that journalists would later applaud his courage and would attribute his impact on the collective American consciousness to immersion, a necessary tenet of literary journalism. "Letters to Alicia"—ostensibly epistles about Europe, the Middle East, and Vietnam written by Steinbeck to Alicia Patterson, the late wife of Harry F. Guggenheim—appeared from 1965-67 in the weekend supplement to *Newsday,* the newspaper Patterson founded in 1940. From 1966-67, Steinbeck traveled in and wrote about political issues in Vietnam, Thailand, Laos, Indonesia, Hong Kong, Japan, and South Korea. During the war, Steinbeck traveled to Vietnam and was photographed "pushing through a swampy jungle in military fatigues and helmet, looking like a lost soldier from the Italian campaign of World War II," Parini writes. According to Parini, Steinbeck wrote his column about the "daily life of soldiers" and the "smells and sights and sounds of Vietnam" *(Steinbeck* 474).

Work by literary critics is extensive and profoundly helpful to those study-ing Steinbeck's literary journalism; however, media scholars describe journal-ism history and Steinbeck's literary contributions differently. In *John Stein-beck's Nonfiction Revisited,* French writes that "there is a difference between headline hunting and the now more important feature writing. The legendary reporter of old depended on speed, agility, and nerve—qualities in which Stein-beck did not excel—and moved quickly from one story to another . . . Feature writers try to influence the way readers see things" (2). In his 1996 book, French relies on traditional definitions of news coverage: Hard news relays facts; fea-tures interpret.

However, these distinctions—while not the point of French's critical study of Steinbeck—are problematic, even when journalists themselves suggest that they ascribe to them. It can be argued that any writing is about point of view; even a straight news reporter's vantage point plays a role in how he or she relays the "facts" of an event as common as a traffic accident. Hard news may rely on an inverted pyramid and may not be primarily concerned with influencing the reader, but it is written by a person with certain preconceptions. The retelling of an event as mundane as a traffic accident can rely heavily upon where the re-porter is standing, what time of day it is, how many witnesses are available to interview, what groups those witnesses represent, etc.

It is also questionable whether in journalism the feature article has become "more important" than other genres. Features have existed in American journal-ism since at least the penny press era (1830s-1880s), and features are "more important" than straight news only in that they now occasionally appear on page one of American newspapers as human interest stories with news hooks. In fact, the feature article often is relegated to special sections inside the newspaper and treated as a nonessential human interest story.

French also suggests that "Steinbeck came back to the journalism that re-jected his early efforts" and "that journalism came round to providing a new outlet for his particular talents and a new career when he appeared to be running into dead ends as a fiction writer" (2). Journalism did not undergo the transfor-mation French may be suggesting here; instead, Steinbeck eventually availed himself of historically accepted forms of journalism as he developed as a writer and chose to experiment with various genres. Like other writers including Stein-beck, Truman Capote understood the fluid nature of truth-telling, whether he was writing fiction such as *The Grass Harp* or what he believed was the first nonfiction novel, *In Cold Blood.* Historically, journalism and media studies have incorporated the personal essay, travel writing, and the hybrid news-feature. *Travels with Charley* and other works attest to Steinbeck's genius in crossing literary boundaries with courage and with varying degrees of skill.

In spite of its occasionally simplistic distinctions between "art" and "jour-nalism," Parini's biography of Steinbeck provides one of the best descriptions of Steinbeck's interest in journalism. One of the characteristics central to literary journalism is immersion, a writer's commitment to live alongside of his or her sources. Parini writes that Steinbeck "approached the writing of fiction from what could be called a journalistic viewpoint, digging a row between 'art' on the one side and 'journalism' on the other. His Depression-era novels, in particular, possess a distinctly journalistic flavor and might be thought of as part reportage; one senses the 'research' behind them, the fact that the author had actually gone out and met the people he was writing about and tramped the roads beside them" *(Steinbeck* 150). Describing Steinbeck's personal connection with the laborers and migrant workers in Monterey, Parini says that Steinbeck was "more like a reporter or a police detective than a novelist" and that he "prowled the region with a notebook in hand" *(Steinbeck* 151):

> His approach to journalism was highly personal: not so far off from what decades later would be called the New Journalism . . . The statistics issued daily by the Office of War Information did not concern him . . . [During World War II, he] lived with the troops, ate meals with them, walked the streets with them, traveled on the same ships as they did, sat on the edges of their bunks, talked and (mostly) listened. His "columns" were like pieces of short stories, rich in dialogue and description, and each had a slight undertow of plot. *(Steinbeck* 274)

Steinbeck said in a letter quoted by Kathryn Marshall that "the hardest thing about writing is simply to tell the truth" (105), and it is clear that he experimented with various methods of relaying truths throughout his life. From 1925-26, he covered the courts and unimportant events such as "Courtesy Day" for the *New York American,* a William Randolph Hearst newspaper. Parini writes in his biography that Steinbeck, the "cub reporter," was "sent into the streets of Manhattan to find stories, and he did, after a fashion." Parini also writes that "his reporting style, however, was much too florid—full of metaphors and images—to satisfy his editors, and he was dispatched to the federal court, where he would be taken under the wing of a crew of experienced court reporters" (53). Their attempts were to no avail, however, and Steinbeck was fired.

In the end, according to his biographers, Steinbeck failed as a reporter, in part because he identified too closely with his subjects and would not sacrifice their deepest truths. In a *New York Times Magazine* article, "Autobiography: Making of a New Yorker," Steinbeck writes:

> I didn't know the first thing about being a reporter. I think now that the twenty-five dollars a week that they paid me was a total loss. They gave me stories to cover in Queens and Brooklyn and I would get lost and spend hours trying to find my way back. I couldn't learn to steal a picture from a desk when a family refused to be photographed and I invariably got emotionally involved and tried to kill the whole story to save the subject. (Shillinglaw, *America* 34)

In *The True Adventures of John Steinbeck, Writer,* Steinbeck biographer Jackson J. Benson argues that Steinbeck "found himself getting emotionally involved with the people he was supposed to write about and then trying to kill the story to protect the people" (95). Reminiscent of experiences described by Willa Cather, Katherine Anne Porter, and other writers of fiction who turned their backs on journalism, this refusal to remain emotionally separate from his subjects may help to explain Steinbeck's talent for creating sympathetically the realistic characters who cross indistinct lines between fact and fiction in his work. It may be argued that it was the time Steinbeck spent in professional journalism and his obvious gifts for observation and reporting that account for his skill as an ethnographer and for his ability to write novels celebrated as examples of documentary realism.

Travels with Charley in Search of America

Best known for *The Grapes of Wrath*—a novel that relied upon fact and won Steinbeck the 1940 Pulitzer Prize—Steinbeck was later celebrated by the public for *Travels with Charley in Search of America*. This curious four-part book remains a compelling example of Steinbeck's success with nonfiction and serves as what Parini calls an "elegy for a world he has lost" *(Travels* ix), but it is undeniably different from the journalism he produced earlier in his career. Accurately defined as a travel chronicle or travel monologue, *Travels with Charley* is a first-person narrative with a beginning, middle, and end; the journey undertaken by the author contributes its own structure, and as Steinbeck draws conclusions about himself and his homeland, the road trip takes on the narrative significance of a personal quest. Explaining why the pilgrimage is necessary, Steinbeck writes in *Travels with Charley,* "Thus I discovered that I did not know my own country" (5). He tells the reader that going to the "rooftree" of Maine at the beginning of his journey "seemed to give the journey a design, and everything in the world must have design or the human mind rejects it" (50).

Travels with Charley is not simply an elegy for the America with which Steinbeck has lost touch; it is also a poignant record of a man facing his own mortality. With characteristically subtle humor, Steinbeck recreates a conversation with a woman in a restaurant. She gives him directions to Sauk Centre, Minnesota, the birthplace of Sinclair Lewis. The conversation reflects a Steinbeck who has begun to deal with his own physical limitations and to wonder about how he will be remembered:

> "Sinclair Lewis came from there."
> "Oh! Yeah. They got a sign up. I guess quite a few folks come to see it. It does the town some good."
> "He's the first man who told me about this part of the country."
> "Who is?"
> "Sinclair Lewis."
> "Oh! Yeah. You know him?"
> "No, I just read him."
> I'm sure she was going to say "Who?" but I stopped her. "You say I cross at St. Cloud and stay on Fifty-two?"
> The cook said, "I don't think what's-his-name is there any more."
> "I know. He's dead."
> "You don't say." (102)

Published the year he received the Nobel Prize and more popular than even *The Grapes of Wrath*—Benson calls the initial sale "greater than any other Steinbeck book" (913-14)—*Travels with Charley* combines personal essay, travel writing, and political and social commentary. An introspective narrative published six years before Steinbeck's death, *Travels with Charley* is a window into the mind of one of America's pre-eminent writers as he considers his own *raison d'etre*. Called an "act of courage" (881) by Benson, the trip Steinbeck took might have shortened his life, since he had begun experiencing health problems. Steinbeck understood the significance of the pilgrimage he was committed to, going so far as to compare himself to Don Quixote as a picaresque hero. Calling his trip "Operation Windmills," Steinbeck named his specially constructed and equipped vehicle Rocinante after Don Quixote's horse. The comparison between Steinbeck and Don Quixote is especially appropriate, for, as critic Robert De-Mott notes, Steinbeck remained all his life a "sojourner" even though DeMott concedes that the Monterey Peninsula (or perhaps more accurately how Steinbeck remembered the Monterey Peninsula) remained his "spiritual home" (xii).

Alluding to both Miguel de Cervantes' *Don Quixote* and Robert Louis Stevenson's *Travels with a Donkey*, *Travels with Charley* details Steinbeck's cross-country trip with Charles le Chien, or "Charley," his beloved French poodle. Steinbeck left Sag Harbor near the end of Long Island, New York, on Sept. 23, 1960, and spent 11 weeks traveling, interviewing, and taking notes about landscape. The four parts of *Travels with Charley* include preparations for the trip; travels through New England, Maine, and Illinois; travels from New Mexico to California; and final stops in Texas and Louisiana. By the end of his journey, Steinbeck had traveled 10,000 miles through more than 30 states. Toward the end of the journey when the travelers arrived in southern Oregon and stared at the majesty of the redwoods, Steinbeck said, "Look, Charley. It's the tree of all trees. It's the end of the Quest" (144).

Critics debate the tone of *Travel with Charley,* although most of them agree with French. Citing critics who call *Travels with Charley* a "wasteland vision" in which "monster America" wins, French himself considers *Travels with Charley* a decidedly bleak portrait of the nation. To overly emphasize this viewpoint, however, would be to discredit Steinbeck's desire to reacquaint himself with the complexity of America and to revisit its varied landscapes. Even while dealing with his own inevitable physical deterioration, grieving the destruction of open space, and confronting inhumanity and ignorance, Steinbeck finds many aspects of his native land to celebrate. Nathaniel Philbrick correctly argues that *Travels with Charley* "marks Steinbeck's validation of his own continued connection with America" (239).

From the beginning of his journey through New England, Steinbeck is mesmerized by the beauty around him: He revels in the roadside stands "piled with golden pumpkins and russet squashes and baskets of red apples so crisp and sweet that they seemed to explode with juice when I bit into them," the "neat and white-painted" villages, and the "fire" in the fall leaves (23). As one might expect, Steinbeck is at his artistic best when he is describing the natural world he encounters on his journey. In one example, he writes, "The trees rise straight up to zenith; there is no horizon. The dawn comes early and remains dawn until the sun is high. Then the green fernlike foliage so far up strains the sunlight to a

green gold and distributes it in shafts or rather in stripes of light and shade"
(146).

In spite of Steinbeck's love for nature and his admiration for some aspects
of human civilization, it would be difficult to argue that *Travels with Charley* is
a particularly hopeful vision of America. Along with *The Winter of Our Discontent* and *America and Americans, Travels with Charley* is one of three books that
Benson calls a "moral trilogy" (968). There can be no doubt that Steinbeck is
disheartened by much of what he sees from the windows of Rocinante, and, as
noted earlier, it is his stated desire for social and political change that defines
Steinbeck as a literary journalist. "There is throughout his work—even his up-
beat later writings—a pervading sense of waste: wasted hopes, wasted energies,
wasted efforts," writes French. "*Travels with Charley* is finally a melancholy
chronicle about someone who sets out to find America and gets lost himself in a
literal as well as a metaphorical sense" (106). An excerpt from a letter that Steinbeck wrote to his editor supports French's claim: "Over and over I thought we
lack the pressures that make men strong and the anguish that makes men great.
The pressures are debts, the desires are for more material toys and the anguish is
boredom. Through time, the nation has become a discontented land" (Parini,
Steinbeck 428).

Unlike a journalist interested in balance (if not the elusive objectivity), Steinbeck critiques the nation's propensity for violence and hatred, its waste of
natural resources, its lust for profit and industrialization, and the failure of its
people to appreciate its promise. Writing about violence and war, Steinbeck
says of the nation's nuclear capabilities, "And now submarines are armed with
mass murder, our silly, only way of deterring mass murder" (19). Arguing that
"we have overcome all enemies but ourselves" (150), Steinbeck also turns his
horrified gaze on "The Cheerleaders," a group of women in New Orleans who in
1960 "gathered every day to scream invectives at children" (189). The enraged
women, a focal point of local media, wanted to prevent black children from en-
tering Louisiana schools and shouted at the children as they were escorted to
class by law enforcement officials. Comparing the way in which dogs and people relate to the world, Steinbeck satirically writes of Charley, "He doesn't belong to a species clever enough to split the atom but not clever enough to live in
peace with itself" (203).

Second, Steinbeck grieves about the loss of land in the interest of progress.
He compares American cities to "badger holes, ringed with trash—all of them—
surrounded by piles of wrecked and rusting automobiles, and almost smothered
with rubbish. Everything we use comes in boxes, cartons, bins, the so-called
packaging we love so much. The mountains of things we throw away are much
greater than the things we use" (22). He criticizes the highways sweeping across
what were once open spaces, writing, "When we get these thruways across the
whole country, as we will and must, it will be possible to drive from New York
to California without seeing a single thing" (70). One of the most poignant descriptions is of northern California, as Steinbeck writes:

> This four-lane concrete highway slashed with speeding cars I remember as a
> narrow, twisting mountain road where the wood teams moved, drawn by steady

mules . . . This was a little little town, a general store under a tree and a black-smith shop and a bench in front on which to sit and listen to the clang of ham-mer on anvil. Now little houses, each one like the next, particularly since they try to be different, spread for a mile in all directions. That was a woody hill with live oaks dark green against the parched grass where the coyotes sang on moonlit nights. The top is shaved off and a television relay station lunges at the sky and feeds a nervous picture to thousands of tiny houses clustered like aphids beside the roads. (148)

Steinbeck writes about Washington state with the same horror, and Seattle becomes a metaphor for American industry and mindless sprawl: "I remembered Seattle as a town sitting on hills beside a matchless harborage—a little city of space and trees and gardens, its houses matched to such a background. It is no longer so . . . Everywhere frantic growth, a carcinomatous growth. Bulldozers rolled up the green forests and heaped the resulting trash for burning. The torn white lumber from concrete forms was piled beside gray walls. I wonder why progress looks so much like destruction" (138).

Third, Steinbeck relates encounters with unmotivated Americans who, without meaningful challenges, are lost and frustrated. He describes people "who can drain off energy and joy, can suck pleasure dry and get no sustenance from it. Such people spread a grayness in the air about them" (37). This kind of person, the "new American," is someone who "finds his challenge and his love in traffic-choked streets, skies nested in smog, choking with the acids of indus-try, the screech of rubber and houses leashed in against one another while the townlets wither a time and die" (56).

Fourth, Steinbeck rails against industry and the media that have turned a blind eye to the plight of the earth. "The rivers were full of logs, bank to bank for miles, waiting their turn at the abbatoir to give their woody hearts so that the bulwarks of our civilization such as *Time* magazine and the *Daily News* can sur-vive, to defend us against ignorance" (57-58), he writes. Steinbeck also accuses media, which should be at the forefront of social and environmental progress, of being interested only in supplying the public with superficial information. He argues that newspapers contain "more opinion than news so that we no longer know one from the other" (206).

Ultimately, though, Steinbeck understands that *Travels with Charley* is less about America *per se* than it is about a vision of America refracted through his own gaze. "This monster of a land, this mightiest of nations, this spawn of the future, turns out to be the macrocosm of microcosm me" (159), he writes. It is this admission that most conclusively forms the basis for understanding *Travels with Charley* as literary journalism. In addition to advocating social and political change, Steinbeck sees no reason to apologize for using an intensely personal point of view. Setting himself apart from the journalists who cover daily events, he offers a strong argument for his place as a literary journalist and for his reli-ance upon point of view:

> I've always admired those reporters who can descend on an area, talk to key people, ask key questions, take samplings of opinions, and then set down an orderly report very like a road map. I envy this technique and at the same

time do not trust it as a mirror of reality. I feel that there are too many realities. What I set down here is true until someone else passes that way and rearranges the world in his own style. In literary criticism, the critic has no choice but to make over the victim of his attention into something the size and shape of himself.

And in this report I do not fool myself into thinking I am dealing with constants. A long time ago I was in the ancient city of Prague and at the same time Joseph Alsop, the justly famous critic of places and events, was there. He talked to informed people, officials, ambassadors; he read reports, even the fine print and figures, while I in my slipshod manner roved about with actors, gypsies, vagabonds. Joe and I flew home to America in the same plane, and on the way he told me about Prague, and his Prague had no relation to the city I had seen and heard. It just wasn't the same place, and yet each of us was honest, neither one a liar, both pretty good observers by any standard, and we brought home two cities, two truths. (59-60)

In addition to first-person point of view, one of the common characteristics of literary journalism is the recording and recreation of dialogue. Literary journalists such as Truman Capote in *In Cold Blood* may reconstruct dialogue—while adhering to the essence of the conversation—in order to make it more readable and/or unified. Even traditional journalists—bound to a different set of rules—do not include ellipses or other artificial guides to help the reader determine chronology in conversation. Furthermore, journalists who write straight news use excerpts that best relay the themes of the conversation. According to Parini, Steinbeck turns in *Travels with Charley* to "creating characters and dialogue as a novelist would." Parini writes, "For instance, when he crosses the Canadian border near Niagara Falls, he has a lovely, amusing exchange with the customs officer that could easily sit in the text of a short story. Indeed, the dialogue goes on for pages, and there is a beginning, a middle, and an end" *(Travels* xv-xvi). It would be unlikely that Steinbeck transcribed conversations with sources such as the customs officer.

Since the point of a piece of a literary journalism is to communicate a deeper truth, not merely to assemble facts, the exact words are not as important as they would be to a daily newspaper journalist relating the comments of a city manager in a council meeting. Occasionally, Steinbeck admits without apology to the liberties he takes with dialogue. For example, while talking with a young man who is not particularly well-spoken at a gas station next to a "little put-together, do-it-yourself group of cabins" (129), Steinbeck describes New York City and other places he has seen. The young man responds by saying, "One likes to see for one's self." Steinbeck then writes, "I swear he said it" (131).

Such a reference would be unnecessary for a traditional journalist. The reader would assume that the exact words were relayed, and if they were not, it is unlikely that the reader would ever know. While describing a member of "the Cheerleaders" in New Orleans, Steinbeck quotes bystanders crying out, "Come on, move back. Let her through. Where you been? You're late for school. Where you been, Nellie?" Then he writes, "The name was not Nellie. I forget what it was" (193). These asides make it clear that Steinbeck wants to differentiate his text from that of a working journalist covering the event for a local metropolitan newspaper. The woman's name, he suggests, doesn't matter; her prejudice and insensitivity do.

The underlying truths of *Travels with Charley* lie not only in his observations about his homeland but in his awareness of himself. The journey, as we have noted, takes on its own unity, and Steinbeck makes it clear that the pilgrimage itself is the point of the narrative. He begins and ends his journey in New York, and the reward is a new-found awareness of himself and his country. Along the way, he even claims that he has come to terms with his mortality; his death, he says, has become "a fact rather than a pageantry" (157). Early in the book he tells the reader that he is not one of the "map people." He writes, "I was born lost and take no pleasure in being found" (55). Beginning the journey with "gray desolation" (18), Steinbeck continues it against the odds and against the advice of friends. He wants a robust life, or no life at all: "For I have always lived violently, drunk hugely, eaten too much or not at all, slept around the clock or missed two nights of sleeping, worked too hard and too long in glory, or slobbed for a time in utter laziness," he writes. "I've lifted, pulled, chopped, climbed, made love with joy and taken my hangovers as a consequence, not as a punishment. I did not want to surrender fierceness for a small gain in yardage. . . I see too many men delay their exits with a sickly, slow reluctance to leave the stage. It's bad theater as well as bad living" (17-18).

Travels with Charley ends with Steinbeck lost again—geographically, but not necessarily spiritually—in Manhattan: "Every evening is Pamplona in lower New York," he writes. "I made a turn and then another, entered a one-way street the wrong way and had to back out, got boxed in the middle of a crossing by a swirling rapids of turning people . . . And that's how the traveler came home again" (210).

The Grapes of Wrath

Travels with Charley, written at the end of Steinbeck's career, was, ironically, more popular than his masterpiece *The Grapes of Wrath.* The earlier novel, however, is important to a study of Steinbeck's literary journalism because unlike *Travels with Charley,* it illustrates Steinbeck's ability to incorporate actual events in a fictional narrative. Fiction freed him to experiment with chronology, to change names, and to create his own dramatic structure, much like Upton Sinclair did when he wrote *The Jungle.*

The autobiographical narrative about seeking America might have been Steinbeck's most popular work of nonfiction, but his most popular fiction was undoubtedly *The Grapes of Wrath.* Comparing *The Grapes of Wrath* to other documentary epics during the 1930s and 1940s, William Howarth celebrates Steinbeck's best-known novel along with *An American Exodus* by Dorothea Lange and Paul Taylor and *Let Us Now Praise Famous Men* by James Agee and Walker Evans. In "The Mother of Literature: Journalism and *The Grapes of*

Wrath," Howarth writes, "The notion that Steinbeck turned to fiction because it was a higher, truer form of expression betrays either his intellect or his documentary principles. He chose fiction to make his story more artful, not truthful" (83). However, he concludes that *The Grapes of Wrath* "endures as literature because it sprang from journalism, a strong and vibrant mother" (96). Howarth cites specifically the final chapters of the novel, which rely upon events Steinbeck witnessed in 1938 near Visalia, California: "Unusually prolonged rain that winter produced high floods along the local streams, stranding over 5,000 migrant families in homeless destitution. For several days, Steinbeck joined relief efforts there, moving families and caring for the sick" (76).

When *Life* magazine did not run his story on the Visalia floods, Steinbeck published it as "Starvation under the Orange Trees" in the *Monterey Trader* (April 15, 1938). "Starvation under the Orange Trees" became the epilogue for *Their Blood Is Strong* and ends with Steinbeck's apocalyptic words: "Is it possible that this state is so stupid, so vicious and so greedy that it cannot feed and clothe the men and women who help to make it the richest area in the world? Must the hunger become anger and the anger fury before anything will be done?" (Shillinglaw, *America* 87).

Arguing that *The Grapes of Wrath* relied upon "case study, informant narrative, and travel report" (83), Howarth elevates the role of journalistic techniques in the creation of *The Grapes of Wrath.* However, although journalists would celebrate Howarth's thesis, it would be difficult to prove that the novel endures "because" the reader can trace its roots to journalism. Its survival as an American epic is far more complex than that; its literary longevity depends as much on characterization, plot, description, and compelling mythology as it does on its fictionalization of historical events. It may be argued that Tom Joad and Jim Casy would have existed in literature without having had counterparts in "real" life. Still, whether journalism is dismissed or celebrated, it must be a factor in understanding Steinbeck's most enduring novel.

Several experiences and shorter works contributed to Steinbeck's final version of *The Grapes of Wrath.* Early in his career, Steinbeck met George West, an editor for the *San Francisco News,* at the Carmel home of journalist Lincoln Steffens. After he finished *In Dubious Battle*, Steinbeck agreed to do a series on the Dust Bowl migration into rural California for West. He covered the plight of migrant workers for the *News* and in September 1936 published "Dubious Battle in California" in *Nation.* In October 1936, the series was collected as *The Harvest Gypsies* and later yet as *Their Blood Is Strong* (1938), a reprint of *The Harvest Gypsies* with a postscript published by the pro-labor Simon J. Lubin Society. *The Harvest Gypsies* is especially compelling because it includes photographs by Dorothea Lange, one of the Farm Security Administration photographers who became famous for her portrayal of migrant workers and others affected by the plummeting economy.

While being immersed in the events of his time, Steinbeck met figures who were larger than life and who were easily translated into fiction. One such person was Tom Collins, who headed migrant camps in Marysville and Arvin, California, for the federal government. *The Grapes of Wrath* is partially dedicated to

Collins ("To Tom—who lived it"). In the foreword to a manuscript by Collins, Steinbeck writes of the time he met Collins: "Sitting at a littered table was Tom Collins, a little man in a damp, frayed, white suit . . . He had a small moustache, his graying, black hair stood up on his head like the quills of a frightened porcupine, and his large, dark eyes, tired beyond sleepiness, the kind of tired that won't let you sleep even if you have time and a bed" (*Steinbeck* 179). Steinbeck spent a week with Collins and mingled with the Arvin camp residents, never missing an opportunity to interview them.

In 1939, Steinbeck completed the first draft of *The Grapes of Wrath*, an example of literary journalism that tells the story of migrant workers and protects their dignity. The novel was the result of the time Steinbeck spent visiting migrant camps and working through Collins' manager's reports—which included "social and cultural observations on migrant life and individual anecdotes sometimes told in Okie dialect" (ix), according to Charles Wollenberg. The novel deals with a trip by the Joad family from Oklahoma to California and provides a re-enactment of the plight of the displaced farmer that actually began in the 1880s when a severe drought struck the nation.

During the 1890s, rainfall totals dropped, and from 1905 to 1915 farmers had to deal with too much rain and some flooding. Tenant farmers also were being replaced by technologically enhanced methods of growing and harvesting crops. Between 1925 and 1930, the amount of land being cultivated increased by 34 percent because, with the newly invented combine, farmers could harvest as much as they could plant (77), according to Marilyn Coffey in *Natural History*. Overuse of the land meant that topsoil would only remain in place with moisture, and when drought and winds came, dust filled the skies. "Some 300,000 square miles—four times the land area of Nebraska—were damaged by dust or erosion" (80), Coffey said.

By 1930, the nation faced a farming crisis of unprecedented proportions. During the 1930s every state in the nation gained population except the Dakotas, Nebraska, Kansas, and Oklahoma. By 1932, there were 12 million unemployed Americans, 5,000 banks went under, and the national income was cut in half. From 1935 to 1938, between 300,000 and 500,000 Okies arrived in California (xi), according to Wollenberg. Those fleeing Oklahoma, Arkansas, Texas, Nebraska, Kansas, Missouri, and other states were known collectively and pejoratively as "Okies." Soundly despised because they were considered ignorant and dirty, "Okies" were ineligible for social relief and were homeless. They were attacked by vigilantes and by local police. Coffey writes:

> Small wonder, then, that when the dust storms of the 1930s rolled over the Plains—their turbulent black clouds pitching and heaving thundersqualls that showered dust instead of rain—some feared they were witnessing the apocalypse. The land, which had seemed so clearly defined, began to move: from field to field, from county to county, from state to state. The distinction between land and sky, once so clear, became blurred as earth rose up to dance before the wind in a dozen different guises. Thousands of tons of soil, once indisputably wed to the land, rose and invaded the stratosphere. Such a reversal of the physical world was shocking. (72-73)

Because of what he observed in the migrant camps, Steinbeck argued for a state agricultural labor board, a union for migrant workers, and a program to help migrants resettle on small family farms. The Resettlement Administration, succeeded by the Farm Security Administration, established 15 camps to aid the migrant workers before the program was terminated after World War II, but the camps were not adequate. In *The Harvest Gypsi*es, Steinbeck's advocacy journalism is particularly apparent:

> The squatters' camps are located all over California. Let us see what a typical one is like. It is located on the banks of a river, near an irrigation ditch or on a side road where a spring of water is available. From a distance it looks like a city dump, and well it may, for the city dumps are the sources for the material of which it is built. You can see a litter of dirty rags and scrap iron, of houses built of weeds, of flattened cans of paper. It is only on close approach that it can be seen that these are homes. (26)

Steinbeck respects the displaced farmers, and that respect is evident in his description of a typical migrant camp family: "Five years ago this family had fifty acres of land and a thousand dollars in the bank. The wife belonged to a sewing circle and the man was a member of the grange. They raised chickens, pigs, pigeons and vegetables and fruit for their own use; and their land produced the tall corn of the middle west. Now they have nothing" (27). In his biography, Parini writes descriptively and persuasively about why Steinbeck engaged in advocacy journalism after seeing the sights that inspired *The Grapes of Wrath:*

> The reality of the situation startled Steinbeck, who was unprepared for the starkness of what he saw: whole families lived in cardboard boxes or in large disused pipes; indeed, shelters were constructed from anything that came to hand: an old rug, some straw mats, pieces of driftwood. Food was scarce and expensive, and people in some areas were reduced to eating rats and dogs. Babies were dying from lack of adequate nutrition or proper medical services. This was the front line of poverty in America, and Steinbeck was saddened and outraged. (174-75)

The Grapes of Wrath crosses many boundaries: It is effective cultural geography, the study of the processes of human interaction with the landscape and the environment; it describes the geology of the Great Plains; it tells the history of the Dust Bowl era; it relates the sociology of migrant workers; it is documentary, the fusion of reportage and investigative methods of the social sciences; it is folklore; it is philosophy; and it is modern mythology. It is also literary journalism.

In his 1962 Nobel Prize acceptance speech, Steinbeck argues for writing that is accessible to the masses of educated Americans. He writes, "Literature was not promulgated by a pale and emasculated critical priesthood singing their litanies in empty churches—nor is it a game for the cloistered elect" *(America* 172). Not everyone agreed. After Steinbeck received the Nobel Prize, Parini writes that the decision to bestow the prize on Steinbeck was "ridiculed . . . by a few well-known academic critics and a handful of journalists who refused to believe that a writer with a popular following could be any good" *(Steinbeck* xix).

In a study of Steinbeck's literary journalism, it is especially important to realize that Steinbeck never argues for life in an ivory tower. The writer, he said in his Nobel Prize acceptance speech, is "charged with exposing our many grievous faults and failures, with dredging up to the light our dark and dangerous dreams, for the purpose of improvement." And since according to Steinbeck, "man himself has become our greatest hazard and our only hope" (Shillinglaw, *America* 174), the contemporary writer—whether that writer is a novelist or a reporter—must "celebrate man's proven capacity for greatness of heart and spirit—for gallantry in defeat, for courage, compassion, and love" (Shillinglaw, *America* 173). Steinbeck's challenge to the writer of fiction is also his challenge to the journalist. Our "faults and failures" and our moments of "greatness of heart and spirit" (Shillinglaw, *America* 173) appear in American newspapers as well as in the pages of novels. Literary journalism is one of the genres in which writers celebrate our strengths and chastise us for our failures, and Steinbeck should be included among its ranks.

Walt Whitman, Edgar Allan Poe, Katherine Anne Porter, Eudora Welty, and John Steinbeck are representative of one thread of literary journalism: those who began their careers in journalism but gained their reputations by writing fiction. In Chapter 3, we meet three women who are representative of the other thread: those who began their careers in journalism and remain best known for their extended nonfiction. One of them, Joan Didion, has written fiction, but both Sara Davidson and Susan Orlean are known primarily as writers of nonfiction. All three merit more recognition for their contributions to the history of literary journalism.

Chapter 3.
Women in American Literary Journalism

Turning and turning in the widening gyre
The falcon cannot hear the falconer;
Things fall apart; the centre cannot hold;
Mere anarchy is loosed upon the world.
The blood-dimmed tide is loosed, and everywhere
The ceremony of innocence is drowned;
The best lack all conviction, while the worst
Are full of passionate intensity. (158)

"The Second Coming"
William Butler Yeats

The women featured in this chapter share both the ability to use a personal voice while developing universal themes and the ability to employ narratives from real life and real time in mythopoetic ways. Their work is allegorical. Their work provides a contextualized social history. Their prose approaches the lyricism of poetry. And although Joan Didion, Sara Davidson, and Susan Orlean merit serious discussion no matter what their gender, the fact remains that since the time Tom Wolfe included only two women (Barbara Goldsmith and Joan Didion) in his classic book *The New Journalism,* the names ordinarily associated with literary journalism have been those of men.

At the center of the best of literary journalism stands Joan Didion, who writes as a participant-observer about growing up in California in the 1950s, about the tumult in America in the 1960s, and about more recent political and cultural events. Didion's work is described by critics as highly personal and as profoundly apocalyptic. Polish journalist Ryszard Kapuscinski is among those who discuss the challenges a literary journalist faces when he or she recreates an event through a personal lens, as Didion does:

> The traditional trick of literature is to obscure the writer, to express the story through a fabricated narrator describing a fabricated reality. But for me, what I have to say is validated by the fact that I was there, that I witnessed the event. There is, I admit, a certain egoism in what I write, always complaining about the heat or the hunger or the pain I feel, but it is terribly important to have what I write authenticated by its being lived. You could call it, I suppose, personal reportage, because the author is always present. I sometimes call it literature by foot. (Campbell n.p.)

Didion, Davidson, and Orlean write about spiritual disintegration in a world in which the center does not hold, and their narrators, although wise, are never quite omniscient. Of the three, Didion most often concerns herself with the role of media in creating reality for readers and viewers. In *The Last Thing He Wanted,* Didion discusses news as fact, as fiction, and as tales. Of one of her characters, she writes, "It occurred to her that possibly what was misleading was the concept of 'news' itself, a liberating thought" (30).

In "Notes Toward a Definition of Journalism: Understanding an Old Craft as an Art Form," G. Stuart Adam discusses the highly personal nature of some forms of journalism, both in the subjects they reveal and in the personal vantage point of the reporter himself or herself. He emphasizes the emotion that drives the news, even when the emotion appears to have been neutralized by a carefully controlled inverted pyramid news story: "Journalism is primarily about the events that the mysteries of passion or a competition or love or hating produce— a fight, a foreclosure, a marriage, a war. It is about the manifest rather than the hidden, the objective rather than the subjective" (24).

Not surprisingly, in the section of his article entitled "Meaning: Myth, Metaphor, Explanation," Adam discusses Didion: "Didion's method of explanation focuses on the cultural as distinct from the psychological. For Didion, what is unconscious resides not in the soul . . . but in society's primary texts or media. What is unconscious in human beings is ambient in the culture" (41). Arguing that many journalism texts are mythic and metaphoric, Adam writes that works by writers such as Didion, Davidson, and Orlean "can therefore be read more as literature than as social science" (42).

This highly personal, profoundly spiritual, and phenomenological approach to writing often suggests an intense relationship between reporter and subject, as discussed earlier. For some critics, having such a relationship revealed in the text is more honest than the vague objectivity of conventional media. A rising star in literary journalism and a frequent contributor to the *New York Times Magazine,* Adrian Nicole LeBlanc reveals just such a relationship with her sources in *Random Family: Love, Drugs, Trouble, and Coming of Age in the Bronx,* a novel she spent 10 years researching and writing. Of her sources, Le-

Blanc writes: "The hardships of these young people and their families are not unusual in their neighborhoods. Neither are their gifts" (406). Given her compassion for and connection to her sources, it is not surprising that LeBlanc has a B.A. in sociology from Smith College (in addition to a master's of philosophy and modern literature from Oxford University and a master of law studies from Yale Law School); her personal interest in her subjects and her understanding of their plight becomes obvious within the first few pages of *Random Family.* Her admiration for and investment in them connects LeBlanc to the three women writers featured in this section of *Settling the Borderland: Other Voices in Literary Journalism,* especially Davidson and Orlean, who share openly their attitudes about those whom they portray.

Joan Didion

Disciples of Joan Didion have imitated her for many years, many of them carving out their own place and their own style in the literary world. In an article entitled "Didion's Daughters," Katie Roiphe writes: "I don't think that I have ever walked into the home of a female writer, aspiring writer, newspaper reporter, or women's magazine editor and not found, somewhere on the shelves, a row of Joan Didion books" (100). A lengthy one-paragraph tribute to Didion from Roiphe's article is worth relaying here:

> On the cover of one of the books is a famous photograph of Didion, stick thin, hair blowing, brow furrowed, eyes hidden behind enormous black sunglasses, looking as if she needs a cigarette. She was the embodiment of everything cool in sixties journalism. Her writing was stylish, ironic, neurotic, and felt. Her sharp tone cut through the pretensions and weirdness of the times, but she also cried as she walked down the street and had migraine headaches and could barely get out of bed. That was her persona—bruised, fragile, harboring a mysterious sorrow that had something, but not everything, to do with the world around her. Didion wrote about murderers and fanatics and 5-year-olds doing acid. She wrote, "I am so physically small, so temperamentally unobtrusive and so neurotically inarticulate that people tend to forget that my presence runs counter to their best interests." She did clipped irony and she did sentences swelling with portent. Hers was the quivering, sensitive sensibility of a generation, and still her words reverberate through our magazines and newspapers, her quirky, distinctive, oddly formal writing style borrowed and imitated, echoed and incorporated until it becomes simply the way we write. And it isn't a fleeting fashion. Nearly 40 years after her first essays appeared in places like *The Saturday Evening Post,* we still imitate Joan Didion, and if we don't imitate Joan Didion, we imitate the people who imitate Joan Didion. Her rhythms are so mesmerizing, her insights so impressive, her personality so perversely appealing that they lodge in the mind. It's no different from the boom of British authors writing like Martin Amis, or novelists drawing on Hemingway and Mailer, or painters drawing on Corot, but it is testimony to the power of Didion's style and the strength of her voice that it echoes into the casual pieces of this, the next century. (100)

Roiphe lists Meghan Daum, Maureen Dowd, Sarah Kerr, Elizabeth Kolbert, Susan Orlean, and Anna Quindlen as "disciples," arguing that male writers tend to imitate Tom Wolfe more: "There are also male writers who imitate Didion, though more of them borrow from Tom Wolfe. Think of all of those articles you've read in *GQ* and *Esquire* with such Wolfian sound effects as 'Splat!' and internal free associations and liberal spatterings of exclamation points" (136).

At the center of Didion's work is the dread and despair an individual feels in the face of the unpredictable universe. The tone of her essays and nonfiction novels often communicates anxiety and fear: "It is the season of suicide and divorce and prickly dread, wherever the wind blows" (3), writes Didion in the first paragraph of "Some Dreamers of the Golden Dream." Didion describes natural disasters such as Santa Ana winds, mud slides, wildfires, and earthquakes. She writes about a changing and often frightening political landscape with sometimes wry but always biting tone. She writes of existential loneliness, true love, tragedy, and human destiny. As a journalist, she is a master of detail.

Didion has always been a self-conscious writer committed to perfecting her art, and she knew early in life that she wanted to be a writer. Didion credits Ernest Hemingway, Joseph Conrad, and Henry James with being her literary ancestors. Of Hemingway, she said he taught her "how sentences worked":

> When I was fifteen or sixteen I would type out his stories to learn how the sentences worked. I taught myself to type at the same time. A few years ago when I was teaching a course at Berkeley I reread *A Farewell to Arms* and fell right back into those sentences. I mean they're perfect sentences. Very direct sentences, smooth rivers, clear water over granite, no sinkholes. *(Women Writers at Work* 410)

Devoted to a study of literature since her youth, Didion received a B.A. degree in English from the University of California at Berkeley in 1956. At 22, she was hired by *Vogue* and worked in New York City; the job was the result of a literary award she won at Berkeley.

Her credits are rich and varied. Married for many years to the late playwright John Gregory Dunne, Didion and her husband wrote the screenplays for "A Star Is Born" and "Up Close and Personal." Didion is well known for her columns and essays in The *Saturday Evening Post, Esquire,* and other magazines. Although she has published several novels and collections of essays, she is perhaps most famous for *After Henry, A Book of Common Prayer, Democracy, Joan Didion: Essays and Conversations, The Last Thing He Wanted, Miami, Play It As It Lays, Run River, Salvador, Slouching Towards Bethlehem,* and *The White Album.* As noted in Chapter 1, Didion recently published *The Year of Magical Thinking,* which is destined to be one of her most beloved books and a classic example of memoir.

Didion's work can be divided into particular genres, time periods, or themes. In *Settling the Borderland,* it is most helpful to consider her contribution in terms of the concepts around which she organizes a particular essay, novel, or collection. These concepts include American political movements, attitudes, figures, and symbols; California as the final American frontier; and the significance of one's personal vantage point in making meaning and sustaining community.

American Politics

Didion can be deeply personal, as she is in *The Year of Magical Thinking,* or seemingly detached and analytical as she is in the 2001 book *Political Fictions.* In *Political Fictions,* she deals with the allegorical nature of the American political system with intensity and profound concern. Didion reveals that her essays are designed to show "the ways in which the political process did not reflect but increasingly proceeded from a series of fables about American experience" (7). Her powerful narratives combine scathing political commentary with an allegorist's desire to leave no symbol unturned. When she unveils who actually voted in the 2000 election, she sends a damning message about American political figureheads and about the place from which they derive their power. She writes:

> Fifty-three percent of voters in the 2000 election . . . had . . . incomes above $50,000. Forty-three percent were suburban. Seventy-four percent had some higher education; forty-two percent had actual college degrees. Seventy percent said that they invested in the stock market. That this was not a demographic profile of the country at large, that half the nation's citizens had only a vassal relationship to the government under which they lived, that the democracy we spoke of spreading throughout the world was now in our own country only an ideality, had come to be seen, against the higher priority of keeping the process in the hands of those who already held it, as facts without application. *(Political Fictions* 17-18)

Her concerns with American political process do not stop with politicians themselves but with those in the shadows who describe and deliver events and personalities to the American public—the journalists themselves. She writes:

> American reporters "like" covering a presidential campaign (it gets them out on the road, it has balloons, it has music, it is viewed as a big story, one that leads to the respect of one's peers, to the Sunday shows, to lecture fees and often to Washington), which is why there has developed among those who do it so arresting an enthusiasm for overlooking the contradictions inherent in reporting that which occurs only in order to be reported. *(Political Fictions* 30)

And later, in "Political Pornography," Didion ridicules the idea of objectivity in coverage of political events:

> The genuflection toward "fairness" is a familiar newsroom piety, in practice the excuse for a good deal of autopilot reporting and lazy thinking but in theory a benign ideal. In Washington, however, a community in which the management of news has become the single overriding preoccupation of the core industry, what "fairness" has often come to mean is a scrupulous passivity,

an agreement to cover the story not as it is occurring but as it is presented, which is to say as it is manufactured. *(Political Fictions* 207)

Allegory depends upon the creation of character, and Didion is quick to point out that the American political tableau is the home of some of the best narratives of conflict and some of the most compelling characters. "All stories, of course, depend for their popular interest upon the invention of personality, or 'character,'" she writes, "but in the political narrative, designed as it is to maintain the illusion of consensus by obscuring rather than addressing actual issues, this invention served a further purpose" *(Political Fictions* 41-42). Later, she writes:

> In other words, what it "came down to," what it was "about," what was wrong or right with America, was not an historical shift largely unaffected by the actions of individual citizens but "character," and if "character" could be seen to count, then every citizen—since everyone was a judge of character, an expert in the field of personality—could be seen to count. This notion, that the citizen's choice among determinedly centrist candidates makes a "difference," is in fact the narrative's most central element, and its most fictive. *(Political Fictions* 44)

Whether one agrees with Didion's cynicism about the political process or not, there can be no doubt that her vision derives from an understanding that invented narratives produce intense social reaction. As she explains, "The entire attention of those inside the process was directed toward the invention of this story in which they themselves were the principal players, and for which they themselves were the principal audience" *(Political Fictions* 47). In the 1980s, for example, Americans elected former actor Ronald Reagan as president. The public's enchantment with this particular "character" was not lost on Didion. In "The West Wing of Oz," she writes:

> For the "President," a man whose most practiced instincts had trained him to find the strongest possible narrative line in the scenes he was given, to clean out those extraneous elements that undermined character clarity, a man for whom historical truth had all his life run at twenty-four frames a second, Iran-contra would have been irresistible, a go project from concept, a script with two strong characters, the young marine officer with no aim but to serve his president, the aging president with no aim but to free the tyrannized (whether the tyrants were Nicaraguans or Iranians or some other nationality altogether was just a plot point, a detail to work out later), a story about male bonding, a story about a father who found the son he never (in this "cleaned out" draft of the script) had, a buddy movie, and better still than a buddy movie: a mentor buddy movie, with action. *(Political Fictions* 117)

Like *Political Fictions, After Henry* deals with the best and worst of American politics. *After Henry* is broken into geographical sections that deal with everything from political figures and political processes to the importance of what one would take first from a house threatened by fire. The sections are: Washington, D.C., "In the Realm of the Fisher King" about Ronald Reagan; "Insider Baseball" about elections and political mythmaking; "Shooters Inc." about international news; California, "Girl of the Golden West" about Patty Hearst, "Pacific Distances," "Los Angeles Days," "Down at City Hall," "L.A. Noir," "Fire Season," "Times Mirror Square"; and New York, "Sentimental Journeys."

Didion's themes include objective reality, felt experience, social dislocations, disintegration of family, and a need for order. Didion fuses the personal with the public. She believes that American society is nostalgic, romantic and deluded. She argues against the idea that economic growth equals progress. In fact, no human institutions can form the center for a society in spin. To support her central thesis, Didion borrows a phrase from "The Second Coming," both to serve as title for one of her books *(Slouching Towards Bethlehem)* and to provide the theme around which many of her narratives revolve. The phrase "slouching towards Bethlehem" is rich and evocative on many levels; most importantly, the poem "The Second Coming" reflects Yeats's concern with chaos and a lack of a moral center, which is Didion's primary concern as well.

The Final Frontier

Didion's complicated relationship with California provides her with a potent and paradoxical symbol of beauty and human failure. According to an interview with Susanna Rustin in *The Guardian* (May 21, 2005), Didion often writes about the West, "the final frontier where American dreams were supposed to come true" (n.p.). As Rustin writes: "Whether writing on murderers, film stars, activists or the state's water supply, her 'conviction that we had long outlived our finest hour' is inescapable." In fact, Martin Amis calls her "the poet of the Great Californian Emptiness" (Rustin n.p.).

California becomes a character in her work, laden with imagery. In one particularly rich excerpt in the essay "Notes from a Native Daughter," Didion writes:

> In fact that is what I want to tell you about: what it is like to come from a place like Sacramento. If I could make you understand that, I could make you understand California and perhaps something else besides, for Sacramento *is* California, and California is a place in which a boom mentality and a sense of Chekhovian loss meet in uneasy suspension; in which the mind is troubled by some buried but eradicable suspicion that things had better work here, because here, beneath that immense bleached sky, is where we run out of continent. (172)

And in the essay about hippies in San Francisco during the 1960s entitled "Slouching Towards Bethlehem," Didion pulls from William Butler Yeats's well-known poem in describing California and, more broadly, the nation:

> The center was not holding. It was a country of bankruptcy notices and public-auction announcements and commonplace reports of casual killings and misplaced children and abandoned homes and vandals who misspelled even the

four-letter words they scrawled. It was a country in which families routinely disappeared, trailing bad checks and repossession papers. Adolescents drifted from city to torn city, sloughing off both the past and the future as snakes shed their skins, children who were never taught and would never now learn the games that had held the society together. (84)

Slouching Towards Bethlehem illuminates the San Francisco drug culture of the 1960s and other aspects of American life. Of Didion's book, John Hartsock writes:

Didion cultivates such incongruities in her writing precisely because they demonstrate how impossible it is to reduce phenomenal experience into a tidy package or, in other words, to critical closure. In the face of such evidence she records, she is reflecting how she feels, or "what it was to be me" when she confronted the evidence, in this case a kind of disbelief about the circumstances she found. (199)

Given Didion's interest in what constitutes the moral center of the United States, it is clear why she highlights a poem by an author enchanted by and committed to order and form and civilization, a poet who found himself in a world characterized by soullessness and chaos. In the poem cited throughout this chapter, a poem that deals with political unrest in Ireland, Yeats describes the emergence of the anti-Christ, the presence of evil in the world:

Surely some revelation is at hand;
Surely the Second Coming is at hand.
The Second Coming! Hardly are those words out
When a vast image out of *Spiritus Mundi*
Troubles my sight: somewhere in sands of the desert
A shape with lion body and the head of a man,
A gaze blank and pitiless as the sun,
Is moving its slow thighs, while all about it
Reel shadows of the indignant desert birds.
The darkness drops again; but now I know
That twenty centuries of stony sleep
Were vexed to nightmare by a rocking cradle,
And what rough beast, its hour come round at last,
Slouches towards Bethlehem to be born? (158)

Specifically, Yeats is writing in January 1919 about the conflict between the British and Irish. He borrows images of the Second Coming of Christ (Matthew 24) and the appearance of the Antichrist (the Beast of the Apocalypse) as recorded in I John 2:18. Through her use of disruptive, disquieting images, Didion describes California in *Slouching Towards Bethlehem* as a land of terror and the end of humankind rather than the land of enchantment, consumerism, freedom, and hedonism.

One of the most unsettling aspects of Didion's work is its lack of thematic resolution. Hartsock has noted that there is no "critical closure" possible in most works that qualify as literary journalism, and Didion's canon is no exception. Because encapsulating and explaining the 1960s in America—even to those who lived through that decade—is impossible, Didion uses the time period as a metaphor for American ways of being and ways of behaving. Like Didion, Davidson writes of the 1960s and confesses her own inability to summarize the events she witnessed or to make sense of them. Davidson uses her powerful authorial voice to confess in *Loose Change: Three Women of the Sixties:* "I'm afraid I will be criticized for copping out. ('We want to know what you *make* of it all, what this period meant in terms of a society, a culture.') But the truth is, I have not found answers and I'm not sure I remember the questions" (367).

Of Didion, Hartsock writes, "In the end she resists critical closure if she is true to her points of reference" (153). Referring again to a literary journalist's refusal to be embarrassed by her or his subjectivity, Hartsock writes, "Subjectivity alone undoes the lie, and in undoing it literary journalists resist coming to critical closure" (203). Presumably, the "lie" is the implication by traditional journalists that they have understood and encapsulated an event for a reader. In sum, there is no presumption of "knowing" in literary journalism; hence, there are no absolutes and no ultimate conclusion to the story told. One might argue that such a narrative approach more closely mirrors the reality most Americans experience.

Didion is a cultural allegorist, a prophet of the modern day. In "Some Dreamers of the Golden Dream" originally published in the *Saturday Evening Post,* "Didion sets her sights on the shallow promise and Gothic nature of the California dream" (199), Hartsock writes. In "Baudrillardesque Impulses in the Impressionistic Journalism of Joan Didion," Dennis Russell is on the heels of critics who recognize that Didion documents an America that is "socially, politically, and spiritually adrift" (20). His article is helpful to a study of Didion as an allegorist because he also argues that she uncovers the "counterfeit nature of the American narrative" (25). "Her subjects nostalgically and desperately cling to lifestyles, norms, values, and beliefs that long since have crumbled under the weight of their own mythologies," Russell adds, "and in so doing are systematically replicating an America that may never have existed" (28).

A full reading of Didion's fiction *(A Book of Common Prayer, Democracy, Play It As It Lays, Run River,* and *The Last Thing He Wanted)* and her nonfiction *(After Henry, Miami, Political Fictions, Salvador, Slouching Towards Bethlehem,* and *The White Album)* would reveal layer upon layer of allegorical method and characters employed as metaphor. For our purposes, we will turn to "Some Dreamers of the Golden Dream" from *Slouching Towards Bethlehem* because of its similarities to and differences from Davidson's "Real Property," an extended essay important to any analysis of allegory and literary journalism and discussed at length in the second part of this chapter.

Once again, the setting for the complex tale of American values is Southern California, this time the San Bernardino Valley. As Susan Orlean writes in an interview with Joan Didion—the woman who wrote "taut, chilling" essays for *Vogue, The National Review,* the *Saturday Evening Post,* and the *New York Times Magazine*—described California "as a world both real and imagined, at

once the bedrock of familiarity to her as a native and a place that was then frac-
turing into strange, disordered pieces" ("Straight and Narrow" 282).

The first line of "Some Dreamers of the Golden Dream"—"This is a story
about love and death in the golden land"—signals symbolic intent. The allegorical expectation is heightened with Didion's description: "There has been no rain
since April. Every voice seems a scream. It is the season of suicide and divorce
and prickly dread, wherever the wind blows" (3). The reader has little doubt that
the tale of Lucille Maxwell Miller and her husband Gordon "Cork" Miller and
Banyan Street is ominous. Readers familiar with Didion will suspect that the
story about the Millers is about the couple themselves and not about them at all:
"Unhappy marriages so resemble one another that we do not need to know too
much about the course of this one" (8), we're told.

Arrested for the murder of her husband, Miller becomes an ironic symbol of
a world gone mad. Again, the center will not hold. As detectives begin their investigation, so do Didion and the reader. Crimes are nothing if not puzzles, but
the crimes in Didion's work inevitably take on cultural significance. Didion
writes of her lost protagonist and the search for a motive for her crime:

> They set out to find it in accountants' ledgers and double-indemnity clauses and
> motel registers, set out to determine what might move a woman who believed
> in all the promises of the middle class—a woman who had been chairman of
> the Heart Fund and who always knew a reasonable little dressmaker and who
> had come out of the bleak wild of prairie fundamentalism to find what she
> imagined to be the good life—what should drive such a woman to sit on a street
> called Bella Vista and look out her new picture window into the empty Califor-
> nia sun and calculate how to burn her husband alive in a Volkswagen. (15)

Barbara Lounsberry is correct when she calls Miller the "fullest portrait of those
rapt by that particularly persistent American mirage: the Fitzgeraldian dream of
success and love" (109).

The motive for the crime, an affair with the husband of one of her friends,
explains the crime and doesn't explain it at all. The detectives are looking for
simple causes and effects; Didion, as always, is looking for clues to human nature and to madness in the "golden land" (28). In fact, California again becomes
a character in Didion's story, a location that seems to have its own terrible energy. For example, Didion describes the day Miller's trial opens by telling the
reader about a land where "the air smells of orange blossoms" and where a 16-
year-old tries to kill himself:

> January 11, 1965, was a bright warm day in Southern California, the kind
> of day when Catalina floats on the Pacific horizon and the air smells of orange
> blossoms and it is a long way from the bleak and difficult East, a long way
> from the cold, a long way from the past. A woman in Hollywood staged an all-
> night sit-in on the hood of her car to prevent repossession by a finance com-
> pany. A seventy-year-old pensioner drove his station wagon at five miles an
> hour past three Gardena poker parlors and emptied three pistols and a twelve-
> gauge shotgun through their windows, wounding twenty-nine people. "Many
> young women become prostitutes just to have enough money to play cards," he

explained in a note. Mrs. Nick Adams said that she was "not surprised" to hear her husband announce his divorce plans on the Les Crane Show, and, farther north, a sixteen-year-old jumped off the Golden Gate Bridge and lived.

And, in the San Bernardino County Courthouse, the Miller trial opened. The crowds were so bad that the glass courtroom doors were shattered in the crush, and from then on identification disks were issued to the first forty-three spectators in line. (19-20)

Miller was sentenced to life in prison with the possibility of parole and incarcerated in the California Institution for Women at Frontera, near a field where cattle graze and where a sprinkler system irrigates the alfalfa. "A lot of California murderesses live here, a lot of girls who somehow misunderstood the promise" (25), Didion writes. At the end of the narrative, Didion writes of "the golden land where every day the world is born anew" (28). What she suggests, of course, is not that innocence returns to California (or America) but that there are few consequences and no moments of epiphany in a world in which "time past is not believed to have any bearing upon time present or future" (28). Troubling and prophetic, "Some Dreamers of the Golden Dream" is Didion's critique of human nature and a scathing commentary on American life.

Personal Point of View

Reading Didion's work is an adventure in point of view. As she notes in *The Last Thing He Wanted,* "participants in disasters typically locate the 'beginning' of the disaster at a point suggesting their own control over events" (15). Events may be random, but they rarely occur without someone imposing context and explanation. Those who understand the multi-layered significance of an event, for Didion, are those who see into the life of things: "Those who understand it are at heart storytellers, weavers of conspiracy just to make the day come alive, and they see it in a flash, comprehend all its turns, get its possibilities" *(The Last* 55).

Didion does not take herself or her art too seriously, although she understands that the implications of storytelling may be serious indeed. In *The Last Thing He Wanted,* one of her characters says:

> The persona of "the writer" does not attract me. As a way of being it has its flat sides. Nor am I comfortable around the literary life: its traditional dramatic line (the romance of solitude, of interior struggle, of the lone seeker after truth) came to seem early on a trying conceit. I lost patience somewhat later with the conventions of the craft, with exposition, with transitions, with the development and revelation of "character." (73)

And in *Women Writers at Work,* Didion is quizzed about her statement that writing can be a "hostile act." She explains:

> It's hostile in that you're trying to make somebody see something the way
> you see it, trying to impose your idea, your picture. It's hostile to try to wrench
> around someone else's mind that way. Quite often you want to tell somebody
> your dream, your nightmare. Well, nobody wants to hear about someone else's
> dream, good or bad; nobody wants to walk around with it. The writer is always
> tricking the reader into listening to the dream. (407)

Didion remains skeptical about journalism as an objective enterprise and derides
journalists who are too self-conscious and too detached. Rustin focuses on Didion's impatience "with the American press's pretensions to objectivity" when
she writes:

> Reporters "do not want to be thought of as thinking ideologically because there
> is this fixed idea that the essence of 'journalism' is fairness, as if fairness de-
> pends on not having any ideas," she explains. The result, as in the work of Bob
> Woodward, whom she memorably derided in 1996 for writing "books in which
> measurable cerebral activity is virtually absent," is a human interest-driven
> "political pornography." Journalists, she believes, feeling a "lack of real
> power," are easily seduced when they get close to it. And she is bored by to-
> day's renewed emphasis on methods and processes, which she thinks have
> taken the place of bigger questions: "I think journalism as a career has gotten a
> little too full of itself and a lot of these things seem self-serving." (n.p.)

In *The Last Thing He Wanted,* Didion demonstrates not only interdiscipli-
narity but the ability to write fiction that reads like nonfiction. Elena McMahon,
the protagonist, speaks as Didion might speak, calling herself "the not quite omniscient author/ No longer moving fast./ No longer traveling light" (5). Didion's
years as a journalist are apparent in phrases about two Associated Press stories,
which McMahon and others called "history's rough draft" (11). Critiquing news
coverage, McMahon thinks:

> An American hostage who had walked out of Lebanon via Damascus said at his
> press conference in Wiesbaden that during captivity he had lost faith not only
> in the teachings of his church but in God. *Hostage Describes Test of Faith,* the
> headline read, again misleadingly. She considered ways in which the headline
> could have been made accurate (*Hostage Describes Loss of Faith? Hostage
> Fails Test of Faith?),* then put down the *Herald* and studied her father. He had
> gotten old. (29)

Didion reigns as the best-known woman literary journalist, and talented
writers such as Davidson and Orlean pay tribute to her directly and indirectly. In
the April 2002 issue of *Vogue,* Orlean describes Didion as a "person who will
visit El Salvadoran body dumps but is also easily frightened, not by concrete
horrors but by abstractions like failure and loneliness and dislocation" (281-82).
She argues that, along with Tom Wolfe and Norman Mailer, Didion invented a
"new kind of journalism that slipped into and out of anthropology, politics, and
autobiography" (283).

Didion often addresses the role of the journalist in American society and acknowledges her use of first-person point of view. In her preface to *Slouching Towards Bethlehem,* Didion writes, "But since I am neither a camera eye nor much given to writing pieces which do not interest me, whatever I do write reflects, somewhat gratuitously, how I feel" (xv). Even essays about John Wayne are self-reflexive. In "John Wayne: A Love Song," Didion writes about her longing to become the heroine of a Western and her memory of Wayne's words in a film called "War of the Wildcats" in which he tells someone he will build a house "at the bend in the river where the cottonwoods grow" (30):

> And in a world we understood early to be characterized by venality and doubt and paralyzing ambiguities, he suggested another world, one which may or may not have existed ever but in any case existed no more: a place where a man could move free, could make his own code and live by it; a world in which, if a man did what he had to do, he could one day take the girl and go riding through the draw and find himself home free, not in a hospital with something going wrong inside, not in a high bed with the flowers and the drugs and the forced smiles, but there at the bend in the bright river, the cottonwoods shimmering in the early morning sun. (31)

Didion is a literary journalist by trade and by nature. Her distrust of the institutional voice is beautifully articulated in the essay "Slouching Towards Bethlehem," in which she tries unsuccessfully to interview San Francisco police officers about the lost adolescents congregating in the city:

> We are in an interrogation room, and I am interrogating Officer Gerrans. He is young and blond and wary and I go in slow. I wonder what he thinks "the major problems" in the Haight are.
> Officer Gerrans thinks it over. "I would say the major problems there," he says finally, "the major problems are narcotics and juveniles. Juveniles and narcotics, those are your major problems."
> I write that down.
> "Just one moment," Officer Gerrans says, and leaves the room. When he comes back he tells me that I cannot talk to him without permission from Chief Thomas Cahill.
> "In the meantime," Officer Gerrans adds, pointing at the notebook in which I have written *major problems: juveniles, narcotics,* "I'll take those notes."
> The next day I apply for permission to talk to Officer Gerrans and also to Chief Cahill. A few days later a sergeant returns my call.
> "We have finally received clearance from the Chief per your request," the sergeant says, "and that is taboo."
> I wonder why it is taboo to talk to Officer Gerrans.
> Office Gerrans is involved in court cases coming to trial.
> I wonder why it is taboo to talk to Chief Cahill.
> The Chief has pressing police business.
> I wonder if I can talk to anyone at all in the Police Department.
> "No," the sergeant says, "not at the particular moment."
> Which was my last official contact with the San Francisco Police Department. (94)

Didion often employs her personal voice, not only to illuminate political and social issues but to discuss her own impressions of family and life in the microcosm. In "On Keeping a Notebook," Didion writes:

> I think we are well advised to keep on nodding terms with the people we used to be, whether we find them attractive company or not. Otherwise they turn up unannounced and surprise us, come hammering on the mind's door at 4 a.m. of a bad night and demand to know who deserted them, who betrayed them, who is going to make amends. We forget all too soon the things we thought we could never forget. We forget the loves and the betrayals alike, forget what we whispered and what we screamed, forget who we are. (139)

And in "On Self-Respect," Didion again is at her best. Having "lost the conviction that lights would always turn green for me" (143), she writes, "The dismal fact is that self-respect has nothing to do with the approval of others—who are, after all, deceived easily enough; has nothing to do with reputation, which, as Rhett Butler told Scarlett O'Hara, is something people with courage can do without" (143). She writes:

> There is a common superstition that "self-respect" is a kind of charm against snakes, something that keeps those who have it locked in some unblighted Eden, out of strange beds, ambivalent conversations, and trouble in general. It does not at all. It has nothing to do with the face of things, but concerns instead a separate peace, a private reconciliation. Although the careless, suicidal Julian English in *Appointment in Samarra* and the careless, incurably dishonest Jordan Baker in *The Great Gatsby* seem equally improbable candidates for self-respect, Jordan Baker had it, Julian English did not. With that genius for accommodation more often seen in women than in men, Jordan took her own measure, made her own peace, avoided threats to that peace: "I hate careless people," she told Nick Carraway. "It takes two to make an accident."
> Like Jordan Baker, people with self-respect have the courage of their mistakes. They know the price of things. If they choose to commit adultery, they do not go running, in an excess of bad conscience, to receive absolution from the wronged parties; nor do they complain unduly of the unfairness, the undeserved embarrassment, of being named co-respondent. In brief, people with self-respect exhibit a certain toughness, a kind of moral nerve; they display what was once called character, a quality which, although approved in the abstract, sometimes loses ground to other, more instantly negotiable virtues. (145)

In Didion's essay about self-respect, she concludes by writing: "To assign unanswered letters their proper weight, to free us from the expectations of others, to give us back to ourselves—there lies the great, the singular power of self-respect. Without it, one eventually discovers the final turn of the screw: one runs away to find oneself, and finds no one at home" (148).

Personal and provocative, Didion analyzes herself and the world around her through measured prose and layered detail. For example, in "On Going Home," Didion writes about taking her baby to her own family's home:

Questions trail off, answers are abandoned, the baby plays with the dust motes in a shaft of afternoon sun.

It is time for the baby's birthday party: a white cake, strawberry-marshmallow ice cream, a bottle of champagne saved from another party. In the evening, after she has gone to sleep, I kneel beside the crib and touch her face, where it is pressed against the slats, with mine. She is an open and trusting child, unprepared for and unaccustomed to the ambushes of family life, and perhaps it is just as well that I can offer her little of that life. I would like to give her more. I would like to promise her that she will grow up with a sense of her cousins and of rivers and of her great-grandmother's teacups, would like to pledge her a picnic on a river with fried chicken and her hair uncombed, would like to give her *home* for her birthday, but we live differently now and I can promise her nothing like that. I give her a xylophone and a sundress from Madeira, and promise to tell her a funny story. (168)

Whether writing about her child's birthday in "On Going Home," about politics in *Political Fictions* or *After Henry*, about accepting responsibility for one's mistakes in "On Self-Respect," or about packing photographs in preparation for natural disaster in "Fire Season," Joan Didion maintains a central place in the history of American literary journalism. The range of her subjects and the reach of her vision continue to draw and to challenge readers.

Sara Davidson

Unsurprisingly, one of Joan Didion's friends and intellectual and literary soul mates is Sara Davidson. Because Didion is a fifth-generation Californian, she and Davidson connect personally and professionally and celebrate place. For both of them, California is a myriad, magical, and mythical land. American writers including Mark Twain and John Steinbeck have put California on the literary map, but it has taken literary journalists such as Davidson and Didion to round out the picture of sandy beaches, endless sunshine, the spectacular mountains of Yosemite, and the wonder of San Francisco.

Davidson and Didion have, as journalists, added depth and perspective to the American myth of Western expansion and California dreaming. "Real Property" and "Some Dreamers of the Golden Dream" are among their best essays, are representative of their most anthologized and representative work, deal with a state they love and are conflicted about, and help to illustrate the allegorical power of literary journalism. It is impossible not to recognize the similarity in themes found in "Real Property" and "Some Dreamers of a Golden Dream," even though the subject matter and level of self-disclosure are significantly different.

Although we will explore the significance of the essay "Real Property" and the compelling use of symbol and personal point of view in Davidson's work, it is important to acknowledge her most recent contribution, which is a departure from much of her earlier writing. Davidson is comfortable in several genres, including essays, extended nonfiction, screenplays, and other literary forms, and *Leap!: What Will We Do with the Rest of Our Lives?* is a tribute both to her ability to describe her own feelings and to her skills as a reporter.

The Jan. 27, 2007, issue of *Newsweek* featured an article entitled "The First Day of the Rest of My Life," an excerpt from *Leap!* Advertised as "Reflections from the Boomer Generation," *Leap!* is a timely and insightful chronicle about Baby Boomers, who are living longer than previous generations and who have great expectations as they change careers, watch their children becoming young adults, and face their own mortality. With characteristic honesty, Davidson writes about many of the 150 people she interviewed and about herself and her own transitions. In the final section of the book, she writes:

> It's the spring of 2006, and as I sit at my desk, looking out at the lilacs coming into bloom, I feel both hopeful and nervous. When I began working on *Leap!*, I was in free fall, not knowing what I'd do with my time or where and with whom I'd live. I thought I needed to search for a new vocation—teaching? health care? But I've found that what suits me, what I need at the center of my days, is to study and create, regardless of how the work is received . . .
>
> The truth, I must acknowledge, is that I'm not in the same place I was when I began; the incidents and accidents of the past three years have made me half in love with uncertainty. Once again, I have no idea what work I'll do next or what companions will be with me, but I'm not fighting and raging against it. Expectancy is in the air. (284-85)

At publication time for *Settling the Borderland,* Davidson was negotiating a television series based on *Leap!* that is expected to star Goldie Hawn. (Hawn would also produce the series.)

Sara Davidson is no secret to readers who discovered *Loose Change: Three Women of the Sixties* and *Cowboy: A Novel.* Certainly, readers of popular publications such as *Oprah* have encountered Davidson's work more recently. However, like other women in literary journalism, Davidson has not received her just due as an equal to Norman Mailer, Hunter S. Thompson, Tom Wolfe, and other male representatives of the varied and compelling genre.

It is "Real Property," part of a book by the same name, that remains one of Davidson's most compelling literary achievements and an example of the allegorical power and poetic energy of literary journalism alluded to by several scholars, including Thomas B. Connery, John C. Hartsock, John Hellman, John J. Pauly, Norman Sims, and Ronald Weber.

Quoted by Sims, Davidson said that when she first started writing for magazines, Lillian Ross, who wrote for *The New Yorker,* was her literary model: "I was going to do what Lillian Ross had done. She never used the word 'I' and yet it was so clear there was an orienting consciousness guiding you" *(Literary Journalists* 7). She also said she learned from the narrative strategies of Joan Didion, Tom Wolfe, and Peter Matthiessen, author of *The Snow Leopard.*

A reporter and national correspondent for the *Boston Globe* from 1965-1969, Davidson has published more than 70 articles and essays in the *Atlantic, Esquire, Harper's, Life,* the *Los Angeles Times Magazine, McCall's, Mirabella, Ms.,* the *New York Times Magazine, New Woman, Oprah* magazine, *Rolling*

Stone, Spirituality and Health, and other publications. She is best known for the international best seller *Loose Change,* a social history of the sixties told through the lives of three young women who met at Berkeley; *Real Property,* a collection of her early essays; *Cowboy,* a memoir of a relationship; and *Leap!,* a chronicle of Baby Boomers coming of age. She also wrote *Friends of the Opposite Sex* and *Rock Hudson: His Story* and several scripts for television shows such as "Heart Beat," which ran from 1988-89 on ABC, and "Dr. Quinn, Medicine Woman," which ran from 1992-96 on CBS. "Heart Beat" was set at a women's health center run by women doctors and was inspired by a real medical group in Santa Monica, California. During her work on "Dr. Quinn, Medicine Woman," Davidson was head writer and co-executive producer for the television series starring Jane Seymour and created by Beth Sullivan. She has been a guest on "The Today Show," "Larry King Live," and "60 Minutes."

Born in 1943, Davidson is a Phi Beta Kappa graduate of the University of California at Berkeley (1964) with a degree in English. She earned a master's degree in journalism from Columbia University (1965). By the age of 26, she was a freelance magazine writer. Like many literary journalists trained in the study of English and journalism, Davidson is quite self-conscious about her craft and is deeply invested in conversations about the nature of artistic nonfiction, creative nonfiction, literary journalism, the new reportage, personal journalism, parajournalism, art-journalism, essay-fiction, factual fiction, journalit, intimate journalism, or whatever term literary critics prefer.

Working in "The Gray Zone"

One of Davidson's essays, "The Gray Zone," addresses the role of memoir, a particularly rich and problematic category of nonfiction. In the article, Davidson deals generally with the complexity of nonfiction and in particular with the difficulties she has encountered in writing memoir.

She begins with a reference to Patrick Hemingway, editor of his father's *True at First Light,* and with Patrick Hemingway's decision to publish the work as "fictionalized memoir." She then asks the question that drives this study: "When a story has its wellspring in life—in actual events and real people—what constitutes a fictional rendering and what constitutes memoir?" In journalism, she says, the answer matters "absolutely" because reporters have a responsibility not to "invent, change or embellish the smallest detail." In the "gray zone" where she writes, however, the answer for her (and, presumably, for us) is not so clear. She writes:

> When a writer sets out to tell a true story, he immediately finds himself constrained by the fallibility of memory. No one can recall the exact words of a conversation that took place a few days ago, let alone years, even if the writer attempts to recreate that conversation faithfully. In addition, the very process of translating mood, nonverbal signals and emotions into words creates a reality on the page that does not exactly mirror the event in life. But beyond this, the

writer makes a deliberate choice as to how much he will permit himself to take liberties. (49)

Ultimately, Davidson argues for what she calls "not a better system of classification" for nonfiction works but "full disclosure" (50) by authors themselves.

Dealing with the difference between fiction and nonfiction and between the novel and memoir, Davidson writes in her introduction to *Cowboy* that "at one end of the spectrum are works that are entirely imagined, and at the other end, works that purport to be fact. Most, however, are a blend of fact and imagination, and yet a line has been drawn to separate one from the other" (xi). She adds:

> I have long worked in what I perceive as the slippery slope between the two poles, the terrain where we find such entities as the nonfiction novel and the imagined autobiography. In *Loose Change,* published as nonfiction, I wrote about real people and historical events, yet I used fictional techniques—inventing dialogue, rearranging time, and combining scenes for dramatic purpose.
> Then it came to me to write the story in my own voice, as I remembered it, which is not the same as the way it occurred. I tried to convey the experience as strongly as I could, and to that end, I began to add elements and imagine things I could not have known by any other means. To protect the privacy of my children and ex-husbands, I created fictional characters to stand in their stead and speak and act in ways they hadn't. What has resulted is a book that defies categories—a hybrid—and if that sounds like an elaborate dodge, what I can say is that I'm telling you this story in the best and perhaps the only way I can. (xii-xiii)

Davidson knows first-hand the difficulties of writing memoir. In *Loose Change,* she wrote about intimate aspects of her life. Two women and her ex-husband, who are central characters in her novel, read the drafts. Although Davidson had changed the names of many characters and those of the two women, people knew who they were. "Suddenly, something that was all right as a manuscript was not all right when it was being read widely and people were responding to it," Davidson said. "There's one scene where I had a fight with my husband and he slapped me. Well, he started getting crank calls from people who accused him of being a wife beater. It's true, he did slap me. But suddenly he was being vilified, publicly'" *(Literary Journalists* 19). She adds:

> There were people who read it and thought he was a monster. One of the women would be walking down the street and someone would come up to her and say, "My God, I didn't know you had an abortion in your father's office when you were 16!" Relatives of the family would call in horror that she had exposed this kind of thing about herself and her family. The man she had lived with for seven years thought it was a major violation of confidence and trust. He said, "I wasn't living with you to have it become public knowledge. We weren't living our life as a research project." *(Literary Journalists* 20)

Because *Loose Change* was so hurtful to those portrayed in the novel (even though those depicted knew they would appear in the book and had consented), Davidson moved into a kind of disguised memoir when she wrote *Cowboy*. Of *Loose Change,* Davidson wrote, "What bothered me was that I had caused pain to other people, to my husband, to the women, who went through hell," she said. "People say knowing it was about real people heightened their appreciation and relationship to it. They preferred that it was nonfiction. But I do know I would never, never write again so intimately about my life because I can't separate my life from the people who have been in it" *(Literary Journalists* 20). Acknowledging that the women in *Loose Change* had signed releases, Davidson said the fact made it legal for her to use the material, but "emotionally and morally, it's not always so clear cut" *(Literary Journalists* 21).

Davidson altered her point of view and disguised her characters by the time she wrote her next blockbuster, *Cowboy*. In *Cowboy,* she changed names and altered events to protect those about whom she wrote. And she included an "Author's Note": "This book is based on a true story—a love affair I've had with the character whom I call Zack. For reasons of privacy, however, I have placed this story in a fictional context. I've created imaginary characters for the heroine's extended family . . . No relationship should be inferred between these characters in the book and any living persons, nor should incidents about them be taken as fact" (n.p.).

The Search for Meaning

The topics that draw Davidson are as rich and varied as the venues for her work. Although *Loose Change* and *Cowboy* are better known, Davidson's most provocative book is *Real Property*. Richly allegorical, the first essay entitled "Real Property" is drawn from diaries Davidson kept while living in Venice, California, in 1967. The collection in which it appears became a featured selection by the Literary Guild and a best seller. By camouflaging the identities of many of the people whom she interviews, Davidson is able to suggest their representative natures. By juxtaposing the golden paradise of California legend with her own daily reality, she is able to set up political, social, psychological and religious correspondences. The 12 vignettes that comprise "Real Property" can then be understood on multiple levels:

- Introduction to Venice, California
- The history of Marina del Rey and Venice
- Sara Davidson and "Bruce," the "unscarred"
- Davidson's mother and sister and the ironic legacy of real estate
- Real estate as symbolic
- Andy as representative of the changing Hippie movement
- Materialism and marriage
- Dating and connection rituals in Venice

- Israel
- Davidson's real estate "success"
- Comedy on skates
- A drunk in the parking garage

The episodic structure of "Real Property" suggests the fragmentation of the lives she describes. The vignettes include descriptions of Venice; of Marina del Rey; of a man who seems not to have been affected by the pain of those around him; of Davidson's mother and sister and the ironic legacy of real estate; of the symbolic nature of buying and selling real estate as a parable of American priorities; of a man who represents the new Southern Californian; of college women; of dating rituals; of Israel; of financial success; of a skating accident; and of running over a drunken man with her car.

Davidson's allegory is suggestive, not heavily didactic, although there is no doubt about what her opinion of American excess and greed is. She knows she is writing about the "decaying social order" ("Notes from the Land of the Cobra," *Real Property* 213), and she tells the reader in the same essay—a morality play about the Symbionese Liberation Army, Patricia Hearst, and California—that she is writing an allegory that is truer than reality: "What I have come up with are fragments, shards of pathos and humor, and a suspicion that the symbols in this drama may be more potent and meaningful than the reality" ("Notes from the Land of the Cobra," *Real Property* 200).

In both *Real Property* and *Loose Change,* Davidson establishes her authorial voice immediately. The essay "Real Property" begins with the following polemic:

> "Who is the rich man?" asks the Talmud. The question has never seemed more relevant. The answer of the sages is: "He who is satisfied with what he has."
> I live in a house by the ocean with an outdoor Jacuzzi. I owned, until an embarrassing little accident, a pair of roller skates. I still own a volleyball, Frisbee, tennis racket, backpack, hiking boots, running shoes, a Mercedes 240 Diesel and a home burglar alarm system. But I cannot say that I am satisfied. (3)

By questioning her own values, Davidson accomplishes two things: She introduces herself as the central character in her morality play and she encourages readers to identify with her in her quest.

In *Loose Change,* Davidson employs the same technique. Here, too, her self-effacing tone serves to suggest to readers that it is all right if they, too, are unsure about who they are and how they fit into the social order:

> It is the summer of '76 and I am living by the ocean in Southern California. I have fixed up my house as if I intend to stay. I've planted a cactus garden and furnished the rooms with wicker and Mexican tile. People tell me I speak like the natives. They say I look "laid back."
> I don't know. (366)

Davidson's tone remains consistent throughout *Loose Change,* and the conclusion both summarizes and problematizes the issues raised in the nonfiction novel. The anguish of the narrator as she surveys her world is evident when she explains the title of the book ("We had predicted that the center would not hold but it had, and now we were in pieces. 'Loose change,' I told a friend"—366) and when she admits to her own confusion about drugs, the sexual revolution, the civil rights movement, and other phenomena of the sixties: "I'm afraid I will be criticized for copping out. ('We want to know what you make of it all, what this period meant in terms of a society, a culture.') But the truth is, I have not found answers and I'm not sure I remember the questions" (367). In *Loose Change,* as in other works, Davidson defies narrative closure, recognizing that a tidy conclusion to her book suggests that there is a tidy conclusion to the issues that are shaking the foundation of the society.

In "Real Property," Davidson invites the reader into a world defined by real estate sales and shallowness of spirit. She deftly employs cliches, images, and symbols that a reader can identify readily: "What does it mean that everyone I know is looking to make some kind of 'killing?'" Davidson asks. "It means, I think, that we are in far deeper than we know" (6). Describing a man who embodies the cultural attitudes that concern her, Davidson writes:

> He did not want to hear about frustration. He did not want to know about writer's block. He did not think I should feel jealous if he dated other women, and he did not believe a relationship should be work.
> "I think we do too much talking," he said.
> "That's funny. I think we don't do enough." (9)

Like Didion in *Slouching Towards Bethlehem,* Davidson writes of a world in which the core values are unraveling and faith is dissipating, and like Didion and poet William Butler Yeats, she fears that the center will not hold: "Rolling, rolling. The wind is blowing, the palms are blowing and people are blowing every which way. I cannot walk on the boardwalk these days without feeling it in my stomach: something is wrong. There are too many people on wheels. The skaters will fall, the bikers will crash, they will fly out of control and there is nothing to hold onto" (5).

Against this tableau of commercialism and empty social connections lies Davidson's essay about Israel, entitled "Last Days in Sinai." A teaser for that essay appears in "Real Property," where Davidson tells the reader directly that "life in Israel is in diametric contrast to life in Southern California" (27) and that "Israelis are reminded, almost daily, that human life is transient and relationships are not replaceable" (28).

At the end of the essay "Real Property," Davidson expands her description of the real estate boom and the hedonism of the Southern California she knows into a commentary on the nation and on her generation. Like Davidson, literary journalists rarely if ever provide closure. There is a sense of an ending, but not resolution. Davidson writes:

It is a cliché, a joke, something we are past feeling anguished about, but the fact is that a considerable number of people have passed through a door and come out wearing different clothes, and this transformation has taken place almost without comment. People who, in the flowering of the Sixties, gave their children names like Blackberry and Veda-Rama have changed them to Suzy and John. The parents are "getting our money trip together." If they are successful, they are buying homes, Calvin Klein suits and Porsches and sending their kids to private schools to avoid busing.

Not all have come through the door, of course. There are still groups of New Age people in places like Berkeley, Oregon, Hawaii and Vermont. They are still dedicated to social change, still wearing beards and flowing shawls, still holding symposiums where they talk about holistic health care, living closer to the earth and creating communities where people can love each other and share and cooperate. But their numbers are dwindling and few young recruits come along.

Those who have crossed the line cannot help but feel some irony and bafflement about "the people we've become." They retain an awareness, however faintly it is pulsing, that the acquisition of material wealth does not necessarily bring satisfaction, but that awareness is fading rapidly into unconsciousness. (14)

In literary journalism, our very perception of time changes. Because there is no attempt to record breaking events and because the purpose is to look back on an event and analyze its impact, it is especially important to note references to the passage of time. In *Loose Change,* for example, the character Sara said, "We had decided to put my alarm clock in the freezer to see if we could stop time" (62). There is no set purpose to life, so time cannot redeem it.

In a lecture entitled "Literary Journalism: What Are the Rules?" at the University of Colorado in 2002, Davidson argued that her craft is characterized by "natural" language really used by people, saturation reporting, the techniques of fiction, and what she calls "the arc," or a structure in which "the end is as important as the beginning." She quoted Frank Conroy, author of *Stop Time,* who asks of journalism, "Does the writing enter the great stream of literature?" Davidson believes the best journalists employ scene-by-scene description, dialogue ("the strongest way to involve a reader" and describe a character), point of view ("break the taboo of using 'I'"), and being "accurate in spirit" if not "objectively verifiable." Arguing that anything drawn from memory is fiction, Davidson made no apology for employing a personal point of view and suggested that journalists have adhered to their contract with the reader if they provide full disclosure.

Like Didion, Davidson champions the tenets of literary journalism without apology and without hesitation. In "Literary Journalism: What Are the Rules?" Davidson quoted Wright Morris, who said: "Anything processed by memory is fiction." She then introduced the history of literary journalism, suggesting that 1965 was the time of the New Left, the new woman, the new morality, and The New Journalism. Literary journalism "reached a swell" in the 1960s, she said, and was considered "bastard journalism." "The literati saw it as class warfare," she said.

The publication of *In Cold Blood,* which appeared first in *The New Yorker* in serial form, "helped legitimize what we were trying to do," Davidson said. Paying tribute to her colleagues in the field, Davidson listed Joan Didion, John Hersey, Tracy Kidder, Frank McCourt, Lillian Ross, Hunter S. Thompson, Mark Twain, and Tom Wolfe as preeminent examples of the tenets of literary journalism.

But her celebration of the genre of literary journalism comes after a great deal of self-conscious analysis. Davidson's first job was at the *Boston Globe,* where she wrote stories about the election campaign of Richard M. Nixon, about Woodstock, and about a student strike at Columbia University. She also wrote a story about a first-time delegate from Massachusetts. She went water skiing with him. She watched him drink scotch. Then she wrote a story saying he voted the party line over his heart and his conscience.

Readers, politicians, and other journalists retaliated. "I had broken the contract," Davidson said, referring, of course, to the relationship between reporter and source discussed throughout *Settling the Borderland.* However, Davidson said her story was a reaction to the coverage of campaigns for Bobby Kennedy and Nelson Rockefeller, during which she became convinced that she and other reporters "weren't getting much of the story." Reporters, she said, relayed a "manufactured scene," and she subsequently vowed to tell the truth as she understood it, even if a source were unhappy with his or her public portrayal.

Davidson believes reporters can "learn more by watching someone than by listening to their canned speeches." Furthermore, she believes it is "essential" that reporters invade the privacy of their sources. Quoting Tom Wolfe, who said subjects are "specimens in a microscope," Davidson said reporters can't be "stricken with guilt" if they reveal their sources fairly and accurately, acknowledging that reporters are in some part "voyeurs."

According to Davidson, while literary giants were "turning their backs on social realism," journalists were adopting the techniques of Willa Cather, Thomas Hardy, John Steinbeck, and Edith Wharton. She believes that a reporter should become a character in the story instead of "staying pristinely out of the way."

Finally, using Alex Haley's *Roots* as an example, Davidson said writers should tell the truth but not be constrained by what they can learn from talking with a living source. Haley, she said, describes scenes on slave ships and relays the dialogue of those on the ships. To create realistic and truthful scenes and dialogue, he researched oral and written histories and studied traditions and legends. *Roots,* she said, is realistic, not real: It is "not objectively verifiable," but it is "accurate in spirit."

Like other literary journalists whose work is featured in *Settling the* Borderland, Davidson believes the solution to the problem of trust between author and reader is complete disclosure by the author. She measures her contribution to literature by whether she has contributed to the "emotional bedrock of human truth" and has told a story that is so important it "becomes a part of your inner life."

Davidson's awareness of her role as journalist and cultural critic drives her creative work. She is a social observer, and on her web site, she says the "uses the voice of the intimate journalist," drawing material from her life and from the lives of others and "shaping it into a narrative that reads like fiction."

Leap! continues Davidson's tradition of telling the stories of everyday people and of celebrities, such as activist Tom Hayden, singer Carly Simon, spiritual leader Ram Dass, and supermodel Christie Brinkley, with equal parts of emotion and wisdom. While writing *Leap!,* Davidson discovered that "everyone must go through the narrows—the transition to a different phase of life—even if it's only on the physical level" (30). The book covers facing the narrows, hanging onto the past, facing facts and confronting change, giving back to the world around us, reconsidering love and sex, finding helpful rituals, and other issues.

During a presentation to a women's group Sept. 9, 2007, at Mile Hi Church in Lakewood, Colorado, Davidson challenged her audience to consider a time when they felt "stripped of their identity" and when "waves were crashing on you one after another." She said she encountered such a time when she was in her mid-50s and had to redefine herself: "It took a lot to get me on my knees. I asked, 'If I'm not a famous writer, a mother, a lover . . . who am I?'" During this time of soul searching, she learned that "we are not the external roles we play or hope to play."

"I had no kids, no work, no one to see, and nothing to do," Davidson told the group of women. "But I felt I was at the top of my game. I longed for something that would be the fire at the center of my life." She said she gradually realized that she was at heart a reporter, a writer, a translator of events. "I knew I needed to be involved in creative work the way I need air," she said. She knew she wanted to write "for the sheer challenge and joy of the undertaking."

Leap! helped Davidson reach others with both her questions and her discoveries. The theme of the correspondence she has received since the book was published is: "Thank God someone has put a name to what I'm going through. I thought I was the only one." As she interacts with those who have read *Leap!,* Davidson suggests that they learn to celebrate surrender, what she calls "opening your arms to the unknown."

Davidson's search for meaning has helped her clarify her "mission," she said. During a book signing at the Tattered Cover in Denver, Colorado, in 2007, Davidson told the audience that *Leap!* is based on a question she once asked herself: "If [you learned] the world would end in two days, what would you do?" With characteristic humor and personal insight, Davidson—always a journalist—said her answer to herself was, "Take notes."

Susan Orlean

One of the most significant emerging literary journalists is Susan Orlean. Although she is far from the only shining light in her generation, Orlean is particularly appropriate for this chapter because her work, like that of Didion and Davidson, is self-revelatory and deals with universal themes. Furthermore, Orlean's work focuses on personal pilgrimage, on individual courage, on wisdom, and on psychological growth. "To be honest, I view all stories as journeys," Orlean writes. "Journeys are the essential text of the human experience . . . I picture my readers having the same expedition, in an armchair, as they begin reading one of my pieces and work their way through it, ending up with the distinct feeling of having been somewhere else, whether it's somewhere physically exotic or just the 'somewhere else' of being inside someone else's life" (xiv).

Best-selling author of *The Orchid Thief* and *Saturday Night,* Susan Orlean has been a staff writer at *The New Yorker* since 1992. Her articles also have appeared in *Outside, Rolling Stone, Vogue,* and *Esquire.* A discussion of Susan Orlean's *The Orchid Thief,* subtitled *A True Story of Beauty and Obsession,* is appropriate for a study of allegory in literary journalism, if for no other reason than the fact that the nonfiction novel is a compelling example of how literary journalists weave character and didacticism into an extended symbolic system.

Much of Orlean's work falls into the more traditional category of news-features. It is "objective" in the sense that it is fair, even-handed reporting about an event. It is "biased" in the sense that it relies upon personal vantage point. In an essay about her development as a writer, Orlean said she rejected news for features, acknowledging that feature writing is often demeaned:

> I just wanted to write what are usually called "features"—a term that I hate because it sounds so fluffy and lightweight, like pillow stuffing, but that is used to describe stories that move at their own pace, rather than the news stories that race to keep time with events. The subjects I was drawn to were often completely ordinary, but I was confident that I could find something extraordinary in their ordinariness. (x-xi)

One of the best examples of her approach is "Rough Diamonds: Fidel's Little Leagues" that appeared in the Aug. 5, 2002, issue of *The New Yorker.* Although it is a descriptive narrative about Juan Cruz, an 11-year-old "slip of a kid . . . with dark, dreamy eyes, long arms, big feet, and musculature of a grasshopper" (34), it also tells the story of sports in Cuba under the watchful eye of Fidel Castro. Clearly more of a feature article with a long shelf life, "Rough Diamonds" is like *The Orchid Thief* in that it reveals the underside of a society while entertaining the reader with dialogue, description, and narration. As Orlean herself writes, "I didn't want to be a newspaper reporter, because I have never cared about knowing something first, and I didn't want to write only about things that were considered 'important' and newsworthy; I wanted to write about things that intrigued me, and to write about them in a way that would surprise readers who might not have expected to find these things intriguing" (ix).

Some of the people Orlean finds intriguing are featured in a collection entitled *The Bullfighter Checks Her Makeup: My Encounters with Extraordinary People.* They include a 10-year-old boy named Colin Duffy, surfer girls in Maui, a New York real estate broker, controversial ice-skater Tonya Harding, and a woman bullfighter. One of the most provocative essays in the collection that is often anthologized is "The American Man, Age Ten." It is both vintage Susan Orlean and a gem of literary journalism.

Asked to write a profile about then-child actor Macauley Culkin, Orlean convinced her editors to let her write an essay about an average young American male instead of a celebrity. What resulted is a riveting description of what it's like for a young boy growing up in America, from his love of video games, candy, and pizza to his attitudes about marriage, recycling, money, and girls. There is no attempt on Orlean's part to detach herself from her subject; in fact, she acknowledges in the last line of the essay that she has been captured by the child she describes. Wrapping fishing line around various objects in his back yard, Colin goes into the house after dark, leaving Orlean to say: "He dropped the spool, skipped up the stairs of the deck, threw open the screen door, and then bounded into the house, leaving me and Sally the dog trapped in his web" (14).

Describing literary journalism as the "poetry of facts and the art in ordinary life" (xi), Orlean described her quest to bring an average 10-year-old boy to life on the page. In *The Bullfighter Checks Her Makeup,* Orlean writes:

> I liked Colin Duffy right away because he seemed unfazed by the prospect of my observing him for a couple of weeks. He was a wonderful kid, and I still marvel at how lucky I was to have stumbled on someone so endearing, but the truth is that if you set out to write about a ten-year-old boy, any boy would do. The particulars of the story would have been entirely different with a different boy, but the fundamentals would have been the same: An ordinary life examined closely reveals itself to be exquisite and complicated and exceptional, somehow managing to be both heroic and plain. (xii)

Informative, "The American Man, Age Ten" also represents the understated tone employed by many literary journalists as they consciously undercut the formal tone employed by reporters interested in setting themselves up as experts on a particular issue. For example, she writes:

> Psychologists identify ten as roughly the age at which many boys experience the gender-linked normative developmental trauma that leaves them, as adult men, at risk for specific psychological sequelae often manifest as deficits in the arenas of intimacy, empathy, and struggles with commitment in relationships. In other words, this is around the age when guys get screwed up about girls. Elaine and Jim Duffy, and probably most of the parents who send their kids to Montclair Cooperative School, have done a lot of stuff to try to avoid this. They gave Colin dolls as well as guns. (He preferred guns.) (105)

Without telling the reader that the differences between boys and girls are pronounced at Colin's age, Orlean instead shares dialogue and examples. For example, when she asks Colin, "Who's the coolest woman?"—he replies, "None. I don't know" (103). She describes one of Colin's favorite hangouts: "At Danny's, you will find pizza, candy, Nintendo, and very few girls. To a ten-year-old boy, it is the most beautiful place in the world." (103).

The social sphere of the school is no different. Orlean tells the reader that the girls in Colin's class "are named Cortnerd, Terror, Spacey, Lizard, Maggot, and Diarrhea": "'They do have other names, but that's what we call them,' Colin told me. 'The girls aren't very popular'" (104). When asked to analyze why he feels the way he does about girls, Colin replies, "'Girls are different' . . . He hopped up and down on the balls of his feet, wrinkling his nose. 'Girls are stupid and weird'" (104).

The allegorical impact of the essay, however, is not tied to gender issues alone. Orlean makes it clear that she knows she is talking about a white boy in an intact home in the suburbs. She is not so much avoiding social commentary as she is trusting the reader to understand the neighborhood he or she is visiting: "The rest of the town seems to consist of parks and playing fields and sidewalks and backyards—in other words, it is a far cry from South-Central Los Angeles and from Bedford-Stuyvesant and other, grimmer parts of the country where a very different ten-year-old American man is growing up today" (100).

And like many literary journalists, Orlean is a character in her own story. One example is her competition with Colin in a video game she is destined to lose: "We would both be good at Nintendo Street Fighter II, but Colin would be better than me" (99), she writes, as though she expected any other outcome.

Allegory and the Quest for Wisdom

The tone of *The Orchid Thief* is consistent with her earlier work, and in addition to being a character in her story, she also makes clear that she is telling the stories of others in order to better understand herself and her own quest for passion and joy. Her explanation for her pilgrimage to Florida is other people's obsession with orchids, and in the end she will understand her own obsession with telling their stories and deconstructing their fascination with the unique flowers: "Orchids seem to drive people crazy," she writes. "Those who love them love them madly. Orchids arouse passion more than romance. They are the sexiest flowers on earth" (50).

The Orchid Thief is based on a newspaper article Orlean read about John Laroche and three Seminole men, Russell Bowers, Dennis Osceola, and Vinson Osceola, who were arrested with rare orchids they had stolen from a swamp in Florida called the Fakahatchee Strand State Preserve. With typical understatement, Orleans writes, "I wanted to know more about the incident" (6). Knowing more became a 284-page novel. The working title of *The Orchid Thief* was *Passion,* and the novel about rare and beautiful flowers became an internal pilgrimage.

Of her quest, Orleans writes in an interview included at the end of the *The Orchid Thief,* "Obviously at the end of the book, I realize I do have a single-minded passion. It is the passion to be a writer and a reporter. But I think the detachment was to my advantage. I don't like writing about things I am too invested in initially. For me, part of the process of writing is the journey to understanding" (n.p.). Although Orlean's freelance work, which appears often in magazines such as *The New Yorker,* is provocative and revelatory, it is in her longer works that her self-discovery in the act of writing becomes more clear.

Wondering about her own potential to be passionate about life and work, Orlean
writes of her central character, "Laroche's passions arrived unannounced and
ended explosively, like car bombs" (4). She also acknowledges the way in which
she is drawn to his ability to transform the day: "One of his greatest assets is
optimism—that is, he sees a profitable outcome in practically every life situation, including disastrous ones" (5).

   Like California for Davidson and Didion, Florida becomes Orlean's evocative microcosm. Taking the reader with her through her journey of self-
discovery, Orlean writes:

> I was of a mixed mind about Florida. I loved walking past the Art Deco hotels
> on Ocean Drive and Collins Road, loved the huge delis, loved my first flush of
> sunburn, but dreaded jellyfish and hated how my hair looked in the humidity.
> Heat unsettles me, and the Florida landscape of warm wideness is as alien to
> me as Mars. I do not consider myself a Florida person. But there is something
> about Florida more seductive and inescapable than almost anywhere else I've
> ever been. It can look brand-new and man-made, but as soon as you see a place
> like the Everglades or the Big Cypress Swamp or the Loxahatchee you realize
> that Florida is also the last of the American frontier . . . The developed places
> are just little clearings in the jungle, but since jungle is unstoppably fertile, it
> tries to reclaim a piece of developed Florida every day. At the same time the
> wilderness disappears before your eyes: fifty acres of Everglades dry up each
> day, new houses sprout on sand dunes, every year a welt of new highways
> rises. Nothing seems hard or permanent; everything is always changing or
> washing away. (9)

As a woman seeking permanence and understanding in a semiological jungle,
Orlean focuses on setting and character and weaves her tale of growing self-
awareness. She writes:

> That's the way Florida strikes me, always fomenting change, its natural
> landscapes just moments away from being drained and developed, its most
> manicured places only an instant away from collapsing back into jungle. A few
> years ago I was linked to Florida again; this time my parents bought a condo-
> minium in West Palm Beach so they could spend some time there in the winter.
> There is a beautiful, spruced-up golf course attached to their building, with
> grass as green and flat as a bathmat, hedges precision-shaped and burnished,
> the whole thing as civilized as a tuxedo. Even so, some alligators have recently
> moved into the water traps on the course, and signs are posted in the locker
> room saying LADIES! BEWARE OF THE GATORS ON THE GREENS! . . .
>   It has been added to, subtracted from, drained, ditched, paved, dredged, ir-
> rigated, cultivated, wrested from the wild, restored to the wild, flooded, platted,
> set on fire. Things are always being taken out of Florida or smuggled in. The
> flow in and out is so constant that exactly what the state consists of is different
> from day to day. It is a collision of things you would never expect to find to-
> gether in one place—condominiums and panthers and raw woods and hyper-
> markets and Monkey Jungles and strip malls and superhighways and groves of
> carnivorous plants and theme parks and royal palms and hibiscus trees and
> those hot swamps with acres and acres that no one has ever even seen—all
> toasting together under the same sunny vault of Florida sky. Even the orchids

of Florida are here in extremes. The woods are filled with more native species of orchids than anywhere else in the country, but also there are scores of man-made jungles, the hothouses of Florida, full of astonishing flowers that have been created in labs, grown in test tubes, and artificially multiplied to infinity. Sometimes I think I've figured out some order in the universe, but then I find myself in Florida, swamped by incongruity and paradox, and I have to start all over again. (10-11)

To make sense of "incongruity and paradox," Orlean asks a park ranger named Tony to be her guide through the foreign land. Her critical gaze is both external and internal, and when she asks Tony about his work, he explains his fascination with orchids by connecting them to a kind of phenomenological quest. Why does Tony love orchids? He responds by saying, "Oh, mystery, beauty, unknowability, I suppose," he said, shrugging. "Besides, I think the real reason is that life has no meaning. I mean, no obvious meaning. You wake up, you go to work, you do stuff. I think everybody's always looking for something a little unusual that can preoccupy them and help pass the time" (38).

In *The Orchid Thief,* the ghost orchid, "a lovely papery white" (39), becomes the quintessential symbol of perfection and beauty in a flawed universe. As Orlean writes, "The whiteness of the flower is as startling as a spotlight in the grayness and greenness of a swamp. Because the plant has no foliage and its roots are almost invisible against tree bark, the flower looks magically suspended in midair" (39). The purpose of Orlean's quest becomes clear to the reader as it becomes clear to her: "If the ghost orchid was really only a phantom it was still such a bewitching one that it could seduce people to pursue it year after year and mile after miserable mile. If it was a real flower, I wanted to keep coming back to Florida until I could see one. The reason was not that I love orchids. I don't even especially like orchids. What I wanted was to see this thing that people were drawn to in such a singular and powerful way" (40).

What Orlean and the reader discover is the commitment a few followers express about their life's work. Searching for orchids is not a hobby or a weekend distraction. It is a pilgrimage. Orlean writes of their single-minded focus and her own longing: "It was religion. I wanted to want something as much as people wanted these plants, but it isn't part of my constitution. I think people my age are embarrassed by too much enthusiasm and believe that too much passion about anything is naïve. I suppose I do have one unembarrassing passion—I want to know what it feels like to care about something passionately" (41).

In addition to strong first-person point of view, Orlean also reveals both her ability to conduct research and her ability to interview well. The reader learns that orchids are considered "the most highly evolved flowering plants on earth. They are unusual in form, uncommonly beautiful in color, often powerfully fragrant, intricate in structure, and different from any other family of plants" (42). Stopping just short of personifying the mysterious flowers, Orlean adds, "Orchids thrived in the jungle because they developed the ability to live on air rather than soil and positioned themselves where they were sure to get light and water—high above the rest of the plants on the branches of trees. They thrived because they took themselves out of competition. If all of this makes orchids seem smart—well, they do seem smart. There is something clever and unplantlike about their determination to survive and their knack for useful deception and their genius for seducing human beings for hundreds and hundreds of years" (49).

The most important fact about orchids—one that helps to explain Orlean's fascination with them and her growing questions about the nature of obsession and desire—is that orchids "can live forever" (49): "Some orchids at the New York Botanical Garden have been living in greenhouses there since 1898" (49), she tells the reader, adding, "They have outlived dinosaurs; they might outlive human beings" (53).

Throughout the novel, Orlean reminds us why we are on a quest to see the ghost orchid. The journey, both literal and in the pages of a book, is to discover an explanation for our own passions, or at least to discover why other people have them. One explanation is that obsession provides focus:

> The world is so huge that people are always getting lost in it. There are too many ideas and things and people, too many directions to go. I was starting to believe that the reason it matters to care passionately about something is that it whittles the world down to a more manageable size. It makes the world seem not huge and empty but full of possibility. If I had been an orchid hunter I wouldn't have seen this space as sad-making and vacant—I think I would have seen it as acres of opportunity where the things I loved were waiting to be found. (109)

Second, Orlean suggests that the quest also provided a belief in something greater than ourselves, in this case a perfect, albeit fragile, creation: "They sincerely loved something, trusted in the perfectibility of some living thing, lived for a myth about themselves and the idea of adventure, were convinced that certain things were really worth dying for, believed that they could make their lives into whatever they dreamed" (201).

In any case, pursuing the glimpse of a flower required courage and determination. The overwhelming nature of the obsession is, for Orlean, evident in the search itself, since it required venturing into the most inhospitable of all terrains: "The Florida pioneers had to confront what a dark, dense, overabundant place might have hidden in it. To explore such a place you had to vanish into it. I would argue that it might be easier to endure loneliness than to endure the idea that you might disappear" (169).

Laroche becomes the quintessential pilgrim characterized by "benign derangement" (268) and is the "oddball ultimate of those people who are enthralled by non-human living things and who pursue them like lovers" (136). Ultimately, it is Orleans' difference from her protagonist that reassures her. What Orlean discovers is what the reader discovers: The point of the quest has been to see, to possess in some form, a ghost orchid. When Orlean fails to do so, she learns the ultimate lesson in the quest and uses it to comfort the reader:

> In the universe there are only a few absolutes of value; something is valuable because it can be eaten for nourishment or used as a weapon or made into clothes or it is valuable if you want it and you believe it will make you happy.

Then it is worth anything as well as nothing, worth as much as you will give to have something you think you want. It saved all sorts of trouble knowing I wouldn't find a ghost orchid here, since then I didn't even need to look. It was a relief to have no hope because then I had no fear; looking for something you want is a comfort in the clutter of the universe, but knowing you don't have to look means you can't be disappointed. (258)

In the end, Orlean acknowledges her sadness "for anyone who ever cared about something that didn't work out." She writes that she has "realized it was just as well that I never saw a ghost orchid, so that it could never disappoint me, and so it would remain forever something I wanted to see" (281). The essential nature of longing and unrequited love for a person or an object becomes the purpose of the quest.

The power of Orlean's allegory lies in what it teaches us about ourselves, and we meander through the sweltering, humid heat of the Florida swamps in search of an appropriately named ghost orchid. The quest is a religious experience in a world skeptical of religious zeal. In the quest, we find ourselves, or, more precisely, discover that the impossible quest to know ourselves is a worthy pilgrimage.

Journalism as a Diary of the Past

For Susan Orlean, literary journalism is the lens by which news—several men are arrested for stealing orchids—becomes an extended look into the human psyche, into the universal truths of being human. Orlean believes that literary journalism is an art form, and her commitment to her work is revealed when she writes about those whom she has interviewed, those who have transformed her, those who have shown her the permanent in a world of the transitory: "So what I have of them, and always will have, is just that moment we spent together—now preserved on paper, bound between covers, cast out into the world—and they will never get any older, their faces will never fade, their dreams will still be within reach, and I will forever still be listening as hard as I can" *(Bullfighter* xv).

Orlean's work is a study of how to know a person and a place and how to celebrate both. It is also a way of being in the world: Orlean knows herself by interpreting those around her and by connecting with geographic location. In *My Kind of Place: Travel Stories from a Woman Who's Been Everywhere*, Orlean takes the reader from Illinois to Texas to Alabama to New York to Boston to Cuba to France to Japan to Australia to Thailand and elsewhere and from taxidermists to Cuban baseball fans to friends at swimming pools. "Writing is a wonderful life—a marvelous life, in fact—but it is also the life of a vapor, of floating in unseen, filling a space, and then vanishing" (xvi). This is not ordinary tourism; instead, Orlean challenges the reader to visit an unfamiliar place and to know it for the first time. The quest is central not only to *The Orchid Thief* but to the rest of her canon:

It's always a pleasure to revisit a place or, in this case, a story about a place, and it is always fascinating to see what time has done to it. I often keep track of the places and situations I've written about—they stay wired into my consciousness well after I've unpacked my suitcase, filed the travel vouchers, finished the piece. Nothing ever stays the same, of course. The story feels eternal, fixed, and complete, but it is really only a shard of a moment, and, in no time at all, the place will have transformed, the story evolved, the characters changed. (295)

Use of the quest motif heightens the significance of Orlean's observations about the world, but it is not the only one that drives her work. Nothing is inadvertent, accidental, superficial. Seemingly inconsequential descriptions are laden with universal themes, including the passage of time and a quiet sadness at the loss of youth and the uncertainty of the future. In "The Maui Surfer Girls," for example, Orlean addresses much more than what is "cool" about girls who participate in a sport perceived to belong to boys:

At various cultural moments, surfing has appeared as the embodiment of everything cool and wild and free; this is one of those moments. To be a girl surfer is even cooler, wilder, and more modern than being a guy surfer: Surfing has always been such a male sport that for a man to do it doesn't defy any perceived ideas; to be a girl surfer is to be all that surfing represents, plus the extra charge of being a girl in a tough guy's domain. To be a surfer girl in a cool place like Hawaii is perhaps the apogee of all that is cool and wild and modern and sexy and defiant. The Hana girls, therefore, exist at that highest point—the point where being brave, tan, capable, and independent, and having a real reason to wear all those surf-inspired clothes that other girls wear for fashion, is what matters completely. It is, though, just a moment. It must be hard to imagine an ordinary future and something other than a lunar calendar to consider if you've grown up in a small town in Hawaii, surfing all day and night, spending half your time on sand, thinking in terms of point breaks and barrels and roundhouse cutbacks. Or maybe they don't think about it at all. Maybe these girls are still young enough and in love enough with their lives that they have no special foreboding about their futures, no uneasy presentiment that the kind of life they are leading now might eventually have to end. (43)

Because she is a literary journalist and not a detached observer writing about surfing for a conventional medium, Orlean shares her life experiences with her sources and provides both contrast and connection for the reader:

I'd explained I'd grown up in Ohio, where there is no surf, but that didn't satisfy them; what I didn't say was that I'm not sure that at fifteen I had the abandon or the indomitable sense of myself that you seem to need in order to look at this wild water and think, I will glide on top of those waves . . . When I left Maui that afternoon, my plane circled over Ho'okipa, and I wanted to believe I could still see them down there and always would see them down there, snapping back and forth across the waves. (49)

Orlean is in tune with her subjects, yes, but her primary commitment is, quite clearly, to her readers. It is her readers who identify with her pilgrimage, who see new places and new people through her eyes, and who consider their own life choices in the context of a 10-year-old boy mastering video games, a man chasing a ghost orchid, and young girls riding the waves.

Didion, Davidson, and Orlean are far from being the only examples of women literary journalists who are transforming and enriching the genre. Others are mentioned in the conclusion that follows. However, Didion and Davidson helped to define a kind of writing that emphasizes point of view, that relies upon immersion, that employs the techniques formerly presumed to belong to literature, that contains allegorical figures and themes, and that boasts didactic import. Orlean and others are part of their legacy—creating new texts and steering literary journalism into the new century, no doubt—but they are also most certainly in their debt.

Conclusion

It is difficult to get the news from poems,
yet men die miserably every day
for lack of what is found there. (19)

"Asphodel, That Greeny Flower"
William Carlos Williams

During her speech at the Wallace Stegner Award Ceremony Nov. 2, 2005, at the University of Colorado at Boulder, author Terry Tempest Williams said, "I don't know how to write a novel . . . I'm so in love with this life: I can't imagine fictionalizing it." Although *Settling the Borderland: Other Voices in Literary Journalism* emphasizes the thin line between fiction and nonfiction (and the fact that all storytelling occurs through a filter), it is easy to understand Williams' exuberance about life and to celebrate the distinction she makes between telling her own story and telling the story of characters whom she creates. "I have a love affair with the world I live in," Williams said. "Why would I want to write fiction when these are the truths of our lives?" Her environmental concerns and her determination to effect change make being in and of this world essential, but Williams also argues for the pre-eminence of nonfiction. "If I had written *Refuge* as a novel—as fiction—I don't think it would have been as effective because it's true," she added.

One of Williams' statements, though, is especially powerful in the context of *Settling the Borderland*: "You make a contract with your readers that this is true to the best of your knowledge." Her statement is at the heart of this study of

American literary journalism and the contribution that lesser-known writers have made to the genre.

Although it may be more common in a conclusion to review the contribution the study has made, it is more honest to address first what *Settling the Borderland* is not. It is not a how-to book. There are numerous books, including Stephen G. Bloom's *Inside the Writer's Mind: Writing Narrative Journalism* (2002), that will aptly serve this purpose. Bloom's essays about everything from accused murderers to a husband and wife who sign a suicide pact to an afternoon with Dr. Ruth are followed by information about how he learned about the story; his methods for researching, interviewing, organizing, and writing; the impact each piece generated; and suggestions for how to craft nonfiction narratives. An associate professor and head of the master's professional program at the University of Iowa School of Journalism and Mass Communication, Bloom serves an important purpose as he discusses his time as writer for the *Los Angeles Times,* the *Dallas Morning News,* the *San Jose Mercury News,* and other newspapers and diagnoses his success with an example of extended literary nonfiction entitled *Postville: A Clash of Cultures in Heartland America* (2000).

Second, *Settling the Borderland* is not a comprehensive study of women in literary journalism. Like the section about allegory suggests, *Settling the Borderland* focuses on people and specific works that are representative, emblematic, symbolic. However, there are women literary journalists who deserve to be mentioned in this study, and future research will no doubt focus on their contributions. A few examples of these women follow:

One of the most recent is Alexandra Fuller, who wrote the bestseller *Don't Let's Go to the Dogs Tonight* and followed it with *Scribbling the Cat.* The former is a memoir; the latter, a personal narrative about traveling with a soldier through Zimbabwe, Zambia, and Mozambique. As Malcolm Jones Jr. writes, *Scribbling the Cat* is about the "weird intertwining of reporter and subject, and how each bends the story's reality" and is "one of the strangest, best books ever about the ravages of war" (51).

An early and significant writer, Josephine Herbst was a leftist and an advocate for the downtrodden, a novelist-journalist whose work also deserves further investigation by scholars. Her Marxist political perspective led her to write about the lives of working classes from the U.S. to Germany to Cuba to Spain. Having written for liberal magazines between 1929 and 1940, Herbst fell victim to the anti-Communist sentiment in the 1940s and 1950s in the U.S. during the height of her career. Her memoirs were published in a collection entitled *The Starched Blue Sky of Spain and Other Memoirs* (1991). A colleague of Ernest Hemingway and John Dos Passos, she, too, reported from the Loyalist perspective during the Spanish Civil War, publishing her essays in *The Nation* and *Woman's Day.*

Jane Kramer, who immersed herself in the Panhandle of Texas to write "Cowboy," and Adrian Nicole LeBlanc, whose essay "Trina and Trina" is one of the best examples of journalistic instinct and is a celebration of human compassion and connection, deserve extensive recognition for these and other contributions to literary journalism.

Lillian Ross, too, was a pioneer in literary journalism and was acknowledged in Chapter 3 for her influence on Sara Davidson. Reporting for *The New Yorker* for more than 50 years, Ross "stands apart from many other literary journalists with her emphasis on accuracy, her avoidance of reconstructed dialogue, and her disdain for attempts to report the thoughts of subjects" (n.p.), writes James W. Tankard Jr. She is perhaps best known for her "Portrait of Hemingway," which first appeared in *The New Yorker* in 1950, and *Picture,* which deals with movie director John Huston and American filmmaking. Ross is making her way into most lists of significant literary journalists, although Tankard argues that Ross wrote a nonfiction novel years before Capote published *In Cold Blood,* suggesting that she—like many of the women introduced in this study—deserve far more attention.

Since part of the focus of *Settling the Borderland* is to celebrate men who have not received their just due in the scholarly discourse, it is important to mention a few representative male literary journalists omitted from the study, including John Hersey, a reporter and novelist who wrote 23 books in 50 years, including *Hiroshima,* a book that insured his immortality. His introduction to a few Japanese whose lives were utterly changed by the bombing of Hiroshima has assured Hersey a place in the history of literary journalism. In his first paragraph of the chapter "A Noiseless Flash," Hersey writes:

> At exactly fifteen minutes past eight in the morning, on August 6, 1945, Japanese time, at the moment when the atomic bomb flashed above Hiroshima, Miss Toshiko Sasaki, a clerk in the personnel department of the East Asia Tin Works, had just sat down at her place in the plant office and was turning her head to speak to the girl at the next desk. At that same moment, Dr. Masakazu Fujii was settling down cross-legged to read the Osaka *Asahi* on the porch of his private hospital, overhanging one of the seven deltaic rivers which divide Hiroshima; Mrs. Hatsuyo Nakamura, a tailor's widow, stood by the window of her kitchen, watching a neighbor tearing down his house because it lay in the path of an air-raid-defense fire lane; Father Wilhelm Kleinsorge, a German priest of the Society of Jesus, reclined in his underwear on a cot on the top floor of his order's three-story mission house, reading a Jesuit magazine, *Stimmen der Zeit;* Dr. Terufumi Sasaki, a young member of the surgical staff of the city's large, modern Red Cross Hospital, walked along one of the hospital corridors with a blood specimen for a Wasserman test in his hand; and the Reverend Mr. Kiyoshi Tanimoto, pastor of the Hiroshima Methodist Church, paused at the door of a rich man's house in Koi, the city's western suburb, and prepared to unload a handcart full of things he had evacuated from town in fear of the massive B-29 raid which everyone expected Hiroshima to suffer. A hundred thousand people were killed by the atomic bomb, and these six were among the survivors. They still wonder why they lived when so many others died. Each of them counts many small items of chance or volition—a step taken in time, a decision to go indoors, catching one streetcar instead of the next—that spared him. And now each knows that in the act of survival he lived a dozen lives and saw more death than he ever thought he would see. At the time, none of them knew anything. (3-4)

This single paragraph washes over the reader like a wave, devastating in its matter-of-factness. As David Gates notes in Hersey's obituary in *Newsweek,* Hersey "wrote best about the impact of great events on ordinary lives" (70). He won a Pulitzer Prize for his first novel *A Bell for Adano.* Other notable books include *The Algiers Motel Incident* about racial strife in Detroit and *Blues* about fishing off Martha's Vineyard.

Another significant and under-celebrated writer, Denis Johnson has written poetry, short stories, and novels in which he deals with despair and the human condition. His first collection of journalism, entitled *Seek: Reports from the Edges of America and Beyond,* includes some articles published in *Harper's* and *Esquire.* In one essay, "The Militia in Me," Johnson writes sympathetically about America's right-wing movements.

John McPhee, another literary journalist omitted from this study, has received praise for his vast body of work. Hired by *The New Yorker* in 1967, McPhee is a writer who deals often with the environment, geographical location, and nature and is at his best in essays such as "Atchafalaya" and "Travels in Georgia." Using carefully orchestrated flashbacks, McPhee, like Orlean, often describes a journey to unify his narratives; in all things he is a careful architect of truthfulness. McPhee's literary arsenal includes *Oranges*, an account of the citrus industry; *The Pine Barrens,* a social and natural history of a New Jersey wilderness area; *A Roomful of Hovings and Other Profiles and Pieces of the Frame,* collections of articles from *The New Yorker; Coming into the Country* about Alaska; *Basin and Range* about geology; *In Suspect Terrain* about Brooklyn, New York, and other urban areas; and *The Control of Nature.* Brutally exacting, McPhee says he gets "prickly" if accused of making up dialogue: "You don't make up dialogue. You don't make a composite character. Where I came from, a composite character was a fiction" (Sims, "The Literary Journalists" 15).

Joseph Mitchell, who worked in New York as a newspaper reporter and later as a staff writer for *The New Yorker,* belongs in any collection about literary journalism, having inspired many writers of Truman Capote's generation. In *McSorley's Wonderful Saloon* and *The Bottom of the Harbor,* Mitchell collected articles that are a mixture of pathos and comedy (what he called "graveyard humor") and are some of the first essays called literary journalism. *Up in the Old Hotel* is a collection of all of Mitchell's *New Yorker* articles. As Malcolm Jones Jr. wrote in 1992, the book is "an epic of big-city life that shifts between unsentimental celebrations of human gumption and strangely elegiac meditations on death and the burdens of time" (53).

George Orwell's "Shooting an Elephant" is essential in any list of notable pieces of literary journalism. Autobiographical, the essay deals with Orwell's time in Lower Burma when "sneering yellow faces" made his days a nightmare: "All I knew was that I was stuck between my hatred of the empire I served and my rage against the evil-spirited little beasts who tried to make my job impossible" (4). Having destroyed a beast he admired out of fear of humiliation, Orwell calls into question Britain's imperialism and wonders how much cruelty is the result of pride. He writes, "And afterwards I was very glad that the coolie had been killed; it put me legally in the right and it gave me a sufficient pretext for shooting the elephant. I often wondered whether any of the others grasped that I had done it solely to avoid looking a fool" (12).

Although there are many things *Settling the Borderland: Other Voices in Literary Journalism* is not, it incorporates history, theory, and assessment of particular works as a way both to summarize much of the scholarship and creative work to date and to point to future research possibilities. It includes a description of the allegorical import of literary journalism—an emphasis often omitted from studies of the genre—and focuses on phenomenology, or the making of meaning, that drives great works in the genre. It acknowledges the presence of didacticism and celebrates its place in literary journalism, which relies upon the representative nature of characters and the ironic import of geographical locations.

In her final chapter of *Scribbling the Cat,* entitled "The Journey Is Now," Fuller employs didacticism to interpret her work for those who might not have understood the focus she intended or simply to make clear her own personal reasons for having traveled with a soldier through Africa:

> Those of us who grow in war are like clay pots fired in an oven that is overhot. Confusingly shaped liked [sic] the rest of humanity, we nevertheless contain fatal cracks that we spend the rest of our lives itching to fill.
>
> All of us with war-scars will endeavor to find some kind of relief from the constant sting of our incompleteness—drugs, love, alcohol, God, death, truth. K and I, each of us cracked in our own way by our participation on the wrong side of the same war, gravitated to each other, sure that the other held a secret balm—the magic glaze—that might make us whole. I thought he held shards of truth. He thought I held love.
>
> Those of us who grow in war know no boundaries. After all, that most sacred and basic boundary of all (Thou shalt not kill) is not only ignored in war, but outright flaunted and scoffed at. Kill! Slot! Scribble! We (guilty and secret and surviving, and more cunning than the dead) will seep into unseen cracks to find solace. And we will do so without thinking twice, since we are without skins, without membranes, without the usual containments of civilization. We know that life is cheap and that the secret to an inner peace is so dear and so elusive as to be almost unattainable. (250)

Heavily didactic, the conclusion of *Scribbling the Cat* is similar in intent—if not in technique—to the conclusions of other literary journalism texts. The meaning, the moral, the finale, the outcome matter: They are the reason behind the idea, the interviews, the research, and the resulting narrative. They matter absolutely. Raising the social and political consciousness of readers—fulfilling the goals of what was called "muckraking" in American journalism history—remains the domain of literary journalism. Willa Cather, Stephen Crane, Theodore Dreiser, and Upton Sinclair found that they could pursue the higher purposes of narrative best by writing fiction. Joan Didion and John Steinbeck lived in limbo, writing both journalism and fiction. Sara Davidson, Susan Orlean, Tom Wolfe and others have devoted their lives to writing long-form nonfiction. For all of them, the story is the vehicle; social and political awareness (and, in the best of all possible worlds, activism) are the ultimate goals.

Certainly, the conclusion of *Settling the Borderland: Other Voices in Literary Journalism* brings together voices from fiction and nonfiction. Some of those included in the study are startlingly self-reflexive and write not only fiction but also analyze the role of fiction in the world. One of them, Graham Swift, writes in his novel *Waterland* about his belief in the essential nature of the human being as a storytelling animal:

> Wherever he goes he wants to leave behind not a chaotic wake, not an empty space, but the comforting marker-buoys and trail-signs of stories. He has to go on telling stories, he has to keep on making them up. As long as there's a story, it's all right. Even in his last moments, it's said, in the split second of a fatal fall—or when he's about to drown—he sees, passing rapidly before him, the story of his whole life. (63)

Roger Rosenblatt argues something quite similar in "Dreaming the News: Stories Are the Way We Tell Ourselves to Ourselves." There he writes:

> Yet the effect of fiction preceding fact was just that: I began to dream my way into the news. Ordinarily, I would skitter over the papers quickly, the way an animal might take note of possible dangerous places on a journey; it is the stuff I need to know. But now I bored into language; I invented; I expected revelation. What was real became surreal, or perhaps it was that already. I read the news not as the first draft of history but as the first draft of a work of art.
>
> Writers like Truman Capote and Norman Mailer discovered this opportunity a long time ago. But they were approaching the matter from the creative end: How do I dream my way into the wanton murder of a Kansas family, or into Gary Gilmore's frightened, deadly little mind? . . .
>
> So much of living is made up of storytelling that one might conclude that it is what we were meant to do—to tell one another stories, fact or fiction, as a way of keeping afloat. Job's messenger, Coleridge's mariner, the reporter in California all grab us by the lapels to tell us their tale. We do the same; we cannot help ourselves. We have the story of others to tell, or of ourselves, or of the species—some monumentally elusive tale we are always trying to get right. Sometimes it seems that we are telling one another parts of the same immense story. Fiction and the news are joined in an endless chain. Everything is news, everything imagined. (102)

Rosenblatt, who has told many stories himself during his rich career, published "Dreaming the News" in 1997, and the central theme of that essay remains at the heart of his work—and at the heart of *Settling the Borderland: Other Voices in Literary Journalism*. In a 1999 interview, Rosenblatt described the diary entries, poems, letters, and news stories that Jews wrote in the final days of the Warsaw ghetto, even when they knew they would soon die:

> Why did they do it? Why bother to tell a story that no one would hear? And why make the telling of that story their last act on earth? Because it is in us to do so, like a biological fact—because story-telling is what the human animal does, to progress, to live with one another.
>
> Horses run, beavers build dams; people tell stories. Chaucer's pilgrims go back and forth from Canterbury and feel compelled to pass the time by telling

tales. The Ancient Mariner, crazy as a loon, grabs the wedding guest and forces him to listen to an incredible yarn. (n.p.)

Literary journalists, like other tellers of stories, have devoted themselves to a craft that alienates some readers and scholars because it relies upon personal point of view and because it employs techniques that many of them consider to be the particular province of literature. However, their belief in the higher truths of nonfiction and in the power of reality when it is conveyed with description, dialogue, and stream-of-consciousness has gained a growing number of adherents. The importance of allegory and phenomenology in the best works of literary journalism is undeniable, and whether the "lessons" are stated as directly as they are in *Scribbling the Cat* or as subtly as they are in "Some Dreamers of the Golden Dream," human beings will continue to hunger for the stories told to children before bedtime, for the local news, for the commentary that follows national and international disasters, for gossip—for all the once-upon-a-times of our lives.

Works Cited

Abrahamson, David. "Teaching Literary Journalism: A Diverted Pyramid?" *Journalism and Mass Communication Educator* 60.4 (Winter 2006): 430-34.

Adam, G. Stuart. *Notes Toward a Definition of Journalism: Understanding an Old Craft as an Art Form*. St. Petersburg, Fla.: The Poynter Institute for Media Studies, 1993.

Allen, Gay Wilson. *Walt Whitman*. Detroit: Wayne State UP, 1969.

— — —. *The Solitary Singer: A Critical Biography of Walt Whitman*. New York: Grove Press, 1955.

Allen, Michael. *Poe and the British Magazine Tradition*. New York: Oxford UP, 1969.

Associated Press. "Joan Didion To Adapt Memoir Into Play." ABC News Internet Ventures. 5 Jan. 2006. <http://www.abcnews.go.com/entertainment>.

Baker, Carlos. *Hemingway: The Writer as Artist*. Princeton, N.J.: Princeton UP, 1972.

Benson, Jackson J. *The True Adventures of John Steinbeck, Writer*. New York: Viking, 1984.

Berendt, John. "High-Heel Neil." *The New Yorker* 16 Jan. 1995: 38-45.

— — —. *Midnight in the Garden of Good and Evil*. New York: Vintage, 1994.

Bergman, Herbert. "The Influence of Whitman's Journalism on *Leaves of Grass.*" *American Literary Realism: 1870-1910* 3.4 (Fall 1970): 399-404.

Bergman, Herbert, Douglas A. Noverr, and Edward J. Recchia, eds. *The Collected Writings of Walt Whitman: The Journalism.* Vol. 1: 1834-1846. New York: Peter Lang, 1998.

— — —. *The Collected Writings of Walt Whitman: The Journalism.* Vol. 2: 1846-1848. New York: Peter Lang, 2003.

Berner, R. Thomas. *The Literature of Journalism: Text and Context.* State College, Penn.: Strata, 1999.

— — —. *Writing Literary Features.* Mahwah, N.J.: Lawrence Erlbaum, 1988.

Biemiller, Lawrence. "White Suit, Gray Eminence." *The Chronicle of Higher Education* 31 March 2006: A56.

Bohlke, L. Brent, ed. *Willa Cather in Person: Interviews, Speeches and Letters.* Lincoln: Nebraska UP, 1986.

Boynton, Robert S. "Drilling Into the Bedrock of Ordinary Experience." *The Chronicle of Higher Education* 4 March 2005: B10-B11.

— — —. *The New New Journalism: Conversations with America's Best Nonfiction Writers on Their Craft.* New York: Vintage, 2005.

Brasher, Thomas L. *Whitman as Editor of the Brooklyn Daily Eagle.* Detroit: Wayne State UP, 1970.

Bunting, Charles T. "'The Interior World': An Interview with Eudora Welty." *The Southern Review* 8 (Autumn 1972): 711-35.

— — —. "'The Interior World': An Interview with Eudora Welty." *Conversations with Eudora Welty.* Ed. Peggy Whitman Prenshaw. Jackson: UP of Mississippi, 1984. 40-63.

Callow, Philip. *From Noon to Starry Night: A Life of Walt Whitman.* Chicago: Ivan R. Dee, 1992.

Campbell, Deborah. "Can Journalism Be Art?" *The Tyee* 3 April 2006 <http://thetyee.ca/mediacheck/2005/11/01/journalismart>.

Capers, Charlotte. Interview. Mississippi Department of Archives and History. Jackson, Miss. 26 October 1971.

Capote, Truman. *In Cold Blood: A True Account of a Multiple Murder and Its Consequences.* New York: Penguin, 1965.

Chapman, Wes. "Human and Divine Design: An Annotation of Robert Frost's 'Design.'" *The American Poetry Web* 8 March 2006 <http://titan.iwu.edu/~wchapman/american poetryweb>.

Clemons, Walter. "Meeting Miss Welty." *Conversations with Eudora Welty.* Ed. Peggy Whitman Prenshaw. Jackson: UP of Mississippi, 1984. 30-34.

Coffey, Marilyn. "The Dust Storms." *Natural History* Feb. 1978: 72, 74-77, 80-82.

Connery, Thomas B. "Discovering a Literary Form." *A Sourcebook of American Literary Journalism: Representative Writers in an Emerging Genre.* Ed. Thomas B. Connery. New York: Greenwood, 1992. 3-37.

— — —, ed. *A Sourcebook of American Literary Journalism: Representative Writers in an Emerging Genre.* New York, N.Y.: Greenwood, 1992.

— — —. "A Third Way to Tell the Story: American Literary Journalism at the Turn of the Century." *Literary Journalism in the Twentieth Century.* Ed. Norman Sims. New York: Oxford UP, 1990. 3-20.

Cowley, Malcolm, ed. *From Writers at Work: The Paris Review Interviews.* New York: Viking, 1957.

Curtin, William, ed. *The World and the Parish: Willa Cather's Articles and Reviews.* 2 vols. Lincoln: Nebraska UP, 1970.

Davidson, Sara. *Cowboy: A Novel.* New York: Harper Collins, 1999.

— — —. "The First Day of the Rest of My Life." *Newsweek* 22 Jan. 2007: 55-58.

— — —. "The Gray Zone." *Book* July/August 1999: 49-50.

— — —. *Leap!: What Will We Do with the Rest of Our Lives?* New York: Random House, 2007.

— — —. Lecture. "Literary Journalism: What Are the Rules?" School of Journalism and Mass Communication. University of Colorado. Boulder, Colo. 22 Nov. 2002.

— — —. Lecture. Mile Hi Church. Lakewood, Colo. 9 Sept. 2007.

— — —. Lecture. The Tattered Cover. Denver, Colo. 27 April 2007.

— — —. *Loose Change: Three Women of the Sixties.* Berkeley: U of California P, 1977.

— — —. *Real Property.* New York: Pocket Books, 1980.

DeFore, John. "Hoffman Gives Soul to the Role of Capote." *Austin American-Statesman* 28 Oct. 2005: 1E+.

DeMott, Robert. Preface. *Working Days: The Journals of The Grapes of Wrath (1938-41).* By John Steinbeck. Ed. Robert DeMott. New York,: Viking, 1989. xi-xv.

Devlin, Albert J. *Eudora Welty's Chronicle: A Story of Mississippi Life.* Jackson: UP of Mississippi, 1983.

— — —, ed. *Welty: A Life in Literature.* Jackson: UP of Mississippi, 1987.

Dewey, Alvin A. "The Clutter Case: 25 Years Later KBI Agent Recounts Holcomb Tragedy." *Garden City Telegram* 10 Nov. 1984: 1A+.

Didion, Joan. *After Henry*. New York: Vintage, 1992.

— — —. *The Last Thing He Wanted: A Novel*. New York: Vintage, 1996.

— — —. "Notes from a Native Daughter." *Slouching Towards Bethlehem*. New York: Quality Paperback Book Club, 1992. 171-86.

— — —. "On Going Home." *Slouching Towards Bethlehem*. New York: Quality Paperback Book Club, 1992. 164-68.

— — —. "On Self-Respect." *Slouching Towards Bethlehem*. New York: Quality Paperback Book Club, 1992. 142-48.

— — —. *Political Fictions*. New York: Alfred A. Knopf, 2001.

— — —. *Salvador*. New York: Vintage, 1994.

— — —. *Slouching Towards Bethlehem*. New York: Quality Paperback Book Club, 1992.

— — —. "Some Dreamers of the Golden Dream." *Slouching Towards Bethlehem*. New York: Quality Paperback Book Club, 1992. 3-28.

— — —. *The Year of Magical Thinking*. New York: Alfred A. Knopf, 2005.

Donohue, Agnes McNeill, ed. *A Casebook on The Grapes of Wrath*. New York: Thomas Y. Crowell, 1968.

Dreiser, Theodore. *Newspaper Days*. New York: Beekman, 1974.

Eason, David. "The New Journalism and the Image-World." *Literary Journalism in the Twentieth Century*. Ed. Norman Sims. New York: Oxford UP, 1990. 191-205.

Edmondson, Jolee. "Midnight Madness." *Sky* March 1997: 48-57.

Elias, Justine. "After Midnight." *US* Dec. 1997: 89-97, 113.

Eliot, T.S. *The Four Quartets*. New York: Harcourt Brace, 1943.

Ellmann, Richard, and Robert O'Clair, ed. *The Norton Anthology of Modern Poetry*. 2nd ed. New York: W.W. Norton, 1988.

Faulkner, William. *The Sound and the Fury*. New York: Modern Library, 1992.

Fishkin, Shelley Fisher. *From Fact to Fiction: Journalism and Imaginative Writing in America*. Baltimore, Md.: Johns Hopkins UP, 1985.

Fletcher, Angus. *Allegory: The Theory of a Symbolic Mode*. Ithaca: Cornell UP, 1964.

Fowler, Giles. "John Steinbeck." *A Sourcebook of American Literary Journalism: Representative Writers in an Emerging Genre*. Ed. Thomas B. Connery. New York, N.Y.: Greenwood, 1992. 223-30.

Freeman, Jean Todd. "An Interview with Eudora Welty." *Conversations with Eudora Welty.* Ed. Peggy Whitman Prenshaw. Jackson: UP of Mississippi, 1984. 172-99.

French, Warren G. *John Steinbeck's Nonfiction Revisited.* New York: Twayne, 1996.

Frost, Robert. "Design." *The Norton Anthology of Modern Poetry.* Ed. Richard Ellmann and Robert O'Clair. 2nd ed. New York: W.W. Norton, 1988. 262-63.

Fuller, Alexandra. *Scribbling the Cat: Travels with an African Soldier.* New York: Penguin, 2004.

Gates, David. "Literature's Lost Boy: The Self-Destruction of an American Writer." *Newsweek* 30 May 1988: 62-63.

Gilbert, Sandra M., and Susan Gubar, eds. *Norton Anthology of Literature by Women.* New York: W.W. Norton, 1985.

Givner, Joan. *Katherine Anne Porter: A Life.* New York: Simon and Schuster, 1982.

— — —. "Katherine Anne Porter, Journalist." *Katherine Anne Porter.* Ed. Harold Bloom. New York: Chelsea House, 1986. 69-80.

Good, Howard. *Acquainted with the Night.* Metuchen, N.J.: The Scarecrow Press, 1986.

Gray, Paul. "A Man in Full." *Time* 152.18 (2 Nov. 1998): 88.

Greenspan, Ezra. *Walt Whitman and the American Reader.* Cambridge, Mass.: Cambridge UP, 1990.

Hammer, Joshua. "How Two Lives Met in Death." *Newsweek* 15 April 2002: 18-25.

Hartsock, John C. *A History of American Literary Journalism: The Emergence of a Modern Narrative Form.* Amherst: U of Massachusetts P, 2000.

Harvey, Chris. "Tom Wolfe's Revenge." *American Journalism Review* Oct. 1994: 40-46.

Hellman, John. *Fables of Fact: The New Journalism as New Fiction.* Champaign: Illinois UP, 1981.

Hemingway, Ernest. "Monologue to the Maestro." *Esquire* 4 (October 1935): 21, 174A-174B.

Hendrick, George. *Katherine Anne Porter.* New York: Twayne Publishers, 1965.

Herr, Michael. *Dispatches.* New York: Alfred A. Knopf, 1978.

Hersey, John. *Hiroshima.* New York: Alfred A. Knopf, 1946.

Hollowell, John. *Fact and Fiction: The New Journalism and the Nonfiction Novel.* Chapel Hill, N.C.: U of North Carolina P, 1977.

Howarth, William. "The Mother of Literature: Journalism and *The Grapes of Wrath.*" *New Essays on The Grapes of Wrath.* Ed. David Wyatt. Cambridge, Mass.: UP, 1990. 71-99.

Inge, M. Thomas, ed. *Truman Capote: Conversations.* Jackson: UP of Mississippi, 1987.

Jacobs, Robert D. *Poe: Journalist and Critic.* Baton Rouge, La.: LSU Press, 1969.

Johnson, Michael. *The New Journalism: The Underground Press, the Artists of Nonfiction, and Changes in the Established Media.* Lawrence, Kansas: U of Kansas P, 1971.

Jones, Malcolm Jr. "The Paragon of Reporters." *Newsweek* 10 Aug. 1992: 53-54.

— — —. "War Wounds: Alexandra Fuller's Memorable Tangle with a Heart of Darkness." *Newsweek* 17 May 2004: 51.

Kallan, Richard A. "Tom Wolfe." *A Sourcebook of American Literary Journalism: Representative Writers in an Emerging Genre.* Ed. Thomas B. Connery. New York: Greenwood, 1992. 249-59.

Keith, Don Lee. "Eudora Welty: 'I Worry Over My Stories.'" *Conversations with Eudora Welty.* Ed. Peggy Whitman Prenshaw. Jackson: UP of Mississippi, 1984. 141-53.

Kenner, Hugh. "The Politics of the Plain Style." *Literary Journalism in the Twentieth Century.* Ed. Norman Sims. New York: Oxford UP, 1990. 183-90.

Kitch, Carolyn. "The Work That Came Before the Art: Willa Cather as Journalist, 1893-1912." *American Journalism* 14.3-4 (Summer-Fall 1997): 425-40.

Klein, Julia M. Rev. of *The New New Journalism: Conversations with America's Best Nonfiction Writers on Their Craft,* by Robert S. Boynton. *Columbia Journalism Review* March/April 2005 <www.cjr.org/issues/2005/2/ideas-book-klein.asp>.

Kopley, Richard. *Edgar Allan Poe and the Philadelphia Evening News.* Baltimore, Md.: Enoch Pratt Free Library, 1991.

Kroll, Jack. "Truman Capote: 1924-1984." *Newsweek* 3 Sept. 1984: 69.

Kunitz, Stanley J., ed. *Authors Today and Yesterday.* New York.: H.W. Wilson, 1934.

"Lamar Life Radio News." Newsletter. Mississippi Department of Archives and History. Jackson, Miss. Jan. 1932: n.p.

Laucella, Pamela C. "*McClure's:* The Significance of 1906-1912 on Willa Cather and Her Artistic Growth." Association for Education in Journalism and Mass Communication Conf. Washington, D.C. 5-8 Aug. 2001.

LeBlanc, Adrian Nicole. *Random Family: Love, Drugs, Trouble, and Coming of Age in the Bronx.* New York: Scribner, 2003.

— — —. "Trina and Trina." *Literary Journalism: A New Collection of the Best American Nonfiction.* Ed. Norman Sims and Mark Kramer. New York,: Ballantine, 1995. 209-31.

Lopez, Enrique Hank. *Conversations with Katherine Anne Porter: Refugee from Indian Creek.* Boston: Little, Brown, 1981.

Lounsberry, Barbara. *The Art of Fact: Contemporary Artists of Nonfiction.* New York: Greenwood, 1990.

— — —. "Joan Didion's Lambent Light." *The Art of Fact: Contemporary Artists of Non-fiction.* New York: Greenwood, 1990. 107-37.

— — —. "Tom Wolfe's American Jeremiad." *The Art of Fact: Contemporary Artists of Nonfiction.* New York: Greenwood, 1990. 37-64.

Lule, Jack. "Myth and Terror on the Editorial Page: *The New York Times* Responds to September 11, 2001." *Journalism and Mass Communication Quarterly* 79.2 (Summer 2002): 275-93.

Lyon, Peter. *Success Story: The Life and Times of S.S. McClure.* Deland, Fla: Everett/Edwards, 1963.

MacNeil, Robert. *Eudora Welty: Seeing Black and White.* Jackson: UP of Mississippi, 1990.

Malcolm, Janet. *The Journalist and the Murderer.* New York: Alfred A. Knopf, 1990.

Manning, Richard D. "The Other Side." *Northern Lights* 6 (January 1990): 12-14.

Marrs, Suzanne. "Eudora Welty's Photography: Images into Fiction." *Critical Essays on Eudora Welty.* Ed. W. Craig Turner and Lee Emling Harding. Boston: G.K. Hall, 1989. 280-96.

Marshall, Kathryn. "A Quality of Light." *American Way* 1 Oct. 1988: 70-76, 105-6, 108-9.

"Master of His Universe." *Time* 13 Feb. 1989: 90-92.

McGuigan, Cathleen. "Alone With Her Words." *Newsweek* 10 Oct. 2005: 63.

McKenzie, Barbara. "The Eye of Time: The Photographs of Eudora Welty." *Eudora Welty: Critical Essays.* Ed. Peggy Whitman Prenshaw. Jackson: UP of Mississippi, 1979. 386-400.

Meese, Elizabeth A. "Constructing Time and Place: Eudora Welty in the Thirties." *Eudora Welty: Critical Essays.* Ed. Peggy Whitman Prenshaw. Jackson: UP of Mississippi, 1979. 401-10.

Morrison, Toni. "Author Eudora Welty Dies at 92." By Associated Press. *New York Times* 23 July 2001 <http://www.nytimes.com/2001/07/23/arts/AP-Obit-Welty.html>.

Moss, Marilyn Ann. "Theodore Dreiser." *A Sourcebook of American Literary Journalism: Representative Writers in an Emerging Genre.* Ed. Thomas B. Connery. New York: Greenwood, 1992: 143-50.

Nance, William L. *Katherine Anne Porter and the Art of Rejection.* Chapel Hill: U of North Carolina Press, 1963.

Nelson, Jack A. "Mark Twain." *A Sourcebook of American Literary Journalism: Representative Writers in an Emerging Genre.* New York: Greenwood, 1992. 42-53.

Nostwich, T.D. *Theodore Dreiser's "Heard in the Corridors": Articles and Related Writings.* Ames: Iowa UP, 1988.

O'Connor, Flannery. *Mystery and Manners.* New York: Farrar, 1969.

Orlean, Susan. "The American Man, Age Ten." *The Bullfighter Checks Her Makeup: My Encounters with Extraordinary People.* New York: Random House, 2002. 3-14.

— — —. "Introduction: Encounters with Clowns, Kings, Singers and Surfers." *The Bullfighter Checks Her Makeup: My Encounters with Extraordinary People.* New York: Random House, 2002. ix-xv.

— — —. "The Maui Surfer Girls." *The Bullfighter Checks Her Makeup: My Encounters with Extraordinary People.* New York: Random House, 2002. 37-49.

— — —. *My Kind of Place: Travel Stories from a Woman Who's Been Everywhere.* New York: Random House, 2005.

— — —. *The Orchid Thief: A True Story of Beauty and Obsession.* New York: Ballantine, Books, 2000.

— — —. "Reader's Guide." *The Orchid Thief: A True Story of Beauty and Obsession.* New York: Ballantine Books, 2000. n.p.

— — —. "Rough Diamonds: Fidel's Little Leagues." *The New Yorker* 5 Aug. 2002: 34-37.

— — —. "Straight and Narrow: Susan Orlean Gets the Skinny from Joan Didion." *Vogue* 192.4 (April 2002): 281-83.

Orwell, George. "Shooting an Elephant." *Shooting an Elephant and Other Essays.* New York: Harcourt, Brace, and World, 1950. 3-12.

Parini, Jay. Introduction. *Travels with Charley in Search of America.* New York: Penguin, 1997. vii-xxii.

— — —. *John Steinbeck: A Biography.* New York: Holt, 1995.

Paterson, Judith. "Literary Journalism's Twelve Best." *Washington Journalism Review* October 1992: 61.

Pauly, John J. "Damon Runyon." *A Sourcebook of American Literary Journalism: Representative Writers in an Emerging Genre.* Ed. Thomas B. Connery. New York: Greenwood, 1992. 169-77.

— — —. "George Ade." *A Sourcebook of American Literary Journalism: Representative Writers in an Emerging Genre.* Ed. Thomas B. Connery. New York: Greenwood, 1992. 111-19.

— — —. "The Politics of The New Journalism." *Literary Journalism in the Twentieth Century.* Ed. Norman Sims. New York: Oxford UP, 1990. 110-29.

Phelps, Christopher. "How Should We Teach *The Jungle?*" *The Chronicle of Higher Education* 3 March 2006: B10-B12.

Philbrick, Nathaniel. "At Sea in the Tide Pool: The Whaling Town and America in Steinbeck's *The Winter of Our Discontent* and *Travels with Charley." Steinbeck and the Environment: Interdisciplinary Approaches.* Ed. Susan F. Beegel, Susan Shillinglaw, and Wesley N. Tiffney Jr. Tuscaloosa: U of Alabama P, 1997. 229-42.

Plimpton, George. "Capote's Long Ride." *The New Yorker* 13 Oct. 1997: 62, 64-71.

— — —. *Truman Capote: In Which Various Friends, Enemies, Acquaintances, and Detractors Recall His Turbulent Career.* New York: Doubleday, 1997.

— — —, ed. *Women Writers at Work: The Paris Interviews.* New York: Modern Library, 1998.

Poe, Edgar Allan. "The Mystery of Marie Roget." *The Short Fiction of Edgar Allan Poe.* Ed. Stuart and Susan Levine. Indianapolis: Bobbs-Merrill, 1976. 197-225.

— — —. "The Murders in the Rue Morgue." *The Short Fiction of Edgar Allan Poe.* Ed. Stuart and Susan Levine. Indianapolis: Bobbs-Merrill, 1976. 175-97.

Porter, Katherine Anne. *The Collected Stories of Katherine Anne Porter.* San Diego: Harcourt Brace Jovanovich, 1944.

— — —. *The Never-Ending Wrong.* Boston: Little, Brown, 1977.

— — —. *Pale Horse, Pale Rider.* New York: New American Library, 1967.

Prenshaw, Peggy Whitman, ed. *Conversations with Eudora Welty.* Jackson: UP of Mississippi, 1984.

— — —, ed. *Eudora Welty: Critical Essays.* Jackson: UP of Mississippi, 1979.

Reed, Kenneth T. *Truman Capote.* Boston: Twayne, 1981.

Ringle, Ken. "Just Savannah Good Time." *Washington Post* 24 Feb. 1994: C1.

Roberts, Nancy. "Dorothy Day." *A Sourcebook of American Literary Journalism: Representative Writers in an Emerging Genre.* Ed. Thomas B. Connery. New York: Greenwood, 1992. 179-85.

Robertson, Michael. "Stephen Crane." *A Sourcebook of American Literary Journalism: Representative Writers in an Emerging Genre.* Ed. Thomas B. Connery. New York: Greenwood, 1992. 69-79.

— — —. *Stephen Crane, Journalism, and the Making of Modern American Literature.* New York: Columbia UP, 1997.

— — —. "Stephen Crane's New York City Journalism and the Oft-Told Tale." *American Journalism* 9.1-2 (Winter-Spring 1992): 7-22.

Roiphe, Katie. "Didion's Daughters." *Brill's Content* Sept. 2000: 100-103, 136-37.

Rosenblatt, Roger. "Dreaming the News." *Time* 14 April 1997: 102.

— — —. "Journalism and the Larger Truth." *State of the Art.* Ed. David Shimkin and others. New York: St. Martin's Press, 1992. 132-34.

— — —. "The Killer in the Next Tent: The Surreal Horror of the Rwanda Refugees." *The New York Times Magazine* 5 June 1994: cover, 39-42, 44-47.

— — —. "Once Upon a Time" 24 Dec. 1999. *Online NewsHour with Jim Lehrer.* 31 Jan. 2006: n.p. <www.pbs.org/newshour/essays/2000>.

Rubin, Joseph Jay. *The Historic Whitman.* University Park: The Pennsylvania State UP, 1973.

Rubin, Joseph Jay, and Charles H. Brown, ed. *Walt Whitman of the New York Aurora: Editor at Twenty-Two.* State College, Penn.: Bald Eagle Press, 1950.

Russell, Dennis. "Baudrillardesque Impulses in the Impressionistic Journalism of Joan Didion." *Southwestern Mass Communication Journal* 16.1 (2000): 19-28.

Rustin, Susanna. "Legends of the Fall." *The Guardian* 21 May 2005 <http://books.guardian.co.uk>

Schmidt, Peter. *The Heart of the Story: Eudora Welty's Short Fiction.* Jackson: UP of Mississippi, 1991.

Schulman, Norma M. "Wrinkling the Fabric of the Press: Newspaper Opinion Columns in a Different Voice. *Women and Media: Content, Careers, and Criticism.* Ed. Cynthia M. Lont. Belmont, Calif.: Wadsworth, 1995. 55-67.

Sexton, Kathryn Adams. "Katherine Anne Porter's Years in Denver." Thesis. U of Colorado, 1961.

Shillinglaw, Susan, and Jackson J. Benson, ed. *America and Americans and Selected Nonfiction.* New York: Viking, 2002.

Sims, Norman. "The Art of Literary Journalism." *Literary Journalism: A New Collection of the Best American Nonfiction.* Ed. Norman Sims and Mark Kramer. New York: Ballantine Books, 1995. 3-19.

— — —. "The Literary Journalists." *The Literary Journalists: The New Art of Personal Reportage.* Ed. Norman Sims. New York: Ballantine Books, 1984. 3-25.

— — —, ed. *Literary Journalism in the Twentieth Century.* New York: Oxford UP, 1990.

— — —, ed. *The Literary Journalists: The New Art of Personal Reportage.* New York: Ballantine Books, 1984.

Sims, Norman, and Mark Kramer, eds. *Literary Journalism: A New Collection of the Best American Nonfiction.* New York: Ballantine, 1995.

Slote, Bernice, ed. *The Kingdom of Art.* Lincoln: U of Nebraska P, 1966.

Stallman, R.W. *Stephen Crane: A Biography.* New York: George Braziller, 1968.

Steinbeck, John. "John Steinbeck's Acceptance Speech for the Nobel Prize for Literature in 1962." *Vogue* 1 March 1963: 16.

— — —. *The Harvest Gypsies: On the Road to the Grapes of Wrath.* Berkeley, Calif.: Heyday Books, 1988.

— — —. *Travels with Charley in Search of America.* New York: Penguin, 1997.

Steiner, Linda. "Stories of Quitting: Why Did Some Women Journalists Leave the News-room?" *American Journalism* 15.3 (Summer 1998): 89-116.

Stevens, Wallace. "The Idea of Order at Key West." *The Norton Anthology of Modern Poetry.* Ed. Richard Ellmann and Robert O'Clair. 2nd ed. New York: W.W. Norton, 1988. 291-92.

Swift, Graham. *Waterland.* New York: Vintage, 1983.

Talese, Gay. *Fame and Obscurity: Portraits.* New York: World, 1970.

Tankard, James W. Jr. "Lillian Ross: Pioneer of Literary Journalism." Association for Education in Journalism and Mass Communication Conf. Phoenix, Ariz. Aug. 2000.

Toobin, Jeffrey. "American Gothic: What Rushes into the Newsless Void?" *The New Yorker* 73.21 (28 July 1997): 4-5.

Tucker, Mary Louise. "Photography and Photographers." *Encyclopedia of Southern Culture.* Ed. Charles Reagan Wilson and William Ferris. Chapel Hill: U of North Carolina P, 1989. 94-100.

VandeKieft, Ruth M. *Eudora Welty.* New York: Twayne, 1962.

Walsh, John. *Poe the Detective: The Curious Circumstances Behind the Mystery of Marie Roget.* New Brunswick, N.J.: Rutgers UP, 1968.

Webb, Joseph. "Historical Perspective on The New Journalism." *Journalism History* 1 (Summer 1974): 38-42, 60.

Weber, Ronald. *The Literature of Fact: Literary Nonfiction in American Writing.* Athens: Ohio UP, 1980.

Welty, Eudora. *The Collected Stories of Eudora Welty.* New York: Harcourt Brace Jovanovich, 1980.

— — —. "Eudora Welty Interviewed by Davis School Children." Mississippi Department of Archives and History. Davis School. Jackson, Miss. 9 Oct. 1980.

— — —. "One Time, One Place." *The Eye of the Story: Selected Essays and Reviews.* New York: Random House, 1978. 349-55.

— — —. *One Writer's Beginnings.* Cambridge, Mass.: Harvard UP, 1984.

— — —. *Photographs.* Jackson: UP of Mississippi, 1989.

— — —. "A Salute from One of the Family." *A Tower of Strength in the Deep South: 50th Anniversary of the Lamar Life Insurance Co.* Montgomery, Ala.: Paragon Press, 1956.

— — —. *Three Papers on Fiction.* Northampton, Mass.: Metcalf, 1962.

— — —. "A Word on the Photographs." *Twenty Photographs.* Winston-Salem, N.C.: Palaemon Press, 1980.

"Welty Photos Show Another Side of Depression." *The Denver Post* 17 Dec. 1989: 1E.

Westling, Louise. *Eudora Welty.* Totowa, N.J.: Barnes and Noble Books, 1989.

— — —. "The Loving Observer of *One Time, One Place.*" *Welty: A Life in Literature.* Ed. Albert J. Devlin. Jackson: U of Mississippi P, 1987. 168-87.

— — —. *Sacred Groves and Ravaged Gardens: The Fiction of Eudora Welty, Carson McCullers, and Flannery O'Connor.* Athens: U of Georgia P, 1985.

Whitby, Gary L. "Truman Capote." *A Sourcebook of American Literary Journalism: Representative Writers in an Emerging Genre.* Ed. Thomas B. Connery. New York: Greenwood, 1992. 239-48.

Whitman, Walt. *The Complete Writings of Walt Whitman.* Ed. Richard Maurice Bucke, Thomas B. Hamed, and Horace L. Traubel. New York: G.P. Putnam's Sons, 1902.

— — —. *Leaves of Grass: The Deathbed Edition.* New York: Quality Paperback Book Club, 1992.

— — —. "Preface to the 1855 Edition of *Leaves of Grass.*" *The American Tradition in Literature.* Ed. Sculley Bradley and others. Vol. 4. New York: Grossett and Dunlap, 1978. 887-906.

— — —. *The Uncollected Poetry and Prose of Walt Whitman, Much of Which Has Been But Recently Discovered, with Various Early Manuscripts Now First Published.* Ed. Emory Holloway. 2 vols. Garden City, N.Y.: Toronto, Doubleday, Page, 1921.

Whitt, Jan. *Allegory and the Modern Southern Novel.* Macon, Ga.: Mercer UP, 1994.

— — —. "Final Letters to the World: Mark Twain, F. Scott Fitzgerald, John Steinbeck, and Artistic Entropy." *Journal of the American Studies Association of Texas* 38 (November 2007): 1-19.

— — —. "Portrait of an Artist as a Young Woman: Eudora Welty's Early Years in Media." *Southwestern Mass Communication Journal* 15 (1999): 26-38.

— — —. "'To Do Some Good and No Harm': The Literary Journalism of John Steinbeck." *Steinbeck Studies* 3.2 (Fall 2006): 41-62.

— — —. "'The Truth About What Happens': Katherine Anne Porter and Journalism." *Journal of the American Studies Association of Texas* 26 (October 1995): 16-35.

— — —. "'The Very Simplicity of the Thing': Edgar Allan Poe and the Murders He Wrote" *Clues* 15 (Spring/Summer 1994): 29-47.

— — —. "'The Very Simplicity of the Thing': Edgar Allan Poe and the Murders He Wrote." *The Detective in Fiction, Film, and Television.* Ed. Jerome P. Delamater and Ruth Prigozy. Westport, Conn.: Greenwood, 1998. 111-21.

— — —. *Women in American Journalism: A New History.* Champaign: U of Illinois P, 2008.

Williams, Terry Tempest. "Wallace Stegner Award Acceptance Speech." University of Colorado. 2 Nov. 2005.

Williams, William Carlos. "Asphodel, That Greeny Flower." *Asphodel, That Greeny Flower and Other Love Poems.* New York: New Directions, 1994. 9-42.

Wolfe, Tom. *The New Journalism.* New York: Harper and Row, 1973.

— — —. *The Right Stuff.* New York: Bantam, 1980.

Wolcott, James. "The Truman Show." *Vanity Fair* Dec. 1997: 124, 126, 128, 130, 132, 134, 136.

Wollenberg, Charles. Introduction. *The Harvest Gypsies: On the Road to the Grapes of Wrath.* Berkeley, Calif.: Heyday Books, 1988. v-xvii.

Woodress, James. *Willa Cather: Her Life and Art.* New York: Pegasus, 1970.

Wordsworth, William. "Lines Composed a Few Miles Above Tintern Abbey." *The Norton Anthology of English Literature.* Ed. M.H. Abrams. 5th ed. Vol. 2. New York: W.W. Norton, 1986. 151-55.

Yates, Gayle Graham. "An Interview with Eudora Welty." *Frontiers* 9.3 (1987): 100-104.

Yeats, William Butler. "The Second Coming." *The Norton Anthology of Modern Poetry.* Ed. Richard Ellman and Robert O'Clair. 2nd ed. New York.: W.W. Norton, 1988. 158.

Index

About the Author

Author of *Allegory and the Modern Southern Novel* (Macon, Ga.: Mercer UP, 1994), Jan Whitt is an associate professor in the School of Journalism and Mass Communication at the University of Colorado at Boulder.

Having begun her career as a newspaper reporter and editor in Texas, Whitt has written *Women in American Journalism: A New History* for the University of Illinois Press. The manuscript, which is currently in press, won the Mary Ann Yodelis Smith award for feminist scholarship (2005) from the Commission on the Status of Women, a group of scholars in the Association for Education in Journalism and Mass Communication. She also published *Reflections in a Critical Eye: Essays on Carson McCullers* (Lanham, Md.: UP of America, 2007). Current projects include a book on white Civil Rights journalists for UP of Florida and on the television series "The West Wing" for UP of America.

The author of more than 70 articles and book chapters, Whitt publishes in literary, media, and popular culture journals. Her articles appear in *American Journalism, Clues, Journal of the American Studies Association of Texas, Journal of Homosexuality, Journal of Lesbian Studies, Journal of Popular Film and Television, Journal of the West, Journalism Educator,* the *Maine Times, Popular Culture Review, Society of Environmental Journalists Journal, Southern Literary Journal, Southern Studies, Southwestern American Literature,* the *Southwestern Mass Communication Journal, Studies in Popular Culture,* and other publications.

She has published chapters in books that deal with a wide variety of topics, including the history of women's press clubs, women in local television, lesbian publications, Southern literature, detective fiction and film, women and newspapers, American literature, and American television.

Having received teaching and advising awards at Baylor University, the University of Denver, and the University of Colorado at Boulder, Whitt teaches undergraduate and graduate courses in American and British literature, literary journalism, media studies, popular culture, professional writing, and women's studies. Her research focuses on diversity issues in literature and contemporary media.

Whitt completed her B.A. in English and journalism (1977) and her M.A. in English (1980) at Baylor University and earned a Ph.D. in literature at the University of Denver (1985).

A volunteer with Golden Retriever Rescue of the Rockies, Whitt enjoys skiing; running; hiking with her golden retrievers, Mackenzie and Riley; traveling; and reading.